SHAPES OF
NATIVE
NONFICTION

SHAPES OF NATIVE NONFICTION

*Collected Essays by
Contemporary Writers*

Edited by

ELISSA WASHUTA AND THERESA WARBURTON

UNIVERSITY OF WASHINGTON PRESS
Seattle

www.tulalipcares.org

Shapes of Native Nonfiction was supported by a grant from the Tulalip Tribes Charitable Fund, which provides the opportunity for a sustainable and healthy community for all.

23 22 21 20 19   5 4 3 2 1

UNIVERSITY OF WASHINGTON PRESS
www.washington.edu/uwpress

LIBRARY OF CONGRESS CATALOGING-IN-PUBLICATION DATA
Names: Washuta, Elissa, editor. | Warburton, Theresa, editor.
Title: Shapes of Native nonfiction : collected essays by contemporary writers / edited by Elissa Washuta and Theresa Warburton.
Description: Seattle : University of Washington Press, [2019] | Includes bibliographical references.
Identifiers: LCCN 2018047472 (print) | LCCN 2018059193 (ebook) | ISBN 9780295745770 (ebook) | ISBN 9780295745763 (hardcover : alk. paper) | ISBN 9780295745756 (pbk. : alk. paper)
Subjects: LCSH: American literature—Indian authors. | Indians of North America—Literary collections. | Creative nonfiction, American. | American literature—21st century. | American literature—Indian authors—History and Criticism.
Classification: LCC PS508.I5 (ebook) | LCC PS508.I5 S53 2019 (print) | DDC 814/.009897—dc23
LC record available at https://lccn.loc.gov/2018047472

336140814439530

In loving memory of Carol Edelman Warrior,
beloved friend and scholar,
whose work on stories helped shape this collection

CONTENTS

PLAITING

SHAPES OF
NATIVE
NONFICTION

Introduction

Exquisite Vessels

ELISSA WASHUTA AND THERESA WARBURTON

Indigenous peoples understand that there is no difference between the telling and the material. They understand how we all, in fact, live inside and through the narratives we tell and that the importance in telling stories is inseparable from the identity, community, and history they compose and the spiritual, economic, and political realities on which they depend and which they subvert or preserve.

—JOANNE BARKER AND TERESIA TEAIWA, "NATIVE INFORMATION"

Style is simply a way of doing something. The items people make, may they be canoes, houses, masks, or baskets, display regularities and similarities that suggest the makers have followed some set of rules, pattern, and order in their creation. Although a basket is the unique creative product of an individual, its maker followed a set of traditions and cultural conventions that influenced choices throughout the manufacturing process.

—JACILEE WRAY, *FROM THE HANDS OF A WEAVER: OLYMPIC PENINSULA BASKETRY THROUGH TIME*

The basket. The body. The canoe. The page. Each of these vessels has a form, a shape to which its purpose is intimately related. Each carries, each holds, and each transports. However, none of these vessels can be defined solely by their contents; neither can their purpose be understood as strictly utilitarian. Rather, the craft involved in creating such a vessel—the care and knowledge it takes to create the structure and shape necessary to convey—is inseparable from the contents that the vessel holds. To pay attention only to the contents would be to ignore the very relationships that such vessels sustain. Yes, the basket may carry elderberries or trap salmon, but what of the cedar used to weave it? What of the weaver whose skills connect long genealogies of craft and kin? What of the cosmological significance of the elderberries and salmon? Some weavers know how to weave baskets so tightly that water can be boiled in them. How can we think about that water, about the running of rivers and the running of salmon, without thinking of the craft that must go into a vessel that can hold water, whether basket or riverbed? To speak only about the contents of these vessels would be to ignore how their significance is shaped by the vessels that hold them.

Yet it is often on these terms that Native literatures, particularly works of nonfiction, are discussed; as works whose import is related exclusively to their content, a process akin to what Driftpile Cree writer and scholar Billy-Ray Belcourt has described as the impulse toward an "uncovering of a genre of experience from the graveyard of Indigenous history."[1] This impulse reflects the broader tradition of reading Native literatures as a form of "ethnographic reportage," which Cherokee scholar and writer Daniel Heath Justice and non-Native literary scholar James H. Cox have noted has only recently been supplanted by an approach to Native literary criticism that eschews this ethnographic methodology in order to open "new areas of inquiry by shifting the keywords of scholarly conversation from identity, culture, and mediation to history, politics, citizenship, sovereignty, and diplomacy."[2] Though the works in this collection certainly touch on these topics (and more), *Shapes of Native Nonfiction* aims to move beyond an ordering that depends only on content, only on the information that Native authors can provide readers *about* Native peoples. Instead, we bring together the essays here to draw attention to the connection between, as Lenape scholar Joanne Barker and I-Kiribati scholar Teresia Teaiwa put it in the passage we have placed as an epigraph, "the telling and the material," between the content and the form.

For them (and for us), this attention to form (the telling) and how it shapes the content (the material) enables a move away from a focus on a static idea of "Native information" and, instead, emphasizes the dynamic process of "Native in formation." This shift destabilizes the colonial demand for factual information about Native life in favor of a framework that insists upon an understanding of indigeneity as a dynamic, creative, and intentional form which shapes the content that is garnered through its exploration. Here, Barker and Teaiwa lay the groundwork for apprehending the relationship between nonfiction and dynamic form:

> This is native *information*: autobiographical, fictional, anthropological, political, comical, statistical, governmental, theoretical, historical, ethnographic. . . . This is native *in formation*: as we have been informed by, as we are informing, as we are in-formed. It's about process, not stasis. It's not about romanticizing the dead of our history onto the sides of defaced mountains carved up for all time. It's about the way we move with time and with each other.[3]

With this in mind, we have paid special attention to the form of this collection itself in order to mirror the interest in form in the pieces herein. Throughout, we have understood this project as one meant to hold—to hold together and to hold in place. We connected to this deeply through the material vessel of the basket. As both a utilitarian and creative form that is connected to community and the individual, we see the basket not as a metaphor for this collection but rather as a structure (or form) through which to understand how the pieces included here come together in this space. As a practical matter, we also envisioned structuring the collection around the basket as a way to practice responsibility to place. We first conceptualized this project while living on Coast Salish territories in what is currently Washington State. Among Northwest Coast peoples, a wide variety of baskets are used for various purposes, such as root gathering, berry picking, and clamming. Elissa had the chance to hold one of Suquamish elder and master weaver Ed Carriere's baskets through which he told and contained the story of his life. Here we saw the shape of the material connection not only between place and the literary project we undertook but also to the conversation about form that we wanted to bring to the fore. Though written about extensively, the basket has often been of interest as an anthropological rather than a literary object—much like Native nonfiction.

Shape and Nonfiction

A text's form is its visible arrangement, determined by the organization of lines, paragraphs, stanzas, breaks, and other elements. Non-Native narrative theorist Caroline Levine describes the relationship between form and content(s): "Literature is not made of the material world it describes or invokes but of language, which lays claim to its own forms—syntactical, narrative, rhythmic, rhetorical—and its own materiality—the spoken word, the printed page. And indeed, each of these forms and materials lays claim to its own affordances—its own range of capabilities. Every literary form thus generates its own separate logic." Organizing principles, she argues, being abstract, "are iterable—portable. They can be picked up and moved to next contexts."[4] Just as a basket's purpose determines its materials, weave, and shape, so too is the purpose of the essay related to its materials, weave, and shape.

This is clear in the variety of forms and their varied uses throughout this collection. Most of these could be characterized as *lyric essays*, an approach described by non-Native poet Deborah Tall and non-Native essayist John D'Agata as one that "partakes of the poem in its density and shapeliness, its distillation of ideas and musicality of language. It partakes of the essay in its weight, in its overt desire to engage with facts, melding its allegiance to the actual with its passion for imaginative form."[5] This melding is apparent throughout the collection, though in different ways.

For instance, in her essay "Fertility Rites," Hunkpapa Lakota writer Tiffany Midge styles "the cusp of becoming" as both personal narrative and natural (dis)order. Offering glimpses into a journey around wetlands with a "devout amateur mycologist" named Mary, Midge's essay uses the interplay between scientific explanations of plant and animal reproduction and the prevalence of innuendo as the dominant collective monologue on sexuality to explore how language shapes our own senses of becoming. Inuit and Haitian Taino writer Siku Allooloo's piece "Caribou People" invokes a similar approach to the essay as Tall and D'Agata describe it, bringing together personal reflection, a report from an environmental action organization, family history, an interactive web documentary, Canadian history, and poetic language describing the landscape to offer a complex and nuanced glimpse at the evolution of life in Denedeh territory, including both the threats and resilience through which Allooloo experiences the land alongside her people. In each case, the authors depend on what Tall and D'Agata described above as the suturing together of fact and imaginative form, though each author depends on different facts and different forms.

The juncture, then, is not a rote, situated approach to form but rather is an experimentation. As Creek writer Chip Livingston points out in his essay, "I have also recognized other aspects in myself that suggest a somewhat contrary nature," including being mixed. After experimenting with various forms of writing, Livingston turned to the essay since this "contrary nature" meant that "it felt natural to challenge the rigid format" of his previous experience with news writing. In this way, though the authors experiment with form and its relationship to fact differently, there is a cohesion in how the contributors are using this experimentation in order to engage anew topics that overdetermine Native literatures without reifying popular tropes about Native peoples. Livingston's mirroring of mixed identity and the essay form refuses the figure of the "tragic mixed Native" while exploring the exigencies of living alongside multiple histories. By exploring the process of writing and disassociation in "Fairy Tales, Trauma, Writing into Disassociation," Upper Skagit and Nooksack writer Sasha

LaPointe discusses the legacies of violence through a form that refuses the overdetermination of trauma as the singular narrative of Native life, while insisting on recognizing the impact of collective experience on artistic production. And Navajo writer Bojan Louis reframes the uses of anger through a conversation with Antiguan writer Jamaica Kincaid, refusing to assuage the popular desire for either the angry warrior or disappearing Native by noting, "all right violence, you've had your limelight, now it's time for you to take the backseat and observe for the remainder of the trip. As for anger, it can always take the helm while I watch the passing landscape."

Non-Native poet and fiction writer Martha Ronk writes, "The lyric essay is shot through with the sort of semi-coherence that comes from recurring analogy, from an attention to language for its own sake, from the pleasures of the associative around an ill-defined center or shape."[6] This shape is formed by the twining and weaving of disparate parts, remembered and researched, with gaps as hefty as the poem's caesuras. In some cases, this is at the forefront, as in Billy-Ray Belcourt's use of the forward slash to evoke the process of citation in his essay that explores competing and cohabitating experiences of intimate relationships with another person, with oneself, with place, and with history. Or as in Kim TallBear's (Sisseton-Wahpeton Oyate) use of the structure of the 100-word mini essay to begin documenting her "autoethnographic polyamory practice." The sheer number of 100-word essays comes together to formally echo TallBear's desire to reframe promiscuity not as "random and indiscriminate" but as a practice that seeks "abundance through partial connections." The essays she offers as part of her "Critical Poly 100s" then are incomplete but echo Ronk's focus on semi-coherence not as a literary shortcoming but as an important contribution of the nonfiction essay.

Within the contours of this collection, such gaps characteristic of the lyric essay bring to mind those woven into a clam basket, which features wide spaces between woven cedar roots to allow water and sand to flow through while clams remain in the basket. This heightened awareness of the text's visual aspects works against the outmoded idea of Native nonfiction as nothing but a transcription of something that could have been or was delivered orally, a form that has drawn special attention due to the popularity of texts like John G. Neihardt's *Black Elk Speaks* as well as myriad transcriptions of famous speeches like those attributed to Nez Perce leader Chief Joseph and Duwamish leader Chief Seattle.[7] The writers and anthropologists who wrote Native life-stories were motivated by an impulse to capture *everything* about Native life before the complete vanishing they saw as inevitable. The gaps of the lyric essay can serve as resistance, the writer's refusal to catalog the details of their own lives for audience consumption. The lyric essay's associative leaps, from personal experience to researched material and back, show a breadth of experience and understanding that defies the diminishing into nonexistence through which settlement is structured.

While cultural appropriation is often an assimilative act when practiced by a subordinate group, the lyric essay can resist assimilation through the form-enabled boundaries between fragments and the overtness with which the "borrowed" or referenced material is included. For instance, in her essay "To the Man Who Gave Me Cancer," Cherokee writer and scholar Adrienne Keene references the medical language of "*in situ*" or "in its original place" to explore the confluence of abnormal cells that are "out of place" and what indigeneity looks like in the contemporary moment, drawing on the legacies of ancestors while keeping in mind the legacy of descendance. This mirrors vessels like huckleberry gathering baskets, which are often assembled from a weave of various materials, such as cedar bark and beargrass. Lyric essays are usually composed of several strands: lines of inquiry, subjects, or sources, while material from other sources appears alongside the narrator's experience and rumination. In basketmaking, visibly distinctive materials are used to make patterns; in the lyric essay, the differences in content and style from section to section are essential components of the form, creating tension through juxtaposition. These connections between creative nonfiction and basket weaving are notable. For instance, some Northwest Coast Native weavers combine traditional methods with innovative approaches to form, such as a basketry-covered light bulb or cedar-woven cowboy boots. This application of traditional methods to a non-traditional shape resonates with what Brenda Miller and Suzanne Paola have called the "hermit crab essay," or an essay created within the shape of another form.[8]

We conceive of the essay as an exquisite vessel, one that evidences the delicate balance of beauty and pain. The "exquisite" character of this vessel invokes simultaneously an exquisite work of art and the exquisite ache of an intense sensation. By bringing to the fore a focus on form, in both the structure and the concept of the collection, we use the term *exquisite vessel* not just to name the work done herein but to draw attention to form as a creative and literary practice of reverence for the exquisite in its most literal sense of something carefully sought out.[9] To *essay* is to try, test, and practice.[10] The form of the essay, then, is a fitting site for the experiential and sometimes painful work of seeking answers. Many of the essays contained herein linger in these painful places, exploring the legacies of trauma and violence extending from personal to collective inheritance. Many are haunting, and few offer easy answers. Such is the possibility of form-conscious nonfiction, though. To write nonfiction is to render experiences, memories, observations, and interpretations through prose, a process necessitating writer agency and allowing for emotional depth and transformation—not only of the narrator figure but of the writer who essays.

For Native writers, who have long operated within a literary sphere in which most depictions of Native lives are created by non-Natives, nonfiction allows for a revision of the dominant cultural narratives that romanticize Native lives and immobilize Native emotional responses: the essay is the work of feeling and thinking. It is the flux of a character, not a frozen image of one. As Bojan Louis writes,

Colonized people are murdered, raped, silenced, dehumanized, removed, extracted, have had their tongues and eyes cut out, have been fed to dogs, are made to hate themselves and their community members, assimilated, lied to, and on and on and on. A decolonized person seeks to shout, scream, relinquish their hurt and hatred, become the navigator of their self-image, obtain productive and healthy positions in and for the greater good of their communities; they look toward the future while continually waking up to the past.

This collection demonstrates that, here and elsewhere, Native writers don't shy away from experimenting with form in order to explore the painful and the violent. However, they refuse a voyeuristic obsession with tragedy as the ultimate possible contribution of Native literatures to the broader field. Instead, these essays evoke Louis's shout, scream, and relinquishing, all the while insisting on the recognition that Native writers offer innovative, astute, and transformative literary interventions that extend beyond either nostalgia or lamentation of a romanticized past and forever-destroyed future. Both are a myth.

Within this framework, our focus on form-conscious Native nonfiction insists on knowledge as a resource whose coercive extraction is used to narrate settler colonialism in order to normalize its structure. Concern with form has been central to the development of creative nonfiction as a distinct literary practice, especially evident in the explosion of interest in the lyric essay. Miller and Paola, whose work is foundational to our understanding of literary nonfiction generally and the lyric essay specifically, write that consciousness of form requires "placing your allegiance to artifact over experience." That is, form-consciousness serves as resistance against allowing the art of the essay to be collapsed with "the intractable stuff of memory and experience."[11] Form is the work of the imagination, bringing order, intent, and interpretation to the raw material of remembered experience. Of course, the imagination is developed from and situated within a writer's social and political context. Levine argues that forms serve as both aesthetic and social organizing structures: "Literary form does not operate outside of the social but works among many organizing principles, all circulating in a world jam-packed with other arrangements. Each constraint will encounter many other, different organizing principles, and its power to impose order will itself be constrained, and at times unsettled, by other forms."[12] For Native writers, nonfiction offers the opportunity to unsettle our/their positioning within literary publishing by asserting agency in recalling, narrating, organizing, and interpreting experience.

Native Literary Studies / Nonfiction Literary Studies

In addition to innovating the field of creative nonfiction writing and criticism, this collection's focus on form-conscious nonfiction writing also makes important contributions to Native literary studies. In the first place, the explicit focus on collecting contemporary nonfiction writing by Native authors begins to address a lacuna that Osage scholar Robert Warrior first identified in his book *The People and the Word: Reading Native Nonfiction*. As Warrior points out, substantial genealogies of the expansive history of Native writing have been obscured by the near-exclusive focus on fiction and poetry in Native literary criticism.[13] Warrior's literary readings of historical nonfiction texts, like the Osage constitution and newspapers written by Native students in boarding schools, evidences how the scope of Native literary history is expanded when we consider nonfiction texts and how the character of Native history is enriched when we categorize historical documents as literary texts. There is an exciting body of work on early Native writing that continues to enrich this history, including Abenaki scholar Lisa Brooks's work on the use of writing as a form of resistance among Native intellectuals in the colonial era; Cari M. Carpenter and Carolyn Sorisio's work on nineteenth-century writer and activist Sarah Winnemucca's performance, journalistic writing, and speaking tours; and Christine DeLucia's use of hymns in her historical work on King Philip's War and memory.[14]

However, this interest in nonfiction as part of the histories of Native resistance remains mostly focused on the nineteenth century. And the work on nonfiction that extends beyond this time period exists largely in the form of the anthologizing of Native autobiographical writing, which remains relatively limited on the broader scale of collected Native writings as well. By bringing together contemporary nonfiction writing by Native authors, we aim to extend this prominent focus on early Native nonfiction writing to solidify both a genealogy of such work and its transformation over time, while also better documenting the breadth of Native nonfiction writing beyond the autobiographical form. In doing so, we also hope to invite an approach to Native nonfiction that demonstrates the necessity of moving beyond the ethnographic method that we mentioned above. As the authors in this collection embark on the process of carefully crafting interventions that both challenge and expand genre conventions, they also confront the prolific undercurrent of the interpretation and discussion of Native nonfiction writing: the expectation that Native peoples remain as *subjects spoken about* rather than as the *subjects speaking.*

Though certainly present in the discussion of Native fiction and poetry, this method is particularly evident in the study and anthologizing of Native nonfiction writing. The majority of anthologized nonfiction work by Native authors is collected under the auspices of "autobiography," a misnomer because this label customarily applies to work encapsulating the author's entire life up to the point of composition and emphasizes content over craft. In this way, Native autobiography has become a metonym for Native nonfiction. In many of these collections, first-person narrative writing is collected in two particular ways: either as part of a lineage of such writing leading back to the eighteenth century or as a form of writing that can enrich our understanding of both the life experience and creative work of Native writers who otherwise primarily write fiction and poetry.

For us, the singular focus on autobiography represents an important limitation in and of itself. At best, this focus neglects a whole host of other nonfiction writing by Native authors that remains important to the intellectual history of Native literatures. At worst, it perpetuates an ethnographic approach to Native literatures, which assumes a methodological framework grounded in a desire for cultural authenticity that can be easily translated to and for a non-Native reader. Our approach rejects this as the primary purpose of Native literatures in general and of Native nonfiction writing in particular. We agree with Justice and Cox that this shift away from an ethnographic approach is essential to supporting "the intellectual and political sovereignty of indigenous communities and tribal nations" and, with this collection, we seek to remain cognizant of and accountable to the political stakes not only of first-person narrative by Native writers but of nonfiction itself as a creative and intellectual endeavor that engages critically both the substance and shape of story.[15] Our approach, then, moves beyond attempting to create a chronological lineage of Native first-person narratives in order to offer, instead, a glimpse into how contemporary Native authors use nonfiction to challenge conventional knowledge about form, structure, and the production of history. Rather than responding to what Arnold Krupat has referred to as the "virtually irresistible question of whether or to what degree Indian autobiographies give us the 'real' or 'authentic' Indian," we resist this question and push against its assumed centrality to the genre.[16] Instead, we present this collection of form-conscious Native nonfiction as an illuminating example of how contemporary Native authors use form to offer incisive observation, critique, and commentary on our political, social, and cultural worlds rather than only relegating their contributions to descriptive narratives of Native life.

This approach mirrors similar trends in the field of Native literary studies more broadly, particularly the shift away from an interpretive model that centers the settler state. For instance, the ascendancy of literary nationalism as a prominent critical approach urged us to pinpoint particular tribal and national locations as a necessary category of analysis.[17] As Creek scholar Craig Womack has argued, such an approach is necessary because the terms of critical analysis "in regards to analyzing Indian cultures have been owned, almost exclusively, by non-Indians. Radical Native viewpoints, voices of difference rather than commonality, are called for to disrupt the powers of the literary status quo as well as the powers of the state—there is a link between thought and activism, surely."[18] In recent years, this approach has been influential not only to the study of Native literatures but to the study of form within Native literary studies. For instance, works like Anishnaabe writer and scholar Molly McGlennen's *Creative Alliances: The Transnational Designs of Native Women's Poetry* and Cherokee scholar Sean Kicummah Teuton's *Red Land, Red Power: Grounding*

Knowledge in the American Indian Novel offer literary analyses that directly engage the question of form as an intrinsic element of the work that Native literature does in the world. With *Shapes of Native Nonfiction*, we present form-conscious Native nonfiction with this intention, not to offer insight into an insulated view of Native lives but instead to follow in the path laid by Muscogee writer Joy Harjo and Spokane writer Gloria Bird: to "turn the process of colonization around" so that Native literatures "will be viewed and read as a process of decolonization."[19]

It is this latter point that gestures most forcefully toward the broader work that we hope this collection will do. We've given a sense of this collection's contributions to both ongoing conversations and ongoing gaps in the fields of creative nonfiction and Native literary criticism. But this collection also contributes to more expansive conversations about the role of Native literatures in Native and Indigenous studies more broadly. As Justice argues in his recent book *Why Indigenous Literatures Matter,* these bodies of creative work offer important contributions to the world beyond literary circles or academia. He observes, "art without politics descends swiftly into self-referential irrelevance."[20] For him, Native literatures matter not only in the sense of being *relevant* to the world but in the actual *material* of this and future worlds as well. These bodies of work "remind us about who we are and where we're going, on our own and in relation to those with whom we share this world. They remind us about the relationships that make a good life possible."[21] This is also what we hope to emphasize through the focus on both form and nonfiction in this volume, epitomized in the use of the basket as the form of the collection itself. As our second epigraph points out, "although a basket is the unique creative product of an individual, its maker followed a set of traditions and cultural conventions." This process of interaction between the individual, the process of creation, the genealogies of knowledge, and the relationships built through craft is precisely the exquisite work that the authors herein perform. This work creates rather than merely reflects the world. As Tlingit writer Ernestine Hayes reminds us, "Stories perpetuate values of the culture from which they spring." Which world(s), then, are being created herein?

Through the selection of the form-conscious essays that follow, we seek to offer a glimpse into how contemporary Native writers use form as a practice in imaginative world-making to shape the page into a vessel. Most of these essays have been previously published in literary journals, online magazines, and elsewhere. Our intent in reprinting work is to show that while many readers lament the dearth of Native writers of any genre, Native literatures are, in fact, thriving: even with a focus on the lyric essay, we found ourselves overwhelmed by the abundance of exciting work already available to readers. Despite this, Native representation in contemporary nonfiction anthologies remains limited. As Amy Bonnaffons pointed out, the 2003 anthology *The Next American Essay*—edited by John D'Agata and significant in raising the profile of the lyric essay—contained only five essays by writers of color (including Spokane/Coeur d'Alene writer Sherman Alexie) out of thirty-two contributors. Bonnaffons notes that this is "particularly striking when the words 'next' and 'American' are in its title" and, for her, signals "a persistent yet misguided notion in the Academy that 'high art' and 'identity politics' are inherently contradictory."[22] And though Bonnaffons is discussing only one collection here, this is an issue that spans the anthologizing of nonfiction. This misguided notion is the very one that permeates approaches to Native nonfiction described above, which assume that Native authors writing nonfiction must always be explaining their lives as Native peoples. We seek, instead, to carefully curate a collection of nonfiction writing by Native authors that establishes the unique, pivotal work that such authors are doing to explore the boundaries of form in creative nonfiction writing and to challenge popular expectations of Native authors bound to desires borne of anthropological curiosity and colonial representation.

Structure

We've ordered this collection using terms for forms and components of basket weaving. The collection is structured around four particular terms: technique, coiling, plaiting, and twining.

Technique is for craft essays. "Basket makers attain control of technique to the degree that a basket is perceived as a harmonious whole. Such harmony can be achieved only by careful preparation of materials and technical perfection in construction."[23] For instance, Ernestine Hayes details the narrative craft elements of Tlingit oral storytelling to create a genealogy of form-conscious creative nonfiction that extends beyond the written word. In drawing on the practice of storytelling as form, Hayes begins the collection by centering place and land as the foundation upon which experimentation with form occurs.

Coiling is for essays that appear seamless. "Coiling begins at the center of a basket and grows upon itself in spiral rounds, each attached to the round before."[24] Coiled baskets can be woven so tightly that they can hold water; these essays, seamless and generally not fragmented in their approach, are constructed using transitional gestures that unify content far ranging in time, place, and meaning. Deborah Miranda's "Tuolumne" is such an essay, spanning her father's lifetime and beyond and using the Tuolumne River as a central point to which precise, temporally varied moments are attached.

Plaiting is for fragmented essays with a single source. "In plaiting, or checkerwork, two elements are woven over and under each other at right angles." Because the weft and warp are often identical in appearance and material, weft and warp can be indistinguishable in a flat piece, though the weaving itself is visible. For this reason, we apply this term to essays that are segmented in structure and include material from a single source, usually the author's lived experience. This is the case in Michael Wasson's "Self-Portrait with Parts Missing and/or Smeared," an essay that repeatedly offers hard breaks between short, evocative, imagistic segments crafted from memories that span Wasson's life.

Twining is for essays that bring together material from different sources. "Twined work begins with a foundation of rigid elements, or warp rods—around which two, and sometimes three or four, weft elements are woven. The wefts are separated, brought around a stationary warp rod, brought together again, and twisted. The action is repeated again and again, building the basket." We apply this term to lyric essays that combine the author's personal experience and narrator perspective with researched material, such as "Pain Scales Treaties" by Laura Da' where she brings together the pain of illness and the violence of Shawnee removal using the stylistic approach of a work of historical research. Often employing the methods of research-driven modes alongside the interiority of memoir, these essays mimic the flexibility of the twined basket.

Together, the essays described above and the many others collected here form an exquisite vessel. One that we hope remains open while carrying in it, with care, new methods and contexts for understanding the political possibilities of the essay form, the work of the Native nonfiction writer as maker, and both the historical and future shapes of Native nonfiction.

NOTES

1 Billy-Ray Belcourt and Lindsay Nixon, "What Do We Mean by #QueerIndigenousEthics?" *Canadian Art*, May 23, 2018, https://canadianart.ca/features/what-do-we-mean-by-queerindigenousethics.

2 James H. Cox and Daniel Heath Justice, eds., introduction to *The Oxford Handbook of American Indian Literature* (New York: Oxford University Press, 2014), 5.

3 Joanne Barker and Teresia Teaiwa, "Native InFormation," in *Reading Native American Women: Critical / Creative Perspectives*, ed. Inés Hernández-Avila (New York: AltaMira Press, 2005), 125.

4 Caroline Levine, *Forms: Whole, Rhythm, Hierarchy, Network* (Princeton, NJ: Princeton University Press, 2015), 7, 10.

5 Deborah Tall and John D'Agata, "The Lyric Essay," *Seneca Review* (blog), www.hws.edu/senecareview/lyricessay.aspx.

6 Martha Ronk, "Essay as Constellation," *Seneca Review* 37, no. 2 (Fall 2007): 54.

7 John G. Neihardt, *Black Elk Speaks* (Lincoln: University of Nebraska Press, 2014). For more on the speech attributed to Chief Joseph, see Kent Neburn, *Chief Joseph and the Flight of the Nez Perce: The Untold Story of an American Tragedy* (New York: HarperOne, 2006). For more on the speech attributed to Chief Seattle, see Albert Furtwangler, *Answering Chief Seattle* (Seattle: University of Washington Press, 1997).

8 Brenda Miller and Suzanne Paola, *Tell It Slant: Creating, Refining, and Publishing Creative Nonfiction* (New York: McGraw Hill, 2012).

9 From the Latin *exquīsītus*, past participle of *exquīrĕre*, "to search out." *Oxford English Dictionary*, s.v., "exquisite," accessed March 15, 2018, https://en.oxford dictionaries.com/definition/exquisite.

10 From the French *essayer*. See *Oxford English Dictionary*, s.v., "essay," accessed March 15, 2018, https://en.oxforddictionaries.com/definition/essay.

11 Miller and Paola, *Tell It Slant*, 90.

12 Levine, *Forms*, 7.

13 Robert Warrior, *The People and the Word: Reading Native Nonfiction* (Minneapolis: University of Minnesota Press, 2005).

14 Lisa Brooks, *The Common Pot: The Recovery of Native Spaces in the Northeast* (Minneapolis: University of Minnesota Press, 2008); Cari M. Carpenter and Carolyn Sorisio, eds., *The Newspaper Warrior: Sarah Winnemucca Hopkins's Campaign for American Indian Rights, 1864–1891* (Lincoln: University of Nebraska Press, 2015); Christine DeLucia, *Memory Lands: King Philip's War and the Place of Violence in the Northeast* (New Haven, CT: Yale University Press, 2018).

15 Cox and Justice, introduction to *Oxford Handbook of American Indian Literatures*, 8.

16 Arnold Krupat, introduction to *Native American Autobiography: An Anthology* (Madison: University of Wisconsin Press, 1994), 8.

17 For instance, see Jace Weaver, Craig Womack, and Robert Warrior, *American Indian Literary Nationalism* (Albuquerque: University of New Mexico Press, 2006); and Elizabeth Cook-Lynn, *Why I Can't Read Wallace Stegner, and Other Essays: A Tribal Voice* (Madison: University of Wisconsin Press, 1996).

18 Craig Womack, *Red on Red: Native American Literary Separatism* (Minneapolis: University of Minnesota Press, 1999), 5.

19 Joy Harjo and Gloria Bird, *Reinventing the Enemy's Language: Contemporary Native Women's Writings of North America* (New York: W. W. Norton and Company, 1998).

20 Daniel Heath Justice, *Why Indigenous Literatures Matter* (Waterloo, ON: Wilfred Laurier Press, 2018), xx.

21 Justice, *Why Indigenous Literatures Matter*, 6.

22 Amy Bonnaffons, "Bodies of Text: On the Lyric Essay," *Essay Review* (2016), http://theessayreview.org/bodies-of-text-on-the-lyric-essay.

23 Jacilee Wray, ed., *From the Hands of a Weaver: Olympic Peninsula Basketry through Time* (Norman: University of Oklahoma Press, 2012).

24 Descriptions of the practices of basket weaving in this and the following paragraphs are taken from "The Language of Native American Baskets from the Weaver's View," National Museum of the American Indian, http://nmai.si.edu/exhibitions/baskets/subpage.cfm?subpage=tech_tech.

TECHNIQUE

Contemporary Creative Writing and Ancient Oral Tradition

ERNESTINE HAYES

People are storytellers. We tell stories of bears, castles, fires, puppies, roses, and doorways and blood; of men who turn into wolves in the night and women who tame them if they choose. We tell stories of death and birth and happiness and grief. Stories of journeys and returns. Loss. Revenge. Sacrifice. Love. People have been telling stories since first we uttered sounds.

Stories perpetuate values of the culture from which they spring. In this country, fairy tales persisted generations beyond their European origin and now reinforce American values. For example, "Cinderella," with its rags-to-riches lesson, perpetuates the colonial myth that no matter the circumstances of birth, with patience, hard work, tiny feet, and a hand-some prince, any of us—indeed, all of us—can pull ourselves up by our petite bootstraps and become a princess. Another favorite, "Little Red Riding Hood," promotes a lesson of wild dangers surely met on a lone venture into the forest, and it teaches children that wolves are demons bent on eating their grandmothers, ears and all.

The concept of a dangerous unknown is a significant hallmark of sto-ries in America. Enemies, real and imagined, play important roles in shap-ing American values; symbols of threat and gained wealth perpetuated peculiar cultural ideologies for American settlers and continue to do so for their descendants. In popular American culture, stories that reinforce stereotypes, that promote particular values, that extol capitalism, that congratulate the hoarding of wealth and applaud corrupted power are heard wherever colonialism and capitalism have intruded. Which is to say virtually everywhere.

The stories a culture advances remain familiar even when methods of their delivery change. As Vine Deloria Jr. observed, "Instead of gathering around the elders in the evening to hear stories of the tribal past, children today rent a video tape and watch *Star Wars* or horror films."[1] Methods of delivery have expanded, but our reliance on telling stories hasn't changed; it is a characteristic upon which all human societies depend. The movie *Star Wars* and the horror films that figure in Professor Deloria's comment typify the stories that fulfill cultural purposes in the United States. Other American stories feature rockets in the night and flag sewing and brave pioneers who subdue a socially constructed wilderness, who civilize Natives, who deliver proper education and home cooking to unfortunate savages, and who bring about the most evolved, enviable culture built on freedom and equality that the world has ever known.

Or so the stories go.

But Indigenous artists tell different stories and advance different values. Indigenous artists are the storytellers of their generations. Indigenous artists are the history keepers of their generations. Indigenous artists are their generations' witnesses. As much as any fairy tale, those stories remain alive and carry their testimony into the millennia.

The history here recounted took place at the beginning of the Little Ice Age hundreds of years ago in southeastern Alaska in the place that is now called Glacier Bay, the ancestral homeland of the Chookaneidí clan of the Tlingit nation. In the Tlingit social structure, ties to the land are acknowledged by geographical divisions known as kwáans, which remain part of an individual's essential identity regardless of physical residence. Tlingit society also follows strict matrilineal descent, an intangible cultural association as powerful as the geographical tie. Awareness of the significance of place in Tlingit identity and of the crucial worth of young women in the matrilineal system is essential to an appreciation of the portion of Glacier Bay history examined here.

Glacier Bay history involves house groups of the Chookaneidí clan, one of which is the Burnt House, which is said later to have become the Kaagwaantaan clan, to which I belong. It is this cultural association that most directly allows me to cite this history, yet it is important to remember that any reference to this or any story not one's own must be done under the auspices of the group that holds rights to the intellectual property and must always acknowledge that legal ownership.

"The Girl Who Called the Glacier" is among many ancient stories recounted in *Haa Shuká, Our Ancestors: Tlingit Oral Narratives*, a landmark book of narratives told in the original language and translated by Nora Marks Dauenhauer and her husband, Richard Dauenhauer. Two versions of the story of Glacier Bay history are included in the book; one told by Susie James and another by Amy Marvin, both respected elders and acknowledged culture bearers of the Chookaneidí. Nora Marks Dauenhauer is a traditional Tlingit speaker; her husband, now deceased, was an accomplished Tlingit speaker. The stories in *Haa Shuká* were taped as they were told by elders in the Tlingit language and were later translated into the English language. Thorough notes are furnished, a comprehensive introduction prepares the reader for the book's literary challenges, and a brief biography of each elder is appended.

Stories are arranged in chronological order; the first is the story of the migration of the Basket Bay people to the coast. The history of Basket Bay, first related by witnesses to those events, was kept for generation upon generation and remains testimony to the integrity of oral tradition. The final story recounted in *Haa Shuká* is titled "The Coming of the First White Man," representing relatively recent history first told by witnesses who memorialized an ominous event full of portent. The Glacier Bay stories are placed just before the story of the first white men, indicating the approximate period in which these events occurred. In contemporary terms, the dates can roughly be estimated at what would now be approximately the year 1650.

Although the geographical area of what is now Southeast Alaska has undergone intermittent glaciation over several millennia, the most recent significant period of glaciation, popularly known as the Little Ice Age, is estimated to have commenced between six hundred and eight hundred years ago. The ice surge that covered Glacier Bay, which is the subject of this story, is thought to have occurred no less than three hundred years before the present day and may well have occurred earlier. If three hundred years is accepted as a fair estimate, that portion of Chookaneidí history was kept for some twelve generations before being written down by the Dauenhauers.

Haa Shuká describes the land at that place as being comprised of clay-like earth covered with grass, hence the name Chookaneidí—"people from the grassy place." In this part of Chookaneidí history, one family's daughter is in isolation due to menarche, then a customary practice. The girl has been closed off for some time and will soon re-enter public society to take her place in the community. She has remained in a curtained-off area at the back of the house as she learns the responsibilities she will assume as a woman. The story relates that she becomes bored and begins playfully teasing a glacier in the distance, thereby violating a number of cultural prohibitions. This transgression is witnessed by her younger sister, who runs to the front of the house and tells their mother. When the glacier begins to threaten the village in rapid advance, the mother confesses to the community what her daughter has done, whereupon the people realize they must abandon their homes and save themselves.

One of the many ways a storyteller enhances meaning is by showing the degree to which a character cares about an element of setting: an object, a place, a piece of clothing. Characters change and plot advances with transformation in place, objects, conditions, or beliefs, all elements of setting. In "The Girl Who Called the Glacier," interaction with the glacier and the people's reaction to the glacier's advance demonstrates this creative technique.

As a critical component of setting, place is not the stage upon which events occur but is rather an active participant in those events. This acknowledgment of the power inherent in place, which must exist in all elements of setting, appears in oral tradition and in contemporary writing. The glacier that is central to this story is the consciousness-possessing catalyst necessitating flight. When the people leave, they understand that the glacier is a participant in unfolding events, and they are also aware of the reciprocal grief that their absence will cause to the house, to the river, and to the land. Place is not limited to its definition as setting but is an active participant, not only in this story of this glacier's history, not only in an Indigenous way of seeing the world, but in the certainty of all life experience. Landscape, place, and the inspirited, living land is an active participant in our identity, our history, our experience, ourselves as much as any character is a participant in all our stories.

In *Haa Shuká*, Susie James begins the story with an invocation of the land. Her first line, *Gathéeni yóo áwé duwasáakw* names the land, and the second line—*wé haa aaní*—establishes the relationship between the land and the people. This introductory identification of the land explicitly establishes the landscape as a principal actor in the events that are about to unfold and reveals that the land itself is more than setting: the land is also character. The sentient glacier, the girl who calls the glacier, and her grandmother are all principal characters. Upon examination of the girl's precipitating actions, the glacier's response, and the grandmother's choice, the reader asks the question that memorable stories must raise: What happens next?

Plot organizes, structures, and relates a story's events. To hold interest, plot traces the changes from precipitating event to conflict to resolution. In this story, plot emerges as the organization of events that lead to the surprising, inevitable conclusion. The reader's perception of how these events are brought about, how these events lead to other events, and how these events affect the story's characters are illuminated by the story's setting and characters and by a reckoning of what must be the characters' thoughts.

In its relation to self-control and to respect, and in an understanding of the consequences of the violation of social virtues, thought enriches the primary theme, especially in the acknowledged effect of thought on respect and self-control. Dauenhauer directly relates thought to action, explaining the meaning of power and its relation to self-control, pointing out that several of the narratives contained in *Haa Shuká* involve a lack of self-control and a lack of respect for the power residing in non-human manifestations of sentient life.

Implied power is intrinsic to the cultural practice of isolating girls who are approaching menarche. The expression of power is evident in the effect of the girl's words and actions upon the environment in the form of the glacier that responds to her call. The power of the glacier is clearly demonstrated in the people's urgent flight and their reluctant abandonment of the village. The power of the spoken word is evidenced not only in the girl's utterances but also in the persistence of this important history via the spoken word from generation to generation.

Of all the instances of power in the story, the thoughts that prompt the girl's words, which themselves lead to terrible consequences, are perhaps the most convincing. Her power is manifested in speech, illustrating the power and meaning of spoken words. In this history, the girl's words are presented indirectly, but her grandmother, who stays behind in order to restore balance, speaks directly. The narrative by Susie James offers the grandmother's words:

> *This little granddaughter of mine/that broke the taboo*
> *I will take her place/I will take her place.*
> *I will stay in my mother's maternal uncles' house.*
> *I will simply stay/in my mother's maternal uncles' house.*
> *But this granddaughter of mine is a young woman.*
> *Children will be born from her./So you will take her aboard with you.*
> *But whatever happens to my maternal uncles'/house will happen to me.*

These words spoken by the maternal grandmother show that her sacrifice is made with future generations in mind. Her sacrifice not only placates the glacier and mitigates the girl's actions but also ensures the welfare of the community's future generations. Paula Gunn Allen notes in the introduction to *Spider Woman's Granddaughters* that isolation versus community is a characteristic theme of Native writing. This concept of community, validated here, is fundamental to our understanding of the cultural values perpetuated in Indigenous history-keeping. Cultural representations emerge as symbols of worldview and as emblems of cultural values the stories are meant to perpetuate. The witnesses who first memorialized these events and the generations who kept that history alive communicate those enduring values. By the events that are witnessed in this narrative, cultural values are affirmed, and our understanding of an Indigenous worldview is deepened.

All stories, including those memorialized in written work and in oral tradition, reveal the values and norms of the ages and cultures from which they spring—from news items to confessional memoir, from haiku to found poems, from historical fiction to science fiction. The account of this Chookaneidí history is no exception. The stories we read and the stories we tell are not exceptions. The stories we are told are not exceptions.

This American culture tells a story that the long record of Native use and occupation that took place before European contact is "prehistory." Indigenous groups, however, possess histories of thousands of years of occupancy and exodus, relocation and settlement, exploration and discovery, embedded throughout the generations in legal process, artistic declarations, symbolic regalia, and oral tradition at least as accurately and in many cases more accurately than the European system of writing that has been used for so many years to remove rights and appropriate lands. Before colonial contact, Indigenous cultures possessed vigorous legal systems, effective educational systems, efficient health systems, elaborate social orders, elegant philosophical and intellectual insights, sophisticated kinship systems, complex languages, profitable trade systems—every social institution needed for a culture to flourish for thousands of years, not the least of which is a brilliant method of history-keeping that employs elements we now call creative writing.

Tell this story: Had the colonial invasion not taken place, Indigenous people would still be living in the twenty-first century. Our lives would still be modern. Paved roads, airports, and electricity would still occur. Some things would be different. Our children would be receiving educations meant to lead to their success. We would not be so vulnerable to incarceration, alcoholism, poverty. We would be healthy. We would all be speaking our own languages. And we would still be telling our own stories.

We are engaged in the fundamental human activity of telling stories. Around the campfire, in films, on the page, we are witnesses to the events of our world. With our words, we keep the history of our present culture. With our words, we perpetuate our human values. With our words, we clarify our worldview.

We witness.

We witness.

We witness.

NOTE

1 Vine Deloria Jr., "Commentary: Research, Redskins, and Reality," *American Indian Quarterly* (Fall 1991), 460.

Letter to a Just-Starting-Out Indian Writer—and Maybe to Myself

STEPHEN GRAHAM JONES

1. *This isn't the Native American Renaissance.* That was a great and essential and transformative movement without even meaning to be a movement, but that was a different generation, with different issues. You're not resisting falling dead off the back of a horse anymore. You're not resisting people wanting to call you Billy Jack. You're not resisting the invisibility that comes from colonial mythmaking so much as you're resisting the voicelessness that comes from commodification. What you're resisting is headdresses on Reebok shirts. What you're resisting is only being on *Longmire* as some android who can't use contractions. And think about it: if you do stand up and try to fight for the same things those Native American Renaissance writers were fighting for, then you're pretty much saying that they didn't make any headway, that American Indian literature hasn't made any progress.

2. *Don't be an elf.* That's what America wants you to be. Elves are liminal beings. They live close to the spiritual source. They commune with nature. They're stewards of the trees. They belong in the forests. They cry because of Dr. Pepper bottles in the creek. Also, as it turns out, they're made-up, they're not real. If you're an elf, you don't exist, and

like that America's won, who cares if your profile is Che Guevara'd onto a T-shirt. One thing about those profiles: They're silhouettes. They're the shape of us, but it's that End-of-the-Trail mode that says we've come as far as we can, and it was a good fight, but now it's time to die, now it's time to fade into that sunset looming behind us. And it's such a picturesque, compelling image that we even kind of hesitate, don't we? Learn not to hesitate. Be faster than that. Be so fast that the silk-screeners can't capture your image on polyester. Either that or start your own T-shirt shop.

3. *Sometimes the way not to be an elf? It's to write about elves.* Go on, get out there, traffic in the genres typically denied to Indians. That we're not allowed to do fantasy or science fiction and the rest, it's both stereo-typing us and it's primitivizing our writing: It's saying we can't play in the branches that come off literature with a capital *L*. We can't go out on the branches because our literature is still "formative;" it's still in its infancy. Not letting us write for the commercial shelves is saying we have to write "form" before writing free verse, but it's also getting to designate what that form is. Resist that every chance you get. Sneak over the line every time you can. Write where you're not supposed to write, and then move on, do it on the next shelf over too. And the next, on down the line. Leave the whole bookcase red.

4. *Don't ask for permission to do what you do.* I'm not talking about permission from your family or friends, your clan or nation or chosen representative or role model or idol. I'm talking about the critics who give your work the seal of approval, where "approval" means inclusion in the classroom. Yes, it's great to be in the classroom; it's an honor, but it's also great to be everywhere. Really, it's better to be everywhere. If you ask the critics to be the main and only gatekeepers, then you're chaining your work to the trends and fads of criticism—which is to say, you might be setting yourself up for not getting through that gate.

Trick is, don't even worry about the gate. Sneak down the road, jump the fence, and then tell everybody else how to get across as well.

5. *Understand that a lot of the time when your work is discussed, the question being asked about it isn't necessarily going to be Is it good?* So many readers and critics and students and professors, they don't engage the writing as art; they engage it as an ethnographic lens they can use to focus attention on peoples and cultures and issues and crimes and travesties and all the "other" that'll fit in a discussion. Resist this too. Resist this hard. Insist that your work be dealt with as art, not as an entry point to a culture. But understand that the only means you *have* to resist this, it's your writing, it's your art. So write better. Write in ways that refuse to submit to the kinds of discussions that neglect your work's status as real and actual art. Any discussion that doesn't start with Is it good, that means the presumption is that it *is* good, and that presumption, then, it's usually wound up with the fact that you're Indian, meaning the argument is "Indian is good," which is another way of saying "authentic is good." And this is so, so dangerous.

6. *So, don't ask for permission, no. But don't ask for forgiveness either.* You're going to mess up. You're going to say things you wish you hadn't, or that you wish you'd said better. It's part of the nature of writing or speaking aloud that you misspeak, that you write a line you wish you could reel back in. Just keep moving on. Don't let that flubbed line define your career, your stance, your identity. Hide that flubbed line with ten thousand perfect bulletproof timeless lines. Be a different writer each time you turn the page. Anytime you see that dissection pin coming down for the center of your back, close your eyes and roll somewhere else.

7. *Understand that when the audience or the market or the critics refer to you as an "American Indian Writer," that this is an attempt to dismiss you, to*

preserve you on a shelf, to prepare you for display. What you are is a writer who happens to be American Indian—a characteristic that may define you as a person, yes, but you're maybe also a basketball player, or a pretty good carburetor rebuilder, or maybe you can draw hands so delicately that we want to reach into the page to touch them. None of that gets turned into an adjective in front of "Writer," though. Neither should "American Indian" or "Native American" or "Blackfeet" or whatever. Indians having to have pedigrees to get into the show makes racehorses or show dogs of us. And it means we have to carry some version of our registration around with us too.

8. *Understand that the market, the publishing industry, it's going to want to package you as "exotic,"* as somehow foreign and alien on a continent you didn't need anybody's help finding. Always resist this. Always displace that alienness back onto them. But in doing so, be careful of pretending that you didn't cut your own teeth at the cineplex, at the local comic book shop. It's completely okay to let John Rambo be your hero instead of Crazy Horse. To say otherwise is to let America tell you this is for us, this is for you. Take whatever you want, and take it precisely *while* the guards are watching. Dare them to tackle you in the aisle. Then come back the next day with a hat pulled low over your face, do it all over again.

9. *In the same way, don't let people shame you about not being an expert on your own culture.* You don't have to be. Did you sign up to be the official record keeper or historian for your nation, or for all of the nations? You didn't sign up for anything, really. You just happen to be who you are. Maybe you speak your nation's language, maybe you don't. Maybe you grew up on the reservation, maybe you didn't. Maybe your blood's at some level the government prefers, maybe it isn't. Maybe your nation signed a treaty back when, maybe it didn't. Maybe your cheekbones or your hair are what somebody wants to call "wrong." The people who care about that? They're the ones who want to put up a higher fence around

whatever country club they're already in. Trying to meet their criteria, then, it's asking to be let inside, so you can keep others out. Try try *try* not to start playing that game on the page. Yes, if we all still had our language, that would be all right. It wouldn't be bad to, you know, have all our own land back either. Yes, things have been stolen, and yes we need to hold onto things, and how you feel about that will serve as fuel for your words, definitely. Just be wary of ever allowing yourself to think that your "Indian experience" matters any less than any other Indian's experience, or any other model of "Indian experience." That creates hierarchies, which leads to the authenticity shuffle, which is an ugly, ugly dance to do for all the people who really want us to do it. Us doing that dance, it keeps us looking at each other, not the world.

10. *Don't have a checklist to address in your writing.* Yes, *have* a social agenda, a list of grievances. Pissed off is far and away the best place to write from. If you don't have an axe to grind, you don't need to sharpen it with your words. Always keep that axe close at hand. But don't let it reduce your writing to thinly disguised reform. The real reform, it's that you, who are supposed to be invisible, who's supposed to just be a silhouette on a T-shirt, a painting in a motel, a design on a blanket, you have a voice, you can speak, you can make wonderful challenging art. And remember that it's always about the art. If it starts to be about you and your "identity" or any of that, then people aren't engaging your words on the page, they're looking up between every sentence, for you. Write better, then. Make them unable to look up.

11. *Step on everybody's toes in the room, always.* Chances are you're young, can outrun whoever takes offense. But some of those old cats are still pretty fast, too, so be ready to fight as well.

12. *Step on FORM's toes.* Just be prepared for people wanting to read this innovation as a callback to the oral tradition or an appeal to a different aesthetic. Unless that's true—and I've never known it to be—please

don't ratify that. But don't speak against it either, as you'll be protest-ing too loudly, and people will nod, say behind their hands, "Look, the Indian thinks she's trying to be modern, but really she's still ancient." "Ancient" is where the world wants us to be. Ancient things are buried in the past; ancient things belong in museums. You're doing new things on the page. Just keep doing them.

13. *You don't have to be able to define what an Indian is in order to write "Indian."* Putting a definition on us, that's playing their game, that's submitting to being an entry in an encyclopedia. That's saying yes, you drew the boundaries well, I will live just in this little block of text. Instead, just, you know, *write*. If you are Indian, whatever "Indian" might be, then whatever you do, that's Indian as well. You can't *not* do it. It only messes your writing up to try to adopt a persona or put on a headdress to write. When you do that, your voice will probably get all noble and stoic, and then, yes, you may as well be falling dead off the back of a horse. Where you'll land will be a John Wayne movie. And that's a bad place for an Indian to have to spend forever. It's a bad place for an Indian to even spend ten minutes.

14. *You don't have to answer Who are you writing for?* A better question: Who are you writing *against?*

15. *Your writing doesn't have to be "responsible"* as regards representation or culture or any of that. That's not part of your charge as a writer. Your charge as a writer, it's to be sincere, whether you're writing about six-armed Martians or your uncle that time he said he could change the brakes with a blindfold on. Any art that tries to be responsible, it stops being art. Art isn't responsible. Art challenges, art breaks things, art leaves before the tab's been paid. And hopefully it does some good as well. Hopefully it breaks the right things more often than it breaks the wrong things. But sometimes you just have to break everything.

16. I don't know what to call this exactly, but when you meet somebody who's into a certain type of music, say, then you spend the first little bit of discussion establishing your bona fides, don't you? Sure, I know Zep, who doesn't, but let's burrow down in the garage of 1978 some, be sure we're each actually committed to this. Same thing happens when you're from a certain region, or when you grew up without money, or when you play basketball or hunt or used to cheerlead or any of that. It's natural. It's how we judge whether you're worth talking to on this subject. It's how we navigate tastes, so as to avoid blunders later on. All of which is good and fine and unavoidable. But please note that this is happening in American Indian writing more and more, where the first little bit of a piece isn't the writer telling the story but the writer establishing he or she is really Indian by showcasing "expected Indian things," exhibits 1 through 8. This is often cleverly disguised—until you start noticing it. And it seems benign. It's not. What it is is us submitting to the process of legitimization. It's taking a blood quantum test on the page. It's having to "prove" ourselves. It's asking the audience to please now turn to the author photograph, to see if this is a real true Indian or not. And, at that point? You're already losing. Instead just *assume the Indianness.* Of everything. Overwrite the world with *us.* Because we are everywhere. We're in the soil, yes, but we're in the future too. Insist upon that.

17. Please please please *let there be bad Indians?* The cruelest form of essentialism is that which we lay on ourselves. And it's our knee-jerk response, too. Have the Indians be the heroes? Sure, of course. If it feels like resistance, it must be resistance. But if we're always the good guys—which, in Indian stories often translates out to "victim," as being the hero in a trauma drama isn't really the same as putting on a superhero cape and saving the day—then we may as well sign up to be noble as well. And understand that us being the bad guys sometimes, that means that somebody who's not Indian might be a good guy.

Granted, your writing might not be as simple as "Good Guys vs. Bad Guys." But at some level, that's always exactly what it is. Never mind that you used up all your gray crayons drawing this situation out and stole your kids' gray crayons too. Yes, steal back the comic narrative if you can do it honestly—steal back everything you can, then put it in a pile and burn it—but your writing, if it's sincere, then it's going to go where it goes too. Your job as a writer of real words, it's to follow those words, these characters, and to render them so real and so true that the reader forgets she's reading about these supposedly exotic "Indians" with all these complicated, "tragic" issues, and starts instead just reading about people. Gerald Vizenor says that being Indian is an act of the imagination. I've always been drawn to that, but until writing all this out, I don't think I ever really understood it. I'm starting to, though. It's not exclusively an act of the imagination on our part, but on the readers' as well. Through our words, our art, we infect the world with not what we are—we're not a "what"—but with *who* we are.

Funny, You Don't Look Like (My Preconceived Ideas of) an Essay

CHIP LIVINGSTON

Introduction

My approach to the lyric essay is indicative of my approach to many things, sidewinding or crab-walking back and forth in different directions and genres in my progress toward identifying the lyric essay as a form I wanted to work in—in both its short and long formats.

As a mixed-blood person, born from a Creek Indian and French mom and Scottish American dad, I have always known a kind of dual identity in terms of, "I am this one thing, but at the same time, I am also this other thing." And because I have blue eyes and light skin, my mom's family always joked around about my appearance—from saying I was actually the son of the red-headed mailman, which indicated that I didn't really belong, to saying my granny won a bet with a wolf for its eyes, which made me feel special and prized. But it wasn't until second grade that I remember being challenged by white classmates that I couldn't be Indian because I had blue eyes. That's when I truly began seeing myself as two separate things, both white and Native. When I began analyzing in what circumstances I was seen as one thing and in which scenarios I was seen as another, I learned, as children do, how to behave in ways that made me feel most comfortable in one world or another—or maybe it's more accurate for me to say that I learned how to behave in ways that would make me feel, in any way, less uncomfortable.

By second grade I had also learned I was different in terms of gender expectations. And long before I knew the terms *gay* or *two spirit* to identify myself, I knew what behaviors elicited what kinds of responses, or what to hide from whom (my dad) and when (always). But seeing myself as several things that didn't meet the standard classifications, I began to understand some level of hybridization in identity and to project an image of the desired thing, that at times perhaps was misleading or hiding the complete truth.

When I was in seventh or eighth grade, I went with my mother to her new male hairdresser's house, and in that chic, ultra-gay, fashionably restored old salon, I discovered Andy Warhol's *Interview* magazine. At first I was drawn to the quirky style and design, the photo spreads that were elegant and androgynous, artful and erotic, and the whole magazine (and the hairdresser's home salon) seemed to be offering up glimpses of a world I'd never seen. I tried to accompany my mom every time she got her hair done, and I talked her into letting me subscribe to the magazine. At home, I started reading the articles in *Interview*, and I got familiar with the columnists.

When each oversized issue arrived—this was before its current size and format—I'd immediately turn to Christopher Makos's photo spreads to see the cute guys featured, and then I'd turn to Glenn O'Brien's column, Glenn O'Brien's Beat. I wanted to see what he had to say each month. Actually, I didn't really care that much what he talked about; I wanted to see *how* he said it.

I remember very well a particular essay he wrote on the essence of being cool, on being hip, and it made me want to be a journalist. O'Brien's columns were marked by their smart, witty prose and astute assessments of pop culture's extreme edge. And I do remember one line, how O'Brien moved from a description of what was considered "hip" at the time, that when "two hipsters got together, they did the bump." And it was this movement from *hip* as an adjective to *hip* as a noun that shocked and delighted me. It marked a kind of play, this kind of aside and irreverence to a strict following of a thesis, that made me pay attention to O'Brien's essays, which were often segmented or bulleted and marked by wild leaps and breaks in continuity, and unlike any writing I'd yet seen back in the early 1980s.

In journalism school at the University of Florida, I discovered news was not where my writing interests lay, and I ended up majoring in magazine journalism, which let me slide a little from the hard facts-only approach and concentrate on feature stories. But I still wanted to take greater liberties and re-create a whole new story, something not entirely made up but with slight additions of imagination to present something more entertaining. And while the new creation may not necessarily retain its factual accuracy, I saw how the form and arrangement (or rearrangement) of facts could affect or slant the conclusion. And this got me a step closer to the lyric essay. I ended up doing dual degrees, completing a BA in English just after my BS degree in journalism. And by then I'd decided I wanted to be a fiction writer.

I have also recognized other aspects in myself that suggest a somewhat contrary nature, so it felt natural to challenge the rigid format of news writing, but in all of my classes—especially if there was a creative element like a paper or presentation—I was prone to extremely creative interpretations of assignments. A lot of this was honest rebellion, but some of it was just to keep things interesting, for the teachers as well as myself. I didn't want to turn in the same essay on a given subject that everyone else did. I wanted my writing to stand out from the others'.

I remember in graduate school for fiction at the University of Colorado, my professor, Linda Hogan, gave us the assignment to write a one-page story in a novel workshop. When she returned mine to me, she had written across the bottom, "This is a poem." It was the first time I'd written a poem since third grade, and it was entirely unintentional. But my love of lyrical and surprising language and syntax had permeated this short-short story, and Linda's remark resounded in what my fiction might also be considered.

During this same graduate work, the poet Ai was a visiting writer at CU, and she dared me to take her poetry workshop. The first intentional grown-up poem I ever wrote, which was an assignment for that workshop, was a series of fifty dramatic monologues based on the Edgar Lee Masters classic, *Spoon River Anthology*. That assignment became my first published poem, for which I successfully argued to be paid at the higher fiction rate since "it told a story" in fifty voices, and that writing was republished as a short story in my most recent prose collection. And today, knowing what I know about creative nonfiction, and because each of the speakers in my monologue series is based on a real person and what they say is based on what they either said in real life or what I thought they'd say, my piece, titled "Anthology of a Spoon River AIDS Walk," I would consider today to be a lyric essay.

Brenda Miller, in her book *Tell It Slant: Creating, Refining, and Publishing Creative Nonfiction*, talks about shaping the lyric essay as braiding a loaf of challah bread, illustrating how the lyric essay is often an interweaving of several threads loosely associated with a shared topic. But using Miller's braiding metaphor as my transition, I'm going to switch gears now and leave the autobiographical strand of my introduction and switch over to some other writers' interpretations of the lyric essay and ask that you look at some of their creations.

Girl Machine

In 1971 Andy Warhol asked his friend the poet and librettist Kenward Elmslie to write a "think piece" on the film director Busby Berkeley for *Interview* magazine. Berkeley was an avant-garde director and choreographer working in the 1920s to 1940s and, quoting Wikipedia, "was famous for his elaborate musical production numbers that often involved complex geometric patterns. Berkeley's works used large numbers of showgirls and props as fantasy elements in kaleidoscopic on-screen performances."

Elmslie has often spoken about being given this assignment and how he was at a loss on what he should write about him. Now consider that Elmslie was educated at private schools and graduated from Harvard and knew very well how to write an essay. And yet what Elmslie turned in as his essay/

article/think piece on the filmmaker, and what Warhol published, was something titled "Girl Machine," which looked and read very much like a poem.

From "Girl Machine" by Kenward Elmslie

my nerves my nerves I'm going mad
my nerves my nerves I'm going mad
round-the-world
hook-ups
head lit up head lit up head lit up
the fitting the poodle
MGM MGM MGM
MGM MGM MGM
MGM MGM MGM
the fitting the poodle

What a life just falling in and out of
What a life just falling in and out of
swimming pools
xylophones WANTED xylophones
WANTED female singer WANTED
bigtime floorshow   bigtime floorshow
bigtime floorshow   bigtime floorshow

Busby Berkeley
silhouetted in moonlight moonlight
silhouetted in moonlight moonlight
mysterious mirrors
Gold Diggers of Blankety Blank
Clickety Clack   Clickety Clack
swell teeth   not news
swell teeth   not news
woo-woo   woo-woo
woo-woo   woo-woo
Gold Diggers of Blankety Blank
Clickety Clack   Clickety Clack

swell teeth
mysterious mirrors

> mysterious mirrors
> Busby Berkeley
>
> shiny black surfaces
> shiny black surfaces
> shiny black surfaces
>
> a girl machine
> a girl machine
>
> work work work   work work work
> work work work   work work work
> work work work   work work work
> work work work work work
>
> show gets on and is a smasheroo
> show gets on and is a smasheroo
> round-the-world
> hook-ups
>
> Busby Berkeley is the Albert Einstein
> of the movie mu
> Quantum Leap
> Babe Rainbow
> Girl Machine   Girl Machine
> Quantum Leap
> Babe Rainbow
> Girl Machine   Girl Machine

Clearly this creation, on the page, appears visually as a poem, and there's little doubt that it is, in reality, also a poem, but it's become much more than that. It's actually become one of Elmslie's signature performance pieces and has been recorded in various incarnations as a song, has been put to video with artwork by Joe Brainard, and was incorporated into the stage production of *Lingoland*, an off-Broadway review of Elmslie's lyrics and sung poems. But given that it was assigned and received and originally published as an essay, granted an essay by a poet, and granted an essay as classified by the whacky Warhol, and given that "Girl Machine" explores, if somewhat in imitation, the movie musicals it is "reporting on," I think part of what the lyric essay begs readers to do is to be willing to expand our definitions of what's in front of us—or what we're looking at.

Orange Dream

It's probably unfair to present something as initially abstract as "Girl Machine" to exemplify the lyric essay, so consider a piece by Wang Ping called "Orange Dream," in which Ping expounds upon the cultural history of the orange in China.

It begins with two short unpunctuated lines: "Orange trees have roots in the earth" and "We migrants have roots in our souls"—interjecting quickly this resonating duality before launching into a description of the land where the oranges grow and the people who cultivate and revere them. Readers receive the narrative of the orange harvest, the making of the baskets that receive them for transport, as well as the symbolic and culinary significance. We read about oranges through the history of the Chinese dynasties and the movement of China from agriculture to industry. We have the geography of China's rivers and deltas, and we end in literal lyrics of a song sung about orange trees.

Ping's "essay" is clearly closer to what we expect when we think of short creative nonfiction, but Ping calls her creation a poem, and she writes many like them. In many ways, "Orange Dream" isn't so far from the traditional essay, but if it's examined section by section, or paragraph by paragraph, one thing that is evident is the lack of transitions between groups of information. I think a lack of connective tissue among a lyric essay's parts is a significant characteristic of the form—and yet, despite the lack of transitions in "Orange Dream," the sequencing of the elements allows the narrative to flow with rationale.

Another capacity of the lyric essay, which I think Ping's "poem" illustrates, is how well the component parts of the piece can often be taken apart and those individual pieces stand alone and function singularly. Almost every paragraph in "Orange Dream" could be isolated and published independently as an individual micro-nonfiction or prose poem.

If "Orange Dream" were shortened and sectioned, it might read very much like Wallace Stevens's classic poem "Thirteen Ways of Looking at a Blackbird." And vice versa, if Stevens's lines were extended and formatted like prose, published today his work might very well be classified as a lyric essay.

The Way to Rainy Mountain

N. Scott Momaday's classic, *The Way to Rainy Mountain*, though a book-length work of nonfiction, has all the characteristics of an extended lyric essay. For one thing, the text is sectioned and arranged by form rather than linear composition. The text is also braided, following three (or depending on your reading, four or five) strands of context or stories that intermingle and cross over and comment on each other. *The Way to Rainy Mountain* comprises memoir, legend, historical evidence, illustration, and white space.

Momaday uses at least three voices—the autobiographical, the ancestral, and the historical/anthropological—to trace the Kiowa's migrations and forced removal to Oklahoma. The illustrations done by Al Momaday, the author's father, also tell a visual story and can be argued to be a fourth voice in the collage of the Pulitzer Prize–winning author's memoir. The expansive white space and sectioning of the voices has also been widely analyzed for its breath, breadth, and silence.

Definitions by D'Agata and Tall

In 1997 *Seneca Review* began to publish what its editors chose to call the lyric essay. Deborah Tall and John D'Agata wrote the introduction to a special issue on lyric essays, and the following quotes are taken from that introduction:

The lyric essay partakes of the poem in its density and shapeliness, its distillation of ideas and musicality of language. It partakes of the essay in its weight, in its overt desire to engage with facts, melding its allegiance to the actual with its passion for imaginative form.

The lyric essay does not expound. It may merely mention. As Helen Vendler says of the lyric poem, "It depends on gaps. . . . It is suggestive rather than exhaustive."

It might move by association, leaping from one path of thought to another by way of imagery or connotation, advancing by juxtaposition or sidewinding poetic logic.

Generally it is short, concise, and punchy like a prose poem. But it may meander, making use of other genres when they serve its purpose: recombinant, it samples the techniques of fiction, drama, journalism, song, and film.

Storyless, it may spiral in on itself, circling the core of a single image or idea, without climax, without a paraphrasable theme.

The lyric essay stalks its subject like quarry but is never content to merely explain or confess. It elucidates through the dance of its own delving. . . . While it is ruminative, it leaves pieces of experience undigested and tacit, inviting the reader's participatory interpretation.

My Body Is a Book of Rules and Hermit Crab Forms

By these definitions of the lyric essay, Cowlitz memoirist Elissa Washuta provides numerous perfected examples in her linked collection, *My Body Is a Book of Rules*, in which the essays take the shape of a variety of new and familiar forms. Washuta catalogs the drugs she was prescribed and their effects in "Prescribing Information," an essay that becomes much more than a list; we're given the events in the author's life while she is taking the prescriptions and the reasons why she is taking them. In these entries, similar to the overall effect of the influential early books she read in "Preliminary Bibliography," Washuta shares the other aspects of her life—sexuality, music, depression, education, writing, and more. Her essay, "I Will Perfect Every Line Until My Profile Is Flawless," takes the form of a Match.com dating profile—with revelatory footnotes. Another of Washuta's essay, "Sexually Based Offenses," imagines a script for an episode of *Law and Order* as the format for her own reporting of a rape.

Washuta is deftly using what has become known as a hermit crab essay, where the structure already exists and the author moves into it to construct an essay that fits the borrowed form. A short list of possible hermit crab forms that we might use to write about our experiences include:

Treasure maps

Restaurant/movie reviews

Yard sale tags; Craigslist/eBay items

Menus

Recipes

Owner's manuals

Contents labels, warning labels

Customs and border patrol forms

Jokes

Answering machine messages

Vows and other kinds of loyalty oaths

Wedding/Divorce announcements

Family Trees

Card catalog entries

Drug label warnings applied to other aspects of life that need warnings

Census forms

Fairy tales

Horoscopes

How-to guides

Field guides

Crossword puzzles

FAQs

Doctor's notes

To-do lists

Social media feeds

Road atlases

Movie poster taglines

News headlines

Life of a sweater or other clothing items

Tables of contents

Advertisements

Day planners

Course descriptions

Why Use the Lyric Form?

I think it's worth noting that using a prescribed or novel form for an essay provides a certain distance from the subject matter, and that's why I think lyric forms are often appropriate for those difficult-to-write-about moments, like grief.

Another reason to use form is when writing about universal situations that most of us have experienced or witnessed, very likely already read about in a dozen different narratives; the lyric essay is a way to reinvent the wheel, so to speak—to put a new spin on a well-known part of life. They say we authors are always writing the same stories; we're just personalizing it or framing it in different ways.

Conclusion

I started out by discussing how I learned to slip in and out of different identities and how I was drawn to that similar elusiveness of the lyric essay once I identified the genre-crossing creature as I know it. Since "discovering" the form for myself a few years ago, I wanted to write an intentional lyric essay. And when I came back to the United States from Uruguay a few years ago, I came upon a subject I thought would be interesting to write about. The week before our flight, my puppy, who was almost a year old, went into heat for the first time. We flew into Miami, where we rented a car and drove across the country to Colorado, visiting my family on the way, and my dog, poor Frida, really didn't know what was happening inside her body or where I was taking her body, in planes and cars, to visit with nephews and nieces who spoke English and dropped Easter candy on the floor, and hotel rooms with weird smells after days in a car stuffed with suitcases and lamps and anything I could pick up along the way that would fit in a rented SUV—to set up a new home in the States.

And when we finally arrived in Colorado, there was a late April snow, and Frida, still in heat, experienced her first taste of winter, having to pee and poop in cold white stuff that stuck to her feet and fur. I tried to imagine what my dog must have thought, or if she could be given voice, what she might say about the experiences she had flying from South America and driving across North America in her tender emotional and physical state.

For my lyric essay, I thought I'd make it accurate, at least to the itinerary and the images I included in the piece, but since it was from a dog's point of view, I didn't know if it could be considered nonfiction, but anyway, I thought I'd take wild associative leaps. My dog's an artist in her sensibility. She's named after Frida Kahlo. She knows abstraction. And I planned to make it sectional, for each major stop of our journey. And once we found an apartment and moved into it, and once I'd found a desk and got my computer set up on it, I sat down with the intention of writing the lyric essay about Frida's first heat cycle and the trip across the United States.

I was pleased with what I eventually got onto paper and the form it was taking, and once I revised it a few times, I thought it was ready to send out. I had planned to send it to the now-defunct *South Loop Review*, which specialized in lyric essays, but looking at its submission guidelines I saw that the journal was taking a sabbatical while reinventing itself as an online magazine called *(Punctuate)*, and they were not currently taking submissions. I was at a temporary loss, because what I had written I worried would look more like a poem to other editors. But I saw a call for submissions from the online "beast of a literary magazine," *Animal*, looking specifically for creative writing about animals, so I sent my piece about Frida to the poetry editor. I was afraid it was too abstract to be considered an essay in this journal, which I considered pretty traditional if somewhat limited in its content. I got a response in a few weeks from the poetry editor, asking to publish the piece I'd submitted, "The Heat Run."

My lyric essay was going to be published as a poem; there were worse things that could happen, and I like the magazine *Animal*, so I was happy it would find a home there. I said, "Yes, it's available. It's yours and I'm thrilled." And I was—but not as thrilled as I was a couple of months later when I received an email from the poetry editor of *Animal* saying that he had just left an editorial meeting where the nonfiction editor of *Animal* had read my poem and was hoping it might be published as an essay!

So that, I offer in conclusion, was a recent prideful moment: I had written a lyric essay so abstract that I felt almost bashful calling it nonfiction, and yet when it was read incidentally by a nonfiction editor, she fought for the right to rightfully reclassify it. And I offer again now my first intentional lyric essay, "The Heat Run," to conclude this short discussion of the recently popularized nonfiction form.

The Heat Run

VII

That slip in the shower was just enough aquajet punishment on the dwindling blossom to warm back into the frenzy. Washed hot toward the hip shimmy and shoulder dig. Sit. Down. Stay.

VI

Manic spin of new macho. Pre-everything sniff. Pre-bite. Pre-jump, pre-squat, pre-one leg lifted, or stand still and stream. Mark your territory, mark my territory. And thrust just dominance. A dance to balance the whump and bark of preteen masturbation. Everything a growl. Everything purr. Everything whine.

V

Off leash in a mile-high tailspin. Undiapered into iced quicksand. Mountain trail lain down and maintained, browsed, parked. Mud carpet and overhang green. Solar wind fields and sunflower screens. Blood pooling from a leg-shaking sleep but the comforter resoluble. Humanology floorboarded. The pull. The whistle. The stone.

IV

Hotel dramaturges extending corded autos: Salinas. Back at the back of the Days Inn. Kennelled and concreted. Cabbaged. The opposite of prairied. Deflocked and almost desoldiered. Beet-juiced bedspread and eight blankets of credit. Suddenly breasts, suddenly perked, suddenly root-vegged.

III

Little knots tangling, nerves ripening, some kind of delivery and an out-of-the-car giddiness, day ending in Little Rock. First roadside full bloom and this city outskirt no safer than the panhandle. The carsick trick bullshit and good natured-sportiness jetlagged, those Easter nieces not sticking to anything with their sweet fingers and rabbit baskets. Squirrels! Another road this truck packed looking serious. One dog looking like coops are for chickens and, at the same time, where's my coop? This trip unsanctioned and ripped into winter, run wasted on window wheels along the Mississippi. That delta all swampland. All mystery.

II

Blood running cho-cho-cho-cho-co-co-colate. Choclo. Maiz. This in and out a maze of English and Spanish and this southern version of North America dizzying. Even a dog knows the rain drained counterclockwise and now this magnetic pull of centrifugal forest farmland and somehow my family, those nephews almost familiar, those dark haired tías, la abuela con sus árboles de pecan.

I

Starting from swamp, like a creation story—thirty minutes in customs and we come out Americans, that crate of detention to rental car, a pshew of confusion lifted into daybreaking Everglades, sun coming up carp, coming up crawfish, mudpuppy me—rising from overnight jail stories, canines in flight purgatory, this breakfast a birth renewed and spring nation thickening into maturity, my blood-rich beginning cellular, four-footed, fin-and-gilled. Beak-boldened. Song-throated: Here I could sing. And but for my fathers, I would feed alligators.

Nizhoní dóó 'a'ani' dóó até'él'í dóó ayoo'o'oni (Beauty & Memory & Abuse & Love)

BOJAN LOUIS

7 April 2014. **Over the weekend I attended the thirty-first Annual Tucson** Poetry Festival as a representative for a literary magazine of which I will be an editorial staff member. Aside from manning a display table of past issues, I conducted a writing workshop with the mighty Simon J. Ortiz— Acoma intellectual, writer, and poet—aimed at youth and young adult writers, though anyone, of any age, was welcomed to attend. After the workshop, I had lunch with Orlando White, a Diné poet, and he and I attended another workshop facilitated by poet Harryette Mullen. The focus, or at least what began as the focus (we didn't stay for the duration of the workshop), was childhood memories. We, the some forty to fifty workshop participants, were asked to think of our childhoods and engage our five senses, for children remember and associate concrete connections through tactile sensations. We were asked to free write and to describe three to five distinct memories from each one of our individual childhoods.

Colonization and decolonization connote and denote violence. Colonized people are murdered, raped, silenced, dehumanized, removed, extracted, have had their tongues and eyes cut out, have been fed to dogs, are made to hate themselves and their community members, assimilated, lied to, and on and on and on. A decolonized person seeks to shout, scream, relinquish their hurt and hatred, become the navigator of their self-image, obtain productive and healthy positions in and for the greater good of their communities; they look toward the future while continually waking up to the past. Their sleep is disquieted by night terrors. Their patience stilted by exhaustion.

The workshop prompt proved to be difficult, if not impossible. I'm often adverse to friends inquiring about what I was like as child and even more adverse to my parents' recollections of specific events or stories from and of my childhood. Do I remember lying beneath a black Chevy truck (or perhaps it was a GMC) with my dad while he fixed it and pretended that I was helping? Or being ornery on a trip back from visiting my mom's foster parents in Provo, Utah, and pulling over at some nursery where, among the plants, I was in some way calmed? The time at the Navajo Nation fair, fishing trips to Wheatfields Lake, the birth and growth of my sister from an infant to a toddler? No, I remember nothing and respond to these stories with lies about my remembering them because my mom has pictures of most of these moments, and because there are pictures, and because I'm a writer, I can say *yes* there are memories.

In Susan Sontag's essay "An Argument about Beauty," from her posthumous, somewhat unfinished, collection *At the Same Time: Essays and Speeches* published in 2007, she begins with the Catholic Church and Vatican's 2002 scandal of covering up "sexually predatory priests" (3). Sontag quotes Pope John Paul II as telling American cardinals summoned to the Vatican: "A great work of art may be blemished, but its beauty remains; and this is a truth which an intellectually honest critic will recognize." The Church as art, as Beauty beyond fault. I believe Sontag thought as much, agreed that beauty equals consolation. Her son, David Rieff, writes in his foreword: "Did she write to console herself? I believe so, though this is more intuition than grounded judgment" (xiv). I certainly write to console myself, though I've come to realize, and more importantly acknowledge, that through writing and striving to make art I more often than not re-traumatize myself by engaging and going to the dark and ugly memories, which I more easily access than the happy ones that my parents recall. The beautiful notion of childhood; the Diné ideal of hozhó, which can be trans-lated roughly as *the balance of walking and living in harmony, in conjunction with all beings and all things, that each element of the universe has its place and purpose in the* machination *of existence.* Now, *machination* is my word, though I'm fairly certain that it's apt for the translation. Diné bizaad (the Navajo language) directly reflects this ideal in its specificity and precision in regards to who is speaking, your familial and clan relationship to the speaker, when and where they are speaking, in physical relation to whom they are speaking, and in relation to the world, the universe. Essentially, you can't just say shit, as is the case with the absolute beauty and frustra-tion of English (Bilgáana bizaad). Similarly, the Diné idea of balance can be thought of in relation to William Carlos Williams's thoughts on poems being *small machinations.* Every word, space, punctuation, and interaction with the page is intentional, of the utmost importance. One poorly casted cog or wheel and the entire process falls apart, becomes simple thoughts on paper rather than art. Can beauty, then, be all things: the damned, the holy, the sacred, the sacrilegious, the wrecked, the reconstructed, the arti-ficial, and the natural?

We were asked to write for fifteen to twenty minutes, at least that's how long I think it was. For a few minutes nothing came to mind, I envi-sioned a literal blackness, a room and darkness—someone flipping a switch. When I finally wrote, I put this on the page reluctantly:

1. Body blue and your limbs
    taste harsh like rotten kale.
    Not fresh, so there's no sound,
    no crunch but only squish, which
    is word for a sound, but in this
    instance it's a feeling, a verb.
    The idea of pressure upon you.

2. You remember husky, a stolen
   jug of pennies. You remember the
   inability to decipher the noise
   of the dog being poisoned, the
   depth of the burial, and if there
   was even grass.

3. Don't be an idiot, your parents
   didn't make enough to water grass.

Nothing really useful or impressive, though that's what first drafts or free writing become for me, for any writer aware of their consistent and constant failures. There are obvious issues in the above free write. First, I'd already written a poem about my neighbor poisoning our dog and robbing our house, although I didn't include the part about the jug of pennies. Second, being sexually molested/physically abused/abused sexually/molested physically doesn't sound like squish. More like *rip* and *thud*, slow hands clapping. Third, I never ate kale as a child. I didn't eat kale until my late twenties, after I lived in a city, fell in love, and discovered Whole Foods.

In the first chapter of *The Wretched of the Earth*, Frantz Fanon writes, in regards to the colonized, "As soon as they are born it is obvious to them that their cramped world, riddled with taboos, can only be challenged by out-and-out violence." I first read this text in high school after seeing it pictured among a pile of other texts in the liner notes of Rage Against the Machine's newly released CD, at the time, *Evil Empire*. I misunderstood Fanon's thoughts completely, as many younger readers do and as many older "educated" readers still do. Anger is nothing to turn one's head at, to disregard, or to use as an excuse to criticize. Jamaica Kincaid, in her conversation with the *American Reader*, tells her interviewer, in response to a question regarding the mixture of humor and anger in her writing: "There are all sorts of reasons not to like my writing. But that's not one of them. Saying something is angry is not a criticism. It's not valid. It's not a valid observation in terms of criticism. You can list it as something that's true.

But it's not critical." As we say, and others say, on and off the reservation, past and present, *fuckin' A right*. Anger has long been, and used to be, my response to the circumstances of my childhood, ethnic demographic, and creative voice. Always more anger than love, though there was for me, or might have been, an obsession with violence—daggers protruding out of my skull, barbed wire wrapped around my body. My every response was anger, often misdirected, but always refocused upon myself. I sought to understand not only my mental and physical trauma but also historical trauma, both of which I still seek to understand. Love, I believed to be associated with weakness. Pussy ass motherfuckers fell in love. Strong, stoic, the not-giving-a-shit types refused love, refused ideas of heaven, denied the ability of happiness to last. I drank/drink, popped/pop pills, snorted/snort cocaine and crushed pills, smoked/smoke bud, and tried desperately to fuck away the anger, depression, guilt, and suicidal thoughts brewing in my psyche, in my entire being. I've existed in all and in a variety of these fashions from thirteen to thirty-three. I have not found a definite answer, know no absolute. Rather, I've taken the view that my life, my existence is a job; making the continual attentiveness to my partner's emotions and well-being a priority, not solely for her, but for myself as well. I would never have voiced this in my life previously (though that may be inaccurate): I have learned that it's possible to love myself. To say, all right violence, you've had your limelight, now it's time for you to take the back-seat and observe for the remainder of the trip. As for anger, it can always take the helm while I watch the passing landscape.

The excuse that I used in order to leave the "childhood writing" work-shop early was my adverse reaction to the strange and unfamiliar patty-cake sort of activity that ensued after the timed writing exercise. I won't recount the details of the activity because I didn't understand the activity and have no ken of it. I was unable to access anything after the prompt about childhood because it had triggered my non-responsiveness, my retreat. Here is why, which some may have already inferred up to this point, I retreated. Beginning with my early childhood on the Navajo Nation in Window Rock, Arizona, I was sexually and physically abused at the age of three or four by a neighbor who babysat me and her cousin and by an older boy at a Catholic school I attended. After moving to Flagstaff, Arizona, at the age of five or six my abuse continued with another babysitter, whose eldest son welcomed me into his gang (though I wasn't ever actually a gang member aside from his kicking my ass; he was a sixth grader and I in preschool), and finally by two older cousins, first by a female, then a male; all of this until eight, nine, or ten. These years are all blurred to me. And not every instance was of a single occurrence, some lasted summers, some lasted years. I prayed to Jesus, to the Virgin Mary, to God, to the archangels Michael and Gabriel, to the Hopi Kachinas I'd memorized for some reason, and not one answered. So I prayed to Satan, or darkness, the idea and story of being cast out, of being the knower of a knowledge that was poison or a different kind of light. Eventually, I stopped praying, "believing." Christianity, Catholicism, organized religion are systems of colonization. I felt/feel that they made the colonized feel guilty, evil, yearn for forgiveness, judge one another, and base their ideals on an existence that is greater than this earth. Did I mention that I stopped praying, stopped believing? Nowadays, I wake before or with the sun and I pray to it, to the sky, to the earth. I don't always know what I'm saying, but at least I know what each hasn't done to me.

Decolonization and love seem like unlikely partners or unique inner demons. But that, too, is erroneous. Since that workshop, that trigger, I've read and read and read, which is one of the ways that I've taught myself empathy, that and thousands of dollars' worth of counseling, EMDR, failed prescriptions by a clinical psychologist (I was prescribed an experimental delivery system, meaning pill, of Risperdal and a shitload of Xanax after expressing a history of addiction to pharmaceuticals that culminated in my trying to shoot myself at twenty-seven and my gun stovepipe jammed and, having worked up the nerve to transcend the fear of it, shit and vomited all over myself and laid in my kitchen alone for a couple days), and finally cognitive and behavioral therapy. I've learned to forgive myself or to let play that scene in *Good Will Hunting* where Matt Damon's character is having a sort of breakdown and Robin Williams, as the school-of-hard-knocks doctor, consoles Damon's character, telling him something along the lines of *It's not your fault, it's not your fault.* A scene that one of my first girlfriends in high school played for me, as if the simple act of viewing it would dispel the hallucinations, both visual and auditory, that I developed as a result of the years of repressed memories and trauma. Hallucinations that lasted for years, that caused night terrors I still deal with (though significantly less frequently), that helped me hate, that compounded my anger, that led me to two suicide attempts (the first at twenty with Jack Daniels and Demerol, a trip in an ambulance to the ER, stomach pumps, IVs, rehydrating suppositories, and my first required visit to a counselor), that led me to live my life in parentheticals and footnotes, though there are no footnotes here because footnotes are another colonizer, as Junot Díaz illumed to us in *The Brief and Wondrous Life of Oscar Wao.* Decolonization is violent, it is spiritual unrest, it is for me the other side of the river, the western lands. William S. Burroughs, in what is regarded as his finest work since *Naked Lunch* (though this can be argued heatedly), writes in the culminating sections of *The Western Lands* (published 1987 by Penguin Books):

> I want to reach the Western Lands—right in front of you, across the bubbling brook. It's a frozen sewer. It's known as the Duad, remember? All the filth and horror, fear, hate, disease and death of human history flows between you and the Western Lands. Let it flow! My cat Fletch stretches behind me on the bed. A tree like black lace against a gray sky. A flash of joy.
>
> How long does it take a man to learn that he does not, cannot want what he "wants"?
>
> You have to be in Hell to see Heaven. Glimpses from the Land of the Dead, flashes of serene timeless joy, a joy as old as suffering and despair. (257–58)

In a way, and even more so for others, decolonization can be the recognition, the recovering of a time between "filth and horror," "disease and death of human history"; a bold way to say this would be, a time before Columbus, the slave trade, the sugar trade, Christianity, Thanksgiving, Manifest Destiny, massacres, forced walks, displacement, reservations, scorched earth campaigns, boarding schools, oil and coal companies, uranium, superpower, the Washington Redskins and Chief Wahoo, the KXL pipeline, the femicide of Indigenous women, and on and on and on. A time when we were able to kill one another fashionably, with "honor" because fuck all that noble savage bullshit. Humans have beef, sure, but the greater evil will always be greed and "power." "You have to be in Hell to see Heaven." You have to know the devil before you know the savior, and sometimes vice versa, but you have to know the colonizer before comprehending the destruction of angels and the angelic; the acceptance that there's no reward after this life, only this life.

After completely ditching the workshop and opting for a drink outside on the patio of the Hotel Congress, haunted by the myths of John Dillinger, some of us poets sat, talked shit, and negotiated the events for the evening that remained. A writer, not Diné, but Blackfeet from Montana said something along the lines of *you never ask a Native to talk about their childhood. That's Indigenous 101. You think life on the reservation is pretty? Fuck that. Natives never talk about their childhoods.* In the days that I've been composing this, erratically and with disregard to other life obligations, thanks to all the literary triggers, I've thought of two things. The first was triggered by the workshop, of course, and Orlando White himself, though not at that specific moment, but by the memory of the words and images from the first poem, "To See Letters," from his debut collection, *Bone Light.* The speaker's stepfather calling him by his middle name so as to dehumanize him, the speaker's fascination with letters, his physical abuse at the hands of his stepfather, his adolescent ability to forgive, and the final stanza: "When David hit me in the head, I saw stars in the shape of the // Alphabet. Years later, my fascination for letters resulted in poems." This is decolonization. The violence we mirror on ourselves and others nulled.

The second is the hardcore band Converge, whose discography I've listened to exclusively in writing this, but more specifically the song "All

We Love We Leave Behind" from their album of the same name. It's about singer Jacob Bannon's loss of one of his dogs, which he had for the majority of its life. What's important about this for me is that dogs have always been one of the few solaces I've had. I think of protection, love, family. Not property or accessory. I think of the days of sleeplessness and exhaustion. I think that one day I'll figure out how all this happened.

Fairy Tales, Trauma, Writing into Dissociation

SASHA LAPOINTE

Just over two years ago, I walked into my first MFA workshop at the Institute of American Indian Arts with a scattered collection of sections from what I was loosely referring to as the Little Boats story in hand and ready to be critiqued. What I had was a disjointed and fragmented body of memories, the title piece based off a memory in which the imagined vision of boats is the most clear, the most visible thing I can recall. Two years of excavating and exhausting my memory and possibly my heart, I have the draft of a memoir.

The book project I've taken on while pursuing my MFA in creative non-fiction first rooted in me during my time at IAIA as an undergrad. Little Boats came out of an essay assignment asking us to describe our most traumatic memory. I did the work and came to class prepared to workshop my piece and panicked as my classmates went around sharing their stories of moving across country, of terrible break-ups, of pets and loved ones dying. My panic was not a dismissal of these stories; rather, I immediately realized I had overshared.

I stared down at my paper and read the title over and over again while my hands got sweaty and my mouth went dry. Little Boats. Even the title of my piece was my anxiety manifested, a vision that has haunted me since childhood. I wondered why the hell I had chosen to write Little Boats rather than the story of my childhood dog Eyeball falling off a cliff at my grandmother's beach property when we were playing a rowdy game of pirates. Eyeball survived. Everybody cried. We learned about mortality, the dangers of cliff-side play, and the fragility of life. The Eyeball story was a winner.

But I didn't write the Eyeball story. I wrote Little Boats.

In its early stages, Little Boats was just an experiment. It was a letter of apology to my childhood love, a boy I had deeply wounded. It was also a love story, a fairy tale, a parable. It went through many revisions and wore many different masks: witch masks, mermaid masks, wolf masks, and even a comatose Sleeping Beauty mask.

But at its core was my most traumatic memory: me, ten years old, on the Swinomish Reservation, on a water bed, babysitting, falling asleep to a Disney movie and a man, a family friend, a neighbor, enters the bedroom. Abuse occurs.

In an undergrad creative writing class, one of the early drafts was workshopped by a professor whose main critique focused on my "vagueness" in the scene of the initial abuse. *My vagueness.* She's a dear friend who I look up to, a writer who absolutely knows what she's talking about, but I was caught off-guard by her remarks. I understood the need for scene, for details, for particulars, but when it came to my experience of my own abuse, I didn't want someone telling me how to do it.

I went home feeling defeated. I racked my brain for specifics, for the details she claimed were missing, but I couldn't find them. All I found was fog and darkness and shadows in the shapes of little boats along a wall.

While pursuing my MFA I've read a lot powerful nonfiction on the subject of trauma and survival. Susanna Kaysen explicitly recounts being institutionalized in her memoir, *Girl, Interrupted.* Kathryn Harrison speaks openly about surviving an abusive and incestuous relationship with her father in *The Kiss.* Dorothy Allison tackles her own survivor story in *Two or Three Things I Know for Sure.* Her ability to traverse such a large expanse of her life in this short memoir is impressive. She is able to move back and forth in time seamlessly because of her transitions and her focus. Wendy C. Ortiz's book *Excavation* haunted me. Her capacity to embody the thirteen-year-old girl she once was and illustrate the raw and magnified details of her sexual relationship with an adult teacher gripped me like a bad dream.

These authors are confronting harsh subject matter and tackling it with grace. This work is moving, effective, and stunning in its ability to make sense of a traumatic experience. This is an important narrative to have in the world, but it is not the only style of writing that confronts trauma. What I am most interested in, as an abuse survivor, as a woman writing about trauma, as a girl who grew up listening to her tribe's legends and lessons, are the narratives that are using fairy tales, fables, and mythology to address trauma. This realm of storytelling may be based in fantasy and magic, but it can also be examined as a metaphor for what often occurs in many survivors during the experience of trauma: the act of dissociation.

Dissociation in its mildest form can be described as a coping mechanism and often occurs in those who suffer post-traumatic stress disorder. Our bodies are incredible and intelligent things. Of course they've wired in some sort of security system that allows us to check out when things get too scary. It's daydreaming. It's detachment. It's a way to go someplace else, away from the originating trauma. Fairy tales, located outside of our reality, take us to another world. What's interesting about the joining of these worlds, both fairy tale and trauma, is that the intersection resembles the very core of the experience of trauma itself: that daydreaming, that survival, those coping mechanisms can be manifested on the page or the screen.

I experienced dissociation at age ten, when I first suffered abuse. Dissociation took the form of dozens of little boats floating along the wall across from me. The boats came from some place in my mind and surfaced as a distraction, a meditation of sorts manifested in the shape of boats due to the waterbed I was sleeping on and the movement of waves beneath me. For a long time the boats were all I could remember from that night: their paper sails, their delicate smallness. This has fascinated me all throughout my childhood, my adulthood, and now even more so as a writer. The ability to leave one's body, to escape, to go someplace else is powerful and terrifying. The boats were there because I needed them to be. Now, as an adult and as a writer concerned with craft, I need the boats for their language. There are moments in my memoir where I am unable to put into words the details of my abuse. The boats lend themselves to me for the dissociation they represent. For the sake of not being gratuitous, for the sake of my own fragility, it is safer and more effective for me to use the boats.

Perhaps this comes to me intuitively because I am a survivor, or perhaps I have seen and identified with this phenomenon over and over, in popular fiction, fairy tales, and films.

As a girl I cherished what I call the three L's: *Legend*, *The Little Mermaid*, and *Labyrinth*. These were my go-to video rentals on the weekends. I watched them again and again. I fell into them. I love *Labyrinth*. This Jim Henson classic portrayed a young Jennifer Connelly as Sarah, who battled her way through a sinister labyrinth in order to reach her adversary: a hypersexualized, leggings-clad Goblin King, brought to life by David Bowie. Watching the film over and over as a small child, I was able to recognize early on that I could take the film at face value: a magical world opening up to this teenager and sweeping her off into an adventure. Part of me looked deeper and saw a bratty and troubled girl, burdened by the task of caring for her baby brother and desperately seeking escape.

Sarah's character is from a broken home—that much we know. During the night, the Goblin King shows up and kidnaps the baby brother, freeing Sarah from her responsibility while also providing escape from her lonely world. In the labyrinth, Sarah overcomes obstacles, she makes friends, and learns important lessons. The labyrinth provides a world opposite of the one Sarah is familiar with. She's able to triumph over her fears and change her fate. The trauma of the death (or disappearance) of her mother appears in the form of her new baby brother, the concrete evidence of her father's new life and her responsibilities in this new family. The Goblin King takes her world away and replaces it with a fantasy.

It isn't just through film that I observe the connection between fairy tale and trauma. I grew up close to my great-grandmother, Vi Hilbert, who was named a Washington State Living Treasure for her work to preserve the Lushootseed language and stories. I heard stories of a woman she called Aunt Susie, who was an elder when my great-grandmother was just a girl. As a master storyteller and a medicine worker, she had a remarkable influence on my great-grandmother's work, teaching her about the lessons inherent in our culture's legends.

I write a lot about my great-grandmother in Little Boats. I often use her stories and moments I've shared with her as a source of light throughout a dark journey. I was interested to learn more about the woman she learned from, and I picked up the Aunt Susie book, a book that my great-grandmother transcribed and translated from recordings of Aunt Susie's storytelling and interviews.[1] I had thought that my tendency to lean toward the fairy tale was simply born out of a bookworm imagination, a need for my own escape at a young age, a love of all things magical. But it was deeper than that.

Aunt Susie is an ancestor, one I've learned a great deal from through my great-grandmother. Some of the craft tendencies I rely on in my writing are more intuitive than I thought, with ancestral origins. While workshopping Little Boats I often received feedback regarding the dreamlike sequences I fall into. At first this frustrated me. Was I being lazy? Was I trying too hard? Was I simply not ready to write this book? What I've learned after researching Aunt Susie more extensively is: none of the above.

In the following passage from my own work, I depict my reaction to my great-grandmother's passing; in it, I see a connection to one of Aunt Susie's stories.

Coma II: Sleeping Beauty

I fall asleep again. For many days at a time, I sleep. I call into work day after day. I kick the covers away from my body. I toss and turn. The curtains aren't dark enough, and I have to learn to ignore the daylight. Some mornings I hear Brandon at the stove, heating water for tea, trying to get me to eat. With my hand on the doorknob I can almost get to him, I can almost get back to the world. But a wave falls from somewhere, my ceiling maybe? And it crashes over me, reminding me I am still sleeping. My room fills with water again and again. Never waking, I get lonely. I chase a speck of paint, like a white rabbit, across my bedroom wall, convinced if I follow it long enough it will lead me back to the waking world. But my eyes are heavy and I lose the speck of paint again, falling deeper into slumber. I sleep days and weeks away. I sleep my body sore. I sleep through several bill cycles and eventually my mother calls.

"You can't sleep like that." She tells me. I have to see a healer. A medicine worker.

"You're falling into the spirit world and you can't sleep that deep. You need to wake up."

I didn't have a straightforward narrative for what I went through when my great-grandmother passed. The words weren't there in a traditional or conventional sense. All I could do was write the experience I did remember. I wasn't trying to use poetic or flowery language, I talked about it in the only way I could.

Nearly a year after writing that scene, I finally picked up the Aunt Susie book and discovered her passage about being taken away by the salmon people:

I was sick, I was sick for a long time. Spiritually, supernaturally ill.
For the entire salmon season, during all of the runs.
We caught humpback salmon first.
We killed them. Indeed we killed them.
As a consequence, it seems the humpies took me.
They ran off with me (my soul).
There I was sick.
I was medicated (treated) yet I became progressively worse.
It took place there at Hamilton (on the Skagit river).
There I lay (for an indefinite time) until the dog salmon run finished.

I became very thin.
My stomach was compressed.
No food was inside.
I was skinny.
When I would feel it, my face was only bone.
Then I dreamed! I dreamed!
I overheard talking, "Oh you folks had better return that human woman.
You should return her to her human world.
You, the one called Skwayseliwe, will return her."
The leader with a great big canoe was thus identified.
Many other people were on board.
With their red paint cedar bark headdresses on.
I was traveling on the back of the hump of a salmon.
That is how I was canoed.
I was very afraid that I would fall off and drown.
Then I overheard in song:
Unload her now, Skwayseliwe.
You have arrived back in your land.
You will disembark.
You will say to your own grandmother, "Open the door for me.
I came back."
I got off and walked away.
I walked upland, I knocked on the door.
"Open the door, Grandmother. I have arrived."
But they said of me I was crazy (confused they said).
Grandmother said,
"Get a grip on yourself, for you did not just arrive, my dear little one, you
have instead always been here, asleep continuously. Maybe you were
just dreaming."

The story shook me up. I got goose bumps when I read it because Aunt Susie is retelling a moment of dissociation. Whatever the origin of her trauma was, fever, depression, a spiritual sickness, Aunt Susie's only way of making sense of it in words was through the story of her leaving, of her being taken away by the salmon people.

To be brought up around my culture's oral tradition meant to be brought up surrounded by stories. Storytelling is a regular occurrence during our family's gatherings. This innate desire to tell, explore, learn, and teach something through our mythologies, our legends is ancient in us. It's been passed through the generations. My great-grandmother listened to Aunt Susie's stories and passed them on to us. And in these stories and in our own bodies are memories. Cultural and historical memories. The women of my ancestry have survived something. They lived in a time of assimilation, colonization, the loss of their lands and languages. They survived boarding schools and epidemics. These transformative historical experiences left us imprinted. Through the stories passed came an inherent resilience, a strength in the language. The women of my families carried their own traumas, as I have carried mine. Through their stories I've absorbed a language around trauma that allows me to access those fragile moments that sometimes seem too frightening to explore.

NOTE

1 Aunt Susie Sampson Peter, *The Wisdom of a Skagit Elder*, transcribed by Vi Hilbert, translated by Vi Hilbert and Jay Miller, recorded by Leon Metcalf (Seattle: Lushootseed Press, 2005).

COILING

Tuolumne

DEBORAH A. MIRANDA

My father walked out of San Quentin after eight years and somehow ended up at the Tuolumne River. My father's forty-four-year-old body was hardened, callused, scarred, and tattooed with eight years of fighting to breathe, to stay unbroken, or at least alive. He woke up nights in a cold sweat, fists coiled, pumped with adrenaline. Far into old age, he told me, he lived in fear that his release was a mistake, and guards would show up to take him away, lock him back up.

But how did he get from San Quentin to the Tuolumne River, and why? Well, he didn't mean to make that trip. As to why . . .

My father went to see his own father; they hadn't seen each other in a long time. Maybe my dad just wanted to catch up. More likely, he wanted to borrow some money, maybe bum a place to crash until he could find work. My father wasn't afraid of hard work, and right about then, he could use some structure in his day. With all the carpentry skills he'd learned "at college," he'd find work quick.

But these two men, my father, Al, and grandfather, Tom, could not communicate. Oh, they both spoke English. But they also both spoke the language of pain, and for that very reason, could not speak to each other.

I don't know how my father got to his dad's house. He had no money. He had no car. He had nothing. Nothing. Still, in his lonely freedom and state of shock, my father found himself there in Stockton. Maybe Tom was out back in his garden, lifting his prize cantaloupes up on boards so the gophers wouldn't gouge them out from beneath, or maybe he was feeding treats to one of his dear dogs. I'm sure it was hot, the California sun merciless on skin that had not seen much of that particular light for over three thousand days.

Maybe they had coffee. Or a cold beer together. My grandfather was no angel, but he'd never been in prison. I suspect he was shamed by my father's incarceration, but then my father always was the black sheep of the three surviving boys; he would have been used to that. And my father wasn't the first family member incarcerated at San Quentin; his mother's brother, Cesar Robles, convicted of manslaughter, had done time there. He'd killed his wife for her unfaithfulness. My father said Cesar had beheaded her; I'm not sure that part of the story is true. Still, forgiveness was not a family trait. Al and Tom would not have enjoyed this reunion.

And yet at some point Tom said, "Get in the car."

And because he had nowhere to go and no one to go with, my father did. He sat in the passenger's seat of my grandfather's old Ford sedan, waited to see what would happen next. He expected Tom to say something about the prison gang tattoos, the X between my father's eyebrows, the dark blue marks in the crease between thumb and forefinger. Tom said nothing. Just backed out of his driveway, pulled onto the side street, and made his way to a freeway.

They were heading toward the mountains.

When they arrived, Tom steered the car down toward a cluster of tall trees, shaggy pines, and oaks.

The two men stepped out of the car, felt the heat of the engine hanging over the hood, and then the embrace of cool river breath and liquid calls of birdsong. And in the river, the long ancient bodies of salmon returning home, silver and red flashing in the green water, spotted tails pushing hard against the current. It must have been fall; that's when Chinook and steelhead make their return up the Tuolumne.

This is what my father told me, years later.

"The Indians came to this spot," my grandfather said. He might have sounded casual, offhand, or deadly serious.

My father was silent. I do know that. He was stunned by the beauty of that place, the taste of wet air on his tongue, same air of his first breath when he emerged from his mother's womb nearly forty-four years before. Stunned by the song of water, the explosive greens of leaves and pine needles, the scent of life.

And now his father was talking about Indians.

Tom Miranda spent a lifetime being silent about what was written all over his body, his former wife's body, and the bodies of their four boys. Family stories say Tom used to go to Indian dances, make his own regalia, but he never shared any of this with his boys. Indian was a dirty secret.

"You know, you were born near here, up at the Rancheria. I brought you here when you were just a baby. The river, she was a lot faster in those days, before they dammed her; lotta salmon then. Your mother came up here cuz I was away logging, and she had family up here. Her mother died around then, and her grandma was real sick. She needed family to help her with Tommy and Richard. They was just little ones."

My father knew this story. It was his personal creation story, the one that marked him different from everyone else. The sudden November snowstorm, the doctor sent for but stuck on the road, the Indian woman—a cousin? an auntie?—who midwifed Keta. The doctor who finally arrived, exhausted, agreed the hollering dark brown baby was a healthy boy, stepped outside to sign the birth certificate and collapsed, didn't get back up. That baby, never registered with the US government, didn't officially exist until it was time to go to war, and he needed proof he'd been born before he could sign up to die. My father told me that he'd had to go back up to Tuolumne and find that woman who'd delivered him, get her to sign a document.

My father was a little proud of this story. His outlaw birth.

"The Indians used to come here. Catch salmon, big ones. This is the Indian river," Tom went on, looking out over the waters, hands in the pockets of his windbreaker. "You come here when you have questions. You come here when you need—" His voice broke off; maybe he didn't know the word for what he wanted to say. Or maybe he knew the Indian word once but couldn't remember it, or remembered it but knew his son couldn't understand the word even if his father did use it.

I wonder. Was the word *healing, cleansing, rebirth?*

Tom and my father stood there a minute, silent. Then Tom gestured at the river with his chin, an abrupt, sharp jerk. "So." It was a move and a word that said, *Well, it's up to you.*

He wouldn't have touched my father on the shoulder, wouldn't have patted him on the back. The only touch shared between these two men had been blows. Tom turned, walked down the riverbank a ways, left my father to it. When Tom walked away, he carried the remnants of a world with him: languages, dances, tools, materials, songs. Things he never shared with any of his sons. This was the closest he would ever come to attempting that bridge.

This is the Indian river. You come here when you have questions. You come here when you need . . .

My father loved rivers. After he came to live with us in Washington State, that's where he would go when he wasn't drinking, when he had a weekend off. A fishing rod, a battered red tackle box, a thermos of black coffee, and a river—and maybe a chance to be happy. The Puyallup River on the Muckleshoot Reservation was one of his favorites, but he frequented the Green River, the Nisqually, the White, too. He took me once or twice but brought my little brother more often; our father ached for a father-son bond that he didn't quite have the tools to create. If only fatherhood fit in his hands like a good solid hammer and kiln-dried two-by-fours.

I don't know what my father thought as he stood there by the Tuolumne in the cusp between the 1960s and 1970s; whether he prayed, or asked for forgiveness, or wanted to throw himself into the green water and let it decide what to do with his body.

His body.

He carried eight years of hell in that body. Did he think about what had been done to his body in San Quentin? Did he think about what that body had done to others? Did he hate his body for its weaknesses, for its needs, for its fears and angers? Could he even still feel his body anymore? Did he know his body as anything but a weapon, or a target? Did he wonder how long he could bear the weight of his body, heavy with the blood of others, stained with indelible loss and grief, curled tight as a fist around a handful of shame? Was he already thinking about where he could get a beer, start numbing the thousand and one blows to the innocence he'd once known that November night on the Tuolumne Rancheria, swaddled tight against his mother's breast?

Of course, my father had not been innocent in a long time, decades before San Quentin. He knew that.

But my father never told me what he was thinking that day his dad took him back to the river. What I do know is that in 2009, when my father was dying, he gave my brother this command: "Take my ashes back to that river. Scatter me on the Tuolumne." He told our sister Louise the same thing over the phone, calling her in San Jose from his hospice room in Everett, Washington.

Something in that river called him back. Something in that water told him he needed to return to this Indian river one day, even if only as ash. Something told my father that here was the place he would lay down that battered body one last time, his bits of bone and cinders spread on a current that starts as snow somewhere in the Sierras, gathers its power through canyons and gravity, pours like an artery of creation through meadows near the place of his birth, then crosses the Central Valley with its thirst and fertility, is dammed and held captive, joins the San Joaquin River, is dammed again, and finally, weakened in volume but not memory, flows on to the bay and the Pacific Ocean, entering that mother of a story.

Something passed between river and man that day. Was it a promise? A plea? Instruction?

One year after our father's death, my brother fulfilled our father's last wish, and he did it well.

On that day, I could not be there, though I was on a river, too, on the other side of the country with my two children. What I know about this story comes from my siblings, and from the photographs taken by them. I know that Louise loaded up her van: sisters Pat and Rose, our little brother, Al. It was a long drive from San Jose to the nearest part of the Tuolumne. Large stretches of the river were full of trash, the water low and dirty. It made them all sad, to see a beloved river treated so cruelly. Other places were inaccessible for Louise, who uses a cane. They were losing heart when Louise saw a stranger parked nearby and asked him if he knew any good places in the area, somewhere pretty, and easy to get down to the water. It turned out Harry was the right guy to ask. He said, if you go around this park and make a right, go down a couple of lights, make another right, go down around two miles. . . .

Louise told him why they were there, asked if he would be willing to show them the way. He said yes. They jumped in the van to follow. Louise told me, we would have never found this area without him. I think he was sent to guide me. Harry took them to a sweet place where the river ran fast and clear. Our brother walked out and stood, at the edge, smelling. Listening. Feeling. This is the spot, he said.

There, Louise read a prayer she'd composed in Esselen, and they offered abalone and beaded gifts she and Pat had made. Al kicked off his shoes, pulled up the legs of his jeans, skinned off his shirt, waded into the river holding the plastic bag of ashes with both of his big hands. He opened the bag, poured the gray gritty contents out like a cloud onto the surface.

In the pictures Rose took, the plume spreads out, hangs for a moment like a diver streaking downstream. My brother is as brown and broad-shouldered as our father. He stands in the water, sure-footed, watching Al Miranda Sr.'s last mark upon this earth.

Our grandfather had brought his son to that river for guidance during a time of great change. In that moment, even if he could not articulate why, the river was the one thing Tom could offer to a son in need of a ceremony to begin his life over. Now, in a way, that son—our father—had also brought his son to that river, brought three of his daughters, to stand on the bank and say micha eni hikpalala. Together, they reinvented a ceremony for beginning again.

One of these days, I'll go to the Tuolumne too. I'll stand on the bank cut by thousands and thousands of years, by storm, drought, rain.

I'll go because this is an Indian river, our river, and we go there when we have questions, when we have need. We go there for guidance. We go there for cleansing. We go there to say goodbye.

We go there to start over again. We go there because there is one prayer we have never forgotten: water is life.

I Know I'll Go

TERESE MARIE MAILHOT

My father died at the Thunderbird Motel on Flood Hope Road. According to documents, he was beaten over a cigarette or a prostitute. I prefer the cigarette. I considered it an Indian death myself, while walking along the country roads of my reservation. His death intruded, and I could not fathom being a good person when I came from such misery.

He was an anomaly, a drunk savant. He took his colors, brushes, and stool with him when he left. It was harvest and the corn stalks were gold and waving at me. I was constantly waiting, looking out and within. When he left, he was lanky with a paunch, and his hair was black and coarse. He was wearing a baseball T-shirt and jeans covered in rust-acrylic.

As an Indian woman, I resist the urge to bleed out on a page, to impart the story of my drunken father. It was dangerous to be alone with him, as it was dangerous to forgive him, as it was dangerous to say he was a monster. If he were a monster, that would make me part-monster, part-Indian. It's my politic to write the humanity in my characters and to subvert the stereotypes. Isn't that my duty as an Indian writer? But what part of him was subversion?

*

Our basement smelled like river water and cedar bough. He carved and painted endlessly in the corners of the room. I sat in his lap, watching him paint ornate Salish birds in striking red and black.

"You see?" he said. "What is that?"

"Eagle," I said.

"Mother," he said.

He was soft looking sometimes. I liked to sleep in the crook of his neck. He smelled like Old Spice and bergamot. His hands shook when he was not drinking, and when I held them, he seemed thankful. He delighted in my imagination when my mother was too busy. The grass was high on our lawn when I took the hose to our well and let it run.

"What are you doing?" he said.

"I'm a gas-man filling up a tank," I said.

"Silly." He tickled me.

Once, I packed my bags, mimicking my mother. With a bag of dolls and wooden cars, I told him I was leaving. I told him I would not come back until he stopped drinking. He promised me he would stop and then weeks later he left.

*

After the birth of my second son I went to find him. I was brought to the town of Hope, where he was living with his new family. His lawn was ragged. Cars without tires sat on bricks. He answered the door wearing a thin, dirty white shirt. He was jaundiced and his face was gaunt. His hair was mostly black and still coarse. We sat across from each other in lawn chairs in his basement. I resisted the urge to sit poised like him; instead, I held bad posture and slunk in my chair.

"You have my nose," he said. "My big honker. I missed you."

I said I missed him, feeling awful that it was true.

"The best thing I could do was leave."

"I know," I said.

"Your mother was a good woman. I told her I was an asshole, and she took me in like a wounded bear."

"I know."

A month after this he showed up at my house with a white documentary filmmaker. I answered the door but could not let him in the house. My brother was still scared of him, still angry and confused.

"They're doing a documentary about me," he said. "About my art."

I was anxious, standing there with him at my door.

"I know," he said. "I'll go."

*

The National Film Board of Canada debuted the documentary as a piece with immediacy and no external narrative. I'm a woman wielding narrative now, weaving the parts of my father's life with my own. I consider his work a testimony to his being. I have one of his paintings in my living room. *Man Emerging* is the depiction of a man riding a whale. The work is traditional and simplistic. Salish work calls for simplicity because an animal or man should not be convoluted. My father was not a monster, although it was in his monstrous nature to leave my brother and I alone in his van while he drank at the Kent. Our breath became visible in the cold when Dad came back to bring us fried mushrooms. We ate the bar fare like puppies to slop.

*

His smell was not monstrous, nor the crooks of his body. The invasive thought that he died alone in a hotel room is too much. It is dangerous to think about him, as it was dangerous to have him as my father, as it is dangerous to mourn someone I fear becoming.

I don't write this to put him to rest but to resurrect him as a man when public record portrays him as a drunk, a monster, and a transient. I wish I could have known him as a child in his newness. I want to see him with the sheen of perfection, with skin unscathed by his mistakes or by his father's. Before my mother died I asked her if he had ever hurt me.

"I put you in double diapers," she said. "There's no way he hurt you. Did he ever hurt you?"

"No," I said, unsure.

If rock is permeable in water, I wonder what that makes me in all of this? There is a picture of my brother and me next to Dad's van. My chin is turned up, and at the bottom of my irises there is a brightness. My brother has his hand on his hip, and he looks protective, standing over me. I know, without remembering clearly, that my father took this picture, and that not all our times were bad.

Little Mountain Woman

TERESE MARIE MAILHOT

I feel like a squaw, the type white people imagine: a feral thing with greasy hair and nimble fingers wanting.

You have made me feel sick of myself.

I killed a ladybug, and you looked at me like I was wild. I don't think you know how poor I used to be, that my house was infested with ladybugs for so long. My brother and I went mad when they wouldn't stop biting. We tried to swat them with brooms—red and black landed everywhere. They wouldn't leave, and mother wouldn't come home.

I don't think you know how poor that made me feel, a squaw child.

I kill ladybugs whenever I see them. I know that the women you've loved wouldn't do that. They feel lucky. It shames me.

I never get to say the full thing. Like the ladybugs. I don't think you know how I feel with you.

Before I went to the hospital I drove to your home at night. It was December in Mesilla. My moist hand stuck to the door.

You pulled me in and we stumbled to your couch. We sat for minutes in silence, beyond polite conversation, in the dark.

I felt like a voyeur, staring at the things in your house. I wanted them to be mine too. You wouldn't keep a squaw. I think you wanted the other women you were seeing—whole beings.

My thighs were sweaty and your heater was buzzing. I could feel the skin on my neck parting away from itself like arid soil.

Your hands were holding themselves in your lap. You wore old clothes that stayed too long in the corners of your floor. You were dusty and I liked that.

The tips of your fingers felt like wet grapes. I wanted to bite every one. I told you that I needed help and then you asked me to leave. I feel disposable sometimes.

In the hospital they gave me a composition book. I asked for forgiveness.

Letter upon letter, and then I refined that work and what wasn't there was the memory of my father. It was all about you because that's how ignorant I was.

When I got out I could read the dark. I turned the lights off in my kitchen and walked across the tiles, dragging my toes. I had cleaned the place multiple times to feel more alone in the night.

I wondered if your hands were still cold. You reminded me of a broken spring rocking horse and I was all weight.

I reappeared in your life and you were still seeing other women. I feel—sick of myself.

A woman you like plays the banjo and has ethereal hands for the earth. One weekend you and I watch her dog, Rose. The dog eats gluten-free and shits on the floor. I took the feeling that I was being used to the bathroom.

When I feel like a squaw I wash my face with alcohol—toner. There's never enough dirt to constitute the feeling.

A woman you like leaves tennis balls at your place. I searched through your phone and found pictures of her dog, whose name I don't know. It's a small terrier with white fur, and I don't know why she doesn't send pictures of herself. I know that you like that.

Maybe I make myself the squaw, I think. Maybe, this whole time, I should have sent you pictures of my hands.

The things you say to these women—I want that.

I position my arms just so on your couch. I slouch and inhale shorter breaths so I don't expand with too much air. Still, a squaw-feeling. I understand I have sacred blood. I know. They named me Little Mountain Woman. I know that I can pray correctly. I know the tenses and the syllables of every rite and spent hours beneath women who turned soil and made medicine. I know that I'm not ornamental but that I've inherited black eyes and a grand grief small women can't own. I don't think you know I feel this way, but maybe you should know now.

One day I went back to get my earrings from your house and saw you holding Laura in the doorway. I still knocked, not a squaw.

I still can't believe my reserve of water—from my nose and eyes. I have dormant fluid in the body, every woman does. I wonder if I am a cavern or a river.

Once you said that I'm a geyser. A hole in the ground, bursting.

When I became pregnant, the women left. Your fingers feel less full and edible.

I had the baby remembering the women. White women make me feel inferior, but I don't think you know how much. All you see is me killing ladybugs, how could you know the feeling. The *spite* of that feeling.

We compare hurt. I only feel dirty sometimes. I wash my face three or four times in the mirror and let the alcohol sting.

"I want to be pore-less," I say.

You tell me people have pores—that they should.

I feel dormant watching you live fuller than I can. I worry I am a cavern. I've inherited my mother's hollow stomach.

You tell me that my pain feels searing, that I'm missing four layers of skin. Your pain is an empty room. I agree that I'm mercurial and you can be dusty.

When we get married, the officiant says it will be hard.

In marriage—swollen and postpartum, I stare at our bed, which is held up by books. I want to fix it. I strip the bed more often than you like. We wash the sheets. I stare at the doorway where you held her, and I see myself on the other side, a squaw. I wash my face again. Maybe, if you know, I'll feel less of this.

I think you imagined I was all sharp corners and edges. We both know my heart has an extra chamber. I feel more fragile than you know, more squaw and ornamental, like a figurine. I wonder how much you can know. Can you wash me like a saint, born again? From squaw to woman with a face, pores, a body, limbs, history, large heart, older, safer. Can't you wash me or hollow me out for good? Wash me in my own regard and pain and then let it dry out. Let me kill every ladybug and laugh when I do.

Fear to Forget & Fear to Forgive

Or an Attempt at Writing a Travel Essay

BOJAN LOUIS

June/July 2015, Singapore, Singapore

Last night's lightning culled memories, dormant a while now, of my fear of the dark, though it wasn't the complete dark that terrified me but the thick weight of an unseen presence, the dark against the dark, illuminated suddenly (as in movies) by the shake and explosion of a torrential lightning storm. Except last night's downpour was one I've rarely experienced, it being a tropical storm of the equator and not the southwestern desert. Rain fell as if off the end of a river, slammed the metal-covered walkway beneath the apartment window, and I imagined that false sense of shelter creased and folded. Wind threw rain against the window as if to shatter it. I was groggy, much too stuck in dreamland to get up and, I don't know what, hide or sit on the couch in the front room? I worried about the laundry I'd just washed, left piled on the window seat. I'd have to dry it again, carefully pick out glass bits. Still, I did nothing, only listened through my dreams to the hard blasts cracking the night. The rainy season, it seemed, was early in Singapore, though I'd need to google it to be completely sure.

Before this sedated storm sleep experience I'd broken from a fever developed after a late Saturday night out guzzling beers and smoking cigarettes in the Geylang District, which is closer to the east end of the island; there, low rising colonial buildings were lit fluorescent along narrow streets, and the district maintains its scandalous reputation of having been *the* red-light district. I'm left to imagine, or Google, having spent the majority of the get-together in the courtyard and apartment of a gated condominium. Only later, inebriated in a cab, did I realize where I was, or had been, and happily pointed out to my wife that many of the hawker centers were lively, serving soups, noodles, and whatever else in case we wanted to eat. But it was near 4:00 a.m. and navigating a new social space at that hour was out of the question. You know, fuck it, we could (and would) get McDelivery at some point the following afternoon.

The gathering consisted of my wife (a beautiful woman from the American South, or its doormat, Tennessee), a man from London, a man from Belfast, a man from the Yorke Peninsula of Australia ("the Leg" of Australia as it's known), a friend (now friend) of a friend most recently from Seattle, and another woman from New Delhi. International unity. Mostly. What's significant about this, aside from everyone's hometown origins, was each of the ways we'd come to navigate Singapore and its culture based on our personal pasts, historical international relationships, and time spent in the city-state. The obvious historical conflict of territory was between the man from London and the man from Belfast. England and Ireland. One doesn't, or shouldn't, need to think too hard to realize those complexities and historical relationships, the recent elections in Ireland for independence from Britain, for example. To further add to complexity of territory, the woman from New Delhi discussed Kashmir and insisted it "belonged" to India; Pakistan had no claim to it, though some argued that Kashmir belonged to itself, and neither India nor Pakistan (like Bangladesh and its violent fight for independence). However, my first thought was Led Zeppelin, and how surprisingly easy the song is to play on guitar (once I'd figured out the tuning) and what "belonged" means. It's instances such as these that I feel I know little of the world, sometimes nothing. There are people that can recite facts and dates, create a historical timeline, win fucking trivia. But a timeline and facts aren't knowledge per se. I don't know how many times I've tried to discuss this with first-year composition students. Facts are facts: information not synthesized that's easy to manipulate and faulty without context. They are simply things that have been done, as John D'Agata explains somewhere in the intro to *The Next American Essay*, if I'm remembering correctly. I don't know many facts off the cuff, am horrible at trivia. These conversations happened all around me, each person aware that each conversation had the potential to get out of hand because none of it makes sense and, perhaps, no one really knows a goddamned fucking thing.

While I moaned words through the confines of lucid dreaming and lightning flashed around the cracks of the window's large blind, my wife got out of bed to piss, drink water, and close the small window above the shower so the downpour might not enter the apartment. She, too, once we discussed the storm a day or two later, expressed her fear of sitting on the toilet and reaching to shut the window once she finished—old wives' tales, as she called them, of being electrocuted through water in the house whether it be shower, toilet, sink, or rain entering the home. She returned to bed as water seeped in under the front door and we slept late into the afternoon.

We all live with fear, the US, it seems, as a nation, more so than any other. I've spent the majority of my life within its confines: an Indigenous ward in an occupied land. *We're* afraid of Black people, Muslims, Mexicans, China, Russia, North Korea, the Middle East, Africa, Cuba, greasy food and being fat, being too skinny, being wrong, being right or righteous, being accused of being politically incorrect or correct, of teenagers (especially Black teenagers, teenagers of color), of bees or the lack of bees, of not enough people liking our status updates, of reading and critical thought, of not reading enough or of what we read, of thinking for ourselves, of understanding. There, it seems, is something to fear in everything. Gluten is to be feared, whatever the hell it actually is. Sometimes we fear with reason, sometimes without, perhaps mostly without, but largely because "we" revel in ignorance. Wear it like a badge. *We're* proud of the things we don't know. It releases us from being complicit, from responsibility, from acknowledgment and empathy, from following the teachings or the beliefs of *our* religions, values, and mores, etc. Love thy neighbor? Nah, fuck that. They're a thug, a slut, a heathen, a hippie, a Democrat/Republican, a Northerner/Southerner, a this or that _____ of this or that _____. Once we begin to categorize humans we can begin to compartmentalize them as well.

I'm filled with fear. Filled this very moment, typing this essay in a National University of Singapore Starbucks that has a wall of windows overlooking a manicured lawn and trees, dorms and other buildings towering the perimeter. Today it's overcast, humid, and hot. The group behind me is loud and distracting, talking over one another about their research, credentials, the use of libraries around the world, and which are the best: Chicago, Oxford, Shanghai. *Smaller libraries are more focused, but access to an unlimited number of texts is better.* I have no library. My personal library, my symbol of intellectual prowess and girth, is thousands of miles away. So the knowledge and reference base from which I'm writing is simply my own, what's in front of me or easily accessible on the Internet (though I'm reluctant to search for anything to supplement this writing), and what's buried and half exposed in my memory. I've been reading from a Kindle, though I never use the highlight feature because it's unnatural to me. And, anyway, I've been reading novels to pass the time between teaching and working on a fiction collection that I slowly want to abandon for more honest and worthwhile endeavors. This excuse has resulted from frustration and the idea that fiction is entertainment, not a noble pursuit of truth like essays or journalism. But I know, or sense rather, that I'm completely wrong. My fear *is* what-I-know-that-I-don't-know and also what-I-do-know—my experience, my history. Without my books, my library, I have nothing to hide behind.

This isn't the first time that either my wife or I have been to Singapore and Southeast Asia. Three years ago she received the same six-week teaching/writing residency and we spent three months traveling to Bali, North and Central Vietnam, and Cambodia. We'd only dated two months. We wrote, read, fought, fell in and out of love, and nearly broke from one another, for good reason, once we returned traumatized and brokenhearted to the States. I'd fallen in love with her well before I'd actually met her (in that dangerous and romantic way, in that old way): a photo on social media at some event in Arizona where she was visiting ASU's campus from NYC made me think that the possibility of our worlds colliding imminent. At the time, I was living unhappily in Philadelphia with a (mostly present) fiancée who I was growing to resent and falling out of love with, a painful memory and sentence to write, one I've not written until this moment (the resonance of the event still a glacier flipping in my chest). I can't place the exact date or even build a timeline around when I saw the photo of my now-wife. It must have been prior to, or after, the two months I spent at the MacDowell Colony, where I eviscerated the fiction collection I'd written post-MFA and where I also began to compose and collect poetry derived from scraps I'd been writing since my English BA in 2003. Alone in my cabin, I had a couple breakdowns, panic attacks, and eventually made peace with the absolute darkness of the New Hampshire woods by smoking cigarettes and drinking Irish whiskey late into the night, scrawling things I deemed poems. I had developed this magical, fucked-up process of rising early and hungover to work on fiction while alternating days of running two to three miles and lifting at the gym in town just before dinner, after which I'd converse and imbibe with other artists, then work on "poems" late into the night, drunk. I repeated this process with daily two-hour naps. At some point my fiancée visited me, and I felt like I still loved her, but the remaining days in that cabin, and the ones after my return to Philly would drain it all out of me. I was figuring out how to depart, where to depart to, and what to do. Phoenix. I'd return to a city I'd grown to detest and to a job as an electrician working ten- to twelve-hour days, six days a week that would waste me.

I've been typing away at this damned thing for two days now, filled with anxiety, uncertainty, and fear. I want painkillers, my demonic synthetics of old: Xanax, Valium, Percocet, Oxycodone, Soma. That good, good shit. But it's only a notion. My wife has Xanax stashed somewhere in the apartment, pills she was prescribed for flight anxiety, the long haul to get here. I take comfort in the fact that I haven't searched them out, though it's crossed my mind once or twice. In reality, I fear their smallness and potency, the hot breath pressing me down. I'm sitting next to my wife as she works on her writing in the same Starbucks, though it's quieter than the time with the library talkers and sunny outside. Last night, after I finished teaching my portion of an evening creative writing workshop, my wife and I went out to a pub for dinner and a couple drinks. We chatted idly for a while. Our waiter described his brief holiday in KL (Kuala Lumpur, Malaysia) where, he said, it's less overrun with Aussies and Americans, and the street food is more "hygienic," less dodgy than Vietnam or Thailand, though the street food is quite fantastic in those places as well. After he left us, my wife and I immediately made plans to spend a couple nights in KL for the following week. Alone, we shifted our conversation to what each of us was working on, the challenges and frustrations of writing, and the attributes of the Arsenal and Chelsea players on the television over the bar. I rooted for Arsenal because I'm quite fond of Mesut Özil, Santi Cazorla, and Per Mertesacker. Ultimately, they'd lose 2-1. Two Chelsea players (extremely talented) who I dislike scored the winning goals: Eden Hazard and Diego Costa. We talked of this essay, forgiveness and trauma, and how to approach the problems with each, or rather each of our own experiences with forgiveness and trauma. Now, my wife knows nearly everything about my childhood, my past, my addictions, abuse, anger, and struggles. And I know of her past and her losses. Though to say "everything" is to imply that there is nothing left to learn from one another. Of course, that isn't true. We've been married close to four months, together nearly four years, and each time we dig into our psyches and pasts we uncover more doubts, goals, dreams, and fears.

The storms have ceased, the cooler muggy post-rain reprieve has arrived with them, and we've booked our trip to Kuala Lumpur. It's hardly an hour away by plane. Another hour or so cab ride and we're in the city, in the Bukit Bintang neighborhood, the streets web-like and congested, traffic laws for the most part optional. It's got a bustle all its own. Moto riders weave through traffic, taxis honk and swerve for position, there's construction to expand the MRT, and it's Ramadan (it never occurred, or had been taught to me, that Malaysia is a Muslim country). Restaurants prepare buffets and food stalls pop up along the streets and alleyways, ready for those who will break fast after sunset. It smells of cooking meat, fresh fruit, body odor, exhaust, sewer, and garbage. Our hotel is down the street from the high-end fashion mall, the Pavilion, and a block away from Jalan Alor, a street for street food, which, as we learn upon arrival around one or two in the afternoon, comes alive after 6:00 p.m. We find one of the few open places with fans, order dim sum, a couple beers, and a large bottle of water. The food, along with the humid heat, makes for a nap, and so we do.

The following days and evenings lead us to delicious food, malls, narrow colonial streets packed with fakes (Prada, Fendi, Beats, Gucci), 7-Eleven after 7-Eleven, prostitutes who ignore us for the most part, and a helipad that turns into a bar at sunset. There, we take in the far-reaching panoramic view of KL. It's electric, literally, the lights far-spread, the Petronas Towers like some futuristic, fantastic castle. The towers are filled with offices, a mall, and a bar/restaurant, all of which seem to take away from the mystical visage, but who am I kidding? It was fucking amazing to all take in.

The experience and distance from one's "real life" that's had while traveling never alleviates pain and trauma. It will have its moments of being a harsh and brutal reminder. My wife and I are continually aware of this idea. The three months we spent in Southeast Asia in 2012 were, as she's expressed to me, a traumatic experience, no thanks to my verbal assaults, inability to control my emotions, and substance abuse. For three months we shared amazing experiences visiting Hanoi, Halong Bay, Huế, Hội An, Angkor Wat, Bali, and Singapore. But we were trapped. Neither one of us had the funds to change all the fights we'd booked. We—or she, rather—could only survive the long days to our final departure. I struggled to be free of the pain and anger that consumed me, the memories of physical and sexual abuse flooding my every dream. I didn't have a modicum of control over what was destroying most everything around me, myself in particular. The stress and exhaustion of travel abroad would culminate in a huge fight after our return to Arizona during the height of the unbearable desert summer after we'd already struggled so many days and months to stay together. We'd drink too much, scream at one another, I'd push her to the floor like a coward after she backed me into a corner. I'd run away into the hot Phoenix night, she'd call me on my cell, and we'd scream more. I'd return, we'd remind one another of our love, and we'd sleep. Come morning it wouldn't matter. I couldn't—didn't know how to—apologize to her or acknowledge the fear and harm that I'd caused her. I was unable to get beyond my frustration, sadness, and confusion. I'd shake my head at her and drive away. She'd return to Tennessee to be with family, and I'd fly to Philadelphia, rent a small SUV, and drive the few meaningless possessions I left in U-Haul storage back to Arizona. It'd take me five or six days because I didn't want to drive at night and I'd get blackout drunk in every town where I sought out hotels with or near bars. At times, when the road was clear, I'd shut my eyes and let go of the steering wheel. Only once did the vehicle drift, vibrating over the perforations along the road's shoulder, and I nearly lost control. I stopped at a gas station in Oklahoma and vomited in the putrid wet bathroom from hangover, anxiety, and panic. I called a therapist I found on the Internet who specialized in childhood trauma and told him of everything that happened in Sea-Tac and after: my pushing the woman I loved, my inability to cope, and my suicidal thoughts. I needed to make it two more days and call or text him every day until I arrived back to Phoenix.

Fear, and my desire to immerse myself in building my online world literature course for the early modern period, and the need to tackle my professional writer/editor responsibilities have stalled my writing of this essay. It's been over two weeks since I've added anything. I'm all guilt, trapped by memory. In that time, and after the conversation that my wife and I had at the pub in Singapore regarding our previous time spent here, we've traveled through Phú Quốc, Vietnam (an island that probably belongs to Cambodia but was given to the Vietnamese by the French), Ho Chi Minh City (Saigon), and presently Phnom Penh, Cambodia. I've read a couple nonfiction books, a novel, and poems online. During this time my younger sister has traveled to Peru from Arizona for some healing with ayahuasca. I've been with an uneasy mind. She is a significant source of my self-hatred, my inability to forgive, my inability to forget, and my short temper—what I can't seem to get to or say.

I was an angry and erratic child, often morose and cruel to my younger sister, who suffered the consequences of my own suffering and rage as well as her own. Beyond the typical sibling rivalry, I was violent, scared, and sleepless. Unfortunately, we suffered through many similar experiences of abuse, not from our parents (though there are other issues and essays there), but from babysitters and extended family. Our futures were fucked, as were we.

It's impossible to go into any detail. I've been advised not to by many a therapist. I've been advised to move forward. Closing in on my thirty-fifth birthday, it's still difficult. I haven't spoken with my sister for over a year and but a stilted handful of times in previous years. She's been going through a dark time, the specifics of which are unknown to me, to even my parents with whom she still lives. I can't help but feel partly—hell, mostly—responsible.

About three years ago my sister and I had a falling out in Philadelphia. She and my parents were visiting me. My fiancée had recently purchased a house with a roof that had been half-assedly repaired. Tropical storm Irene was drowning and wrecking the East Coast. The ceiling and walls had blistered with rainwater prior to my family's visit. I had to cut an access hole into the attic space to locate the spot where the water showered in. I spent weeks tearing off and rebuilding the roof of the three-story rowhouse from two thirty-five-foot extension ladders. It was slow, frustrating work. At some point, as storms came and went, my fiancée traveled to Mexico for work and a small earthquake shook Philadelphia while I was standing at the peak of the roof. I thought wind had captured the sixty-by-sixty-foot blue tarp and that it was going to damage the decking and shingles. As the earth shook the house, I scrambled across the roof securing the tarp, oblivious to what was happening, thinking that exhaustion and hunger were the cause of the instability I felt.

My family stayed a week. I completed the roof repair with the help and moral support of my father. But everything felt wrong, tense, and humid. Irene hit Philadelphia during their first night. Water poured again into the third floor. I was forced to don my rain gear and harness and ascend the roof to reposition the tarp. Rain blew from every direction, the clouds dense and circling. Green lightning lit the sky, and I felt both an ending and a beginning.

The visit coincided with my sister's birthday. My fiancée had pulled strings to get us all a table at some small, well-renowned Italian restaurant. But as we walked through Rittenhouse Square in Center City, my sister turned and yelled at me, accusing me of never having her back, of thinking her less than or lacking, of being a monster. She hated me. I was supposed to protect her and was never able to.

Once, when we were kids, she told me that she knew I'd abuse my children and probably hit my wife.

I've never been fully able to forgive myself or my abusers, and especially the abusers of my sister. I was forced to watch and participate. I was, I felt, the victim and the assailant. When I pushed my wife, it was confirmation, for me, of my sister's accusation. I've always been no good and on my way to being wholly, completely no good. I can't ever forget or forgive. Anyone or myself. No amount of reassurance has ever been enough. But I'm still alive and filled with hatred, anger, and sadness. I'm also happy and comfortable with the thought that a couple of the people who harmed my sister and myself are suffering, are in pain. I don't forgive them. I want them be present in their pain, to live long and excruciating lives. And as my sister struggles, I struggle. I am present in my pain, hoping to live a long and excruciating life.

The first time I ever traveled abroad, I flew to Prague for a monthlong writing workshop. There, I learned how my name was actually pronounced, the *j* not zha, but a *yawn*. *Bo-yawn*, not *Bo-zhan*. I also learned from two Czech people what it might mean and that it was Croatian, Slavic. One: the fighter or the frightened one. Two: son of thunder. Both appropriate. I'm violent and scared. Preemptive. A product of imperial US cultural values. Also, I am, or have been, an electrician. I was twenty-eight when I learned this, the only knowledge of my name was that my parents chose it as they watched some ski jumper during the 1980 Winter Olympics held in Lake Placid. In Prague I met Arnošt Lustig and Ivan Klíma (the latter on my birthday), two writers who've shaped my writing. Both survived the Holocaust, Russian and German occupation, and exile. Good over evil. In a way, it's what I want. Good over evil. Knowledge over ignorance. Empathy over judgment. I want to learn from and write about these things and believe that it will be enough. It'll be enough.

Fertility Rites

TIFFANY MIDGE

Age ten, and near the cusp of becoming, I discover a pond full of tadpoles in the woods behind the newly built Heather Glen Family Estates. No frogs to kiss and seek my fortune with, just the blind, pale swimmers; all heads and tails flapping in the algae muck. I transplant them to buckets on the back porch, careful to re-create their new home in replica to their old; hauling water from the pond, transplanting moss, grass, pus-yellow swamp rot. I marvel at their design, their spongy slickness, the way they glide and wiggle from one wall of the bucket habitat to the next, with no apparent destination, no goal but to grow into frogs. This is what I hope for: buckets of bullfrogs and horny toads who make deep-throated calls, courting the twilight. This is what I anticipate: meaty legs to harvest and sell, to pickle in old mayonnaise jars.

But the tadpoles always die.

Even replenishing their pond water daily with fresh pond water doesn't help. I bring back more tadpoles, but after a couple of days those died too. I disrupted a fragile ecosystem and can't re-create it like the aphid experiments in Mrs. Louden's science class or the rain forest habitat at Woodland Park Zoo. The pond is an abundant, all-giving womb, a not-to-be-messed-with mother of crawdads, beetles, and dragonflies. And I am a failed incubator, a mad scientist tempting nature and fate, in danger of throwing it all out of balance, sealing my future with every unintended murder. Today, at this stage of life, I don't have children nor will I ever, and I can't help wondering about karma: all those ruined tadpoles, all those poor bastard frogs.

I think of the tadpoles when I think of mushroom hunting.

How one fall I meet Mary, a devout amateur mycologist, just as she's in mid-grope for a cluster of flabby white fruits out at the hillsides by Lake Padden. She likes to defy the guidebooks and plays Russian roulette with her liver with schools of cataloged toxins.

"The guidebooks say these are poisonous, but they haven't been for me." She says, which I hope won't be the words etched on her tombstone.

The State of Alaska's epidemiology bulletin, titled *Hazards of Stalking the Wild Mushroom*, lists common myths about mushrooms. The first old wives' tale being "poisonous mushrooms tarnish a silver spoon." I've been with men like that. Men who tarnished confidence, tainted weeklong intakes of breath saved just for them. Men who were listed in all the field manuals but were overlooked or purposely disregarded just like the hapless characters from a Lifetime movie. It should be that easy; testing your potential mates like scraping a diamond across glass or placing a canary into a mineshaft.

I disclose my secret spot to Mary—a smorgasbord of flesh-toned corals—and she promises she won't touch my pet *Stropharia*, coveted for its cap skirted with lace tatting like a canopy bed. She scrambles down an embankment thinking she'd spied a mass of chicken-fried mushrooms. She's so cavalier uprooting a specimen, a *Jonquil amanita*, just to show me where its cap once met its stem, where the wings now flapped uselessly as skin tags. She strokes the shaft teasingly, then tosses it aside, declaring it,

"No good, it's poisonous," as if she were pronouncing the fate of a eunuch. Her disregard bothers me, this casual evacuation of a mushroom that had grown as large as my hand, through five nights of rain, its genesis a sprite-like exchange of spores and rot, chancing the elements, the hazards of mollusks, to break open through the soil like the fist of a prizefighter—

like the gold-painted Leggs pantyhose egg

hidden from view in the spring grass in the field behind the library. One of five prize eggs that the Sunday school teachers secret away, the eggs you're supposed to trade for a chocolate bunny with ears longer than your pinky. I see that gold egg way before Robby Forsgren comes near it, but I stand observing it dumbly like I'm waiting for a red light to change, all because Miss Pike, within plain view, plots that gold egg in the grass right in front of me and even slips me a conspiring wink that says, *here, take it, it's yours.* But before I can solve my moral dilemma, *that's cheating, isn't it?* Robby Forsgren comes running and dives for my egg like a desperate bridesmaid for the bouquet, then lumbers away, holding it over his head, the coveted chocolate prize all his, the prize I gave away.

AND SO I ANAL DOUCHE WHILE KESHA'S "PRAYING" PLAYS FROM MY IPHONE ON REPEAT

BILLY-RAY BELCOURT

PICTURE THIS: TWO BROTHERS, ONE FINDS IN BOOZE WHAT THE OTHER FINDS IN THE BODIES OF WHITE MEN / REFUSE TO THINK THE CONSEQUENCES OF THESE CRAVINGS AS ANYTHING BUT EQUALLY POISONOUS / I AM NO BETTER THAN HE WHO EATS TOO MUCH OF THE SUNSET / IN FACT ALL I DO IS GNAW AND GNAW AT THE SUN UNTIL MY LIPS ARE SO CRACKED THAT I CAN ONLY SPEAK THE WORLD WRONG / NOWADAYS WHEN ASKED IF I AM HUNGRY, FERAL WORDS DROP FROM MY MOUTH / LIKE *YOU'RE KINDA CUTE, EH* / *NATIVES LIKE YOU ARE ALWAYS UNCUT* / *YOU WERE DIFFERENT, USU-ALLY I CAN'T STOP THINKING ABOUT SOMEONE OR I LOSE INTEREST RIGHT AWAY, YOU WERE SOMEWHERE IN-BETWEEN* / AND MY VOICE ALWAYS STAYS THE SAME SO EVENTUALLY I TOO MISTAKE THE "NOT-I" FOR THE "I" AND NO ONE WARNS YOU ABOUT THE THORNY EDGES OF THE "NOT-I" BECAUSE NO ONE WANTS TO TALK ABOUT INVOLUNTARY EXILE / BECAUSE NO ONE WANTS TO BECOME TRAPPED IN THE CIRCUITRY OF UNBECOMING, WHICH IS PERPET-UAL BECAUSE ATTRITION AND MEMORY OPERATE AT DIFFERENT

TEMPORAL REGISTERS THAN SOMETHING AS TENUOUS AS A PULSE // IF I HAD CATCHPHRASES THEY WOULD PROBABLY SOUND A LITTLE LIKE / *DOES THIS FORESKIN MAKE ME LOOK INDIAN???* / *PLEASE TELL ME IF I HAVE MOURNING BREATH* / *ACTUALLY YOU KNOW WHAT I THINK I WOULD STILL KISS YOU IF YOU HAD MOURNING BREATH I'M SUPER ACCOMODATING LIKE THAT* // I DON'T WANT TO CALL THIS FEELING ANXIETY SO I'LL OPT FOR THE CLUNKIER "NOSTALGIA FOR THE FUTURE" / I THINK THE PRIME MINISTER IS GASLIGHTING ME / I THINK I AM GASLIGHTING ME // I USED TO SAY THAT I WOULD NEVER SPEND MORE THAN 12 HOURS IN AN AIRPLANE BUT NOW I AM DATING AN AUSTRALIAN AND 16 HOURS SOUNDS LIKE A PERFECT OPPORTUNITY TO TALK TO HIM ABOUT ALL OF MY FEELINGS / FOR EXAMPLE LAST WEEK WE WERE HUGGING IN MY BED SUCH THAT MY DICK WAS PRESSED AGAINST HIS AND I SAID SOMETHING LIKE / *I NEED TO LEARN HOW TO MISS YOU LESS* / HE NODDED IN AGREEMENT AS IF I WEREN'T BEGGING HIM FOR MERCY AS IF I HAD SOVEREIGN CONTROL OVER MY EMOTIONS // *ABSENCE IS A HOME AWAY FROM HOME* / I HAVE STARTED RECITING THIS THREE TIMES INTO HIS ARMPIT BEFORE I FALL ASLEEP / HIS THOUGHTS AREN'T NIGHT OWLS LIKE MINE / LATELY I CAN'T STOP THINKING ABOUT HIM OR MAYBE I THINK LESS ABOUT HIM AND MORE ABOUT THE SPACE BETWEEN HIS BODY AND MINE / I INSTALLED THAT SPACE WITH BLOATED MEANING / I MADE A WILDFIRE OUT OF IT / I TRIPPED OVER MY OWN TWO FEET TRYING TO RUN FROM IT // TONIGHT I STARTED TO KISS HIM LIKE I AM ABOUT TO DISSOLVE INTO HIS MOUTH / I HOPE HE LIKES TO SWALLOW / I HOPE HE CAN SPEAK WITH A NEW THROAT // I ABSORB EVERYTHING HE GIVES ME EVEN IF IT IS JUST THE QUIET / LOVE TAUGHT ME HOW TO STARE WITHOUT LOOKING / I DON'T BLINK FOR HOURS / I START TO SMELL LIKE DUST / AND I DISAGREGGATE INTO A BOX OF OLD KEEPSAKES // LIKE ALL GOOD WORSHIPPERS I DO EVERYTHING IN HIS NAME / I DEVOTE BOWEL MOVEMENTS TO HIM / I EXPEL MORE AIR THAN I TAKE IN FOR HIS SAKE // HE STOLE BANALITY FROM ME /

EVERYTHING THICKENS WITH MEMORIES OF HIM AND A COLLEC-
TIVE "YOU" WITH WHICH I AM INDELIBLY MIXED / EVEN THE LIGHT
BULBS GOSSIP ABOUT ME AND YET I CAN'T BRING MYSELF TO STOP
EASEDROPPING // THEY SAY ONLY THE INDIANS DIE YOUNG / OR
WAS IT THE GOOD??? / I ALWAYS FUCK THESE SORTA SAYINGS UP /
SPEAKING OF SAYINGS *HE WAS PRONOUNCED DEAD* IS NOT SIMPLY
A STATEMENT OF FACT / IT IS A PART OF THE CALCULUS OF KILLING
/ THE FIRST TIME HE SAYS HE LOVES ME I BET IT WILL FEEL LIKE
HE IS PRONOUNCING A DEATH / AS IF TO SAY *I LOVE YOU* IS TO SAY
HE WAS PRONOUNCED DEAD MINUTES AFTER / AS IF THE MOMENT HE
INTERPELLATES THE "NOT-I" OF "I LOVE YOU" LETTERS WILL FALL
FLAT ONTO THE FLOOR // TONIGHT HE WANTS ME TO FUCK HIM BUT
I THROW WORDS AT THE WALLS AROUND HIM INSTEAD / AT FIRST
I DON'T NOTICE THE DIFFERENCE // I AM TOO TIRED TO CARRY ALL
OF THESE SYMBOLS / YOU MIGHT THINK THAT I CAN'T TAKE IT AND
YOU'RE RIGHT MY LONELINESS IS KILLING ME JUST THE SAME // I
JOKED ONCE THAT I WAS SO GAY THAT I DIVESTED FROM MEN BUT
IN REALITY I DON'T KNOW HOW TO BE ANYTHING BUT SACRIFICAL
/ I TEND TO PAUSE WHEN DATES ASK IF I AM RELIGIOUS BECAUSE
MY RELATION TO WHITE MEN FEELS ALMOST HOLY / LIKE I AM
DYING FOR THEIR SINS AND EVERY TIME I OPEN MY LEGS IT SOUNDS
SOMETHING LIKE *AMEN* OR *AND ALSO WITH YOU* AND THEN WE
THINK ONLY OF SOME KIND OF HIGHER POWER / ABOUT SOME REA-
SON FOR ALL OF THIS SUFFERING / AND ALL OF THIS WAITING

The Great Elk

RUBY HANSEN MURRAY

I'm on the way to visit Cahokia with the Osage Nation Historical Pres-
ervation Department in a chartered bus that is less than half full. Many
Americans don't know that an agrarian civilization was centered in Illinois
between 600 and 1300 CE. It supported forty thousand people—more than
the population of London at the time. Compulsory labor built a pyramid as
large at the base as the Great Pyramid of Giza. Cahokia became a UNESCO
World Heritage site in 1982, and now schoolkids make yearly field trips.

The Osage are part of the Dhegiha Sioux, one of the groups that built
the monuments and created a complex cultural life, which is why the
Nation takes Osages from Pawhuska to St. Louis most years.

I'm sitting with the elders and archeologists near the front. In the back,
Gwen is beading, and Lana is settled in among fat pillows across from her.
We stop for lunch at a Bass Pro Shop, which appears to be an oversized
hunting lodge on an ordinary thoroughfare in Springfield, Missouri. The
bus circles a large, crowded parking lot before the driver stops at the
imposing doors.

Inside the store, I'm assaulted by stimuli in a space at least four stories
high. The place is a clash of antlers and taxidermied head mounts. Twelve
or more white-tailed bucks are mounted facing different directions on
posts that support upper stories. There's a full-body grizzly, polar bear,
black bear, bighorn sheep, and antelope.

In any direction, from ledges above cabinets, display cases, from the walls, animals either meet my gaze or show their backsides. A post studded with deer antlers stands beside a rack of women's coats.

Upstairs, small human figures file past an enormous bronzed elk that surveys us all. A line of Middle America files up a flight and a half of stairs toward it. The elk looks down on me—the bunched muscles of the rump uphill, the back legs tensed above rocks where it's frozen mid-step. The antlers are curved as gracefully as any ballerina's arms against a blue-and-green panorama of forest and sky. The flight of a hawk is arrested, the undersides of its wing detailed. The elk looks down a narrow nose past its raised chin. I remember elk I've seen skid across the road in front of my truck in the backwoods or climbing up the steep hill from the Columbia River, by Abe Creek.

The elk stands on a rocky ledge by a descending streambed, surrounded by trees in a woodland diorama that curves through the five-hundred-thousand-square-foot store.

People quietly walk before the elk like pilgrims—a couple with arms bared to the heat, a bald man and a woman with a wavy, brown ponytail high on her head. Two children gaze up at the animal.

I think of the time when the Osage people in the stars looked down and saw the whole earth flooded. They sent messengers from two clans: one from the stars and one from the bright-stars to make a way for the people and animals to live on the land.

The messengers spoke to the water spider, the water strider, the white leech, and the dark leech. The insects were gracious; in fact, they offered to make the people live a long time—wrinkled as the ripples on the water. They couldn't help, but they offered to go get the Great Elk, o'pon ton ga. He came and, in the part I like best, threw himself on the surface of the water, not once, but four times.

When the Great Elk stood up, the water was up to the middle of his sides, and the next time he stood up, the water reached the underside of his belly, the next time his knees, and finally the earth was all exposed. The last time, he threw himself down and rolled. He rocked to right himself, like the horses in the pasture next door. I imagine running my hand in the stiff hair of an elk hide, feeling the hairs left behind that will turn into grass.

An elk herd lives near Gearhart on the northern coast of Oregon and goes into the surf from time to time. Those big tan animals with the dark brown capes splash in blue water and foam on sunny days, and that's how I picture the Great Elk thrashing.

This is the way the Omaha anthropologist Frances La Flesche recorded the clan stories that Charles Wah hre she and Shunkamolah told him. Stories that University of Tulsa professor Garrick Bailey collected and reprinted. I wonder if all humans have cellular memory of a flood.

For a moment, seeing the small figures walking before the elk makes me think that white people know the Great Elk too.

The restaurant upstairs, called Hemingway's, is filled with mahogany-inspired furniture and lined with paned windows and an enormous aquarium. In one photo an unshaven Ernest Hemingway, his white hair uncombed, sits at a dining table holding a double shot glass to his lips. He looks at something beside his plate. In another, he's middle-aged, standing beside a marlin, smiling.

We're in the land of sweet tea. The women from Oklahoma are ordering half-sweet and half unsweet. Ted orders a glass of wine and wahoo, a tropical fish.

The only other Bass Pro Shop I've been inside was in Florida. My husband and I were driving the causeway between mangrove swamps and the Florida Keys when we stopped on Islamorada. Beyond a manicured parking strip, a new building held clothing and gear, and in the center of it stood a replica of the *Pilar*, Hemingway's boat. Bass Pro advertises itself as part sporting goods store, part wildlife museum. I remember the egret with black legs, white feathers like lace panties, walking back and forth on the railing by the fishing dock.

Traveling with a group of Osages is like being on a loose family trip, although less stressful than our trips as children. In the 1940s, Osages packed panel trucks full of supplies and sent them ahead to Colorado

Springs, while they followed in their touring cars. After lunch, Ted looks for a place to smoke, and I trail Jackie and her two adult sons looking for sunscreen. An alligator is suspended from the ceiling, its legs and webbed feet extended as if it is swimming. The alligator's white belly, the shadows of grass on the bank, and jagged light on the water make me feel as if I'm underwater.

Alligators aren't native to Missouri, but the store has an alligator pit. Given the restaurant's Hemingway motif, I assume it's a Florida-based chain, but I learn that Johnny Morris started this sporting goods giant from a corner of his father's liquor store here in Springfield, Missouri, in 1972.

I'm looking for inherent logic, but Bass Pro is fantasyland. In this world, big game animals are abundant and guns are unlimited. In fact, 185 muzzle-loading rifles act as balusters on the stairs to the fourth-floor NRA National Sporting Arms Museum.

I leave my friends and start for the bus, but I don't make it outside. Beside the door stands a gleaming white statue of an Indian on his horse that is fully two stories tall. Both are slumped forward, apparently sleeping. The horse's head and neck hang down, and the man is curled over. He's leaning so far forward, it seems he will fall off. I think of a person so drunk he's loose in his body.

The Indian appears to be broken, dispirited, desolate. But when you study the statue, the line of the horse and rider are curved at such a diagonal, it feels dynamic. Braids hang forward off the man's chest near a bright white, muscled arm. The horse's eyes sag half closed, and its tail is blown forward across its legs.

The piece is familiar, of course. *The End of the Trail.* An enormous representation of an Indian man, whose mental, physical, and spiritual inertia are all that keeps him balanced on the horse. A blonde girl who looks to be about ten and her father stand beside me studying the statue.

I don't know why this reproduction is in Missouri. Osage men, like most of our kin, shaved their heads. This appears to be a Lakota man draped in a buffalo robe. I realize I'm being too literal. In a Disney-inspired moment, I think I see a butterfly on the end of one braid, but it's a leather tie.

Jackie and her sons pass between the statue and me. Art is tall and wears a braid down his back.

The little girl says, "Is that an Indian?"

Art looks over his shoulder. I see the question on his face, his raised eyebrows. He glances back at her, as I do, but, like her father, she's gazing up at the statue.

Johnny Morris loves fishing, and he loves the Ozarks, part of our ancestral land. Morris says he was captivated when, as a young man, he found an arrowhead as he crossed a recently plowed field: "It got to me. I started thinking, 'What was life like when the person made this point? What was wildlife like? What was fishing like?' I was standing there in my jeans and my tennis shoes just thinking, 'What did they wear? Did they have on a deerskin crop? Or maybe a buffalo hide? What were they really like?'"

Since then, he's built lodges on nature parks near Branson, Missouri, and at least seventy-seven stores across the country. In 2018 he's worth $5.3 billion according to Forbes. There's an Osage Restaurant at the Top of the Rock, a forty-seven-acre Ozarks Heritage Preserve with a Jack Nicklaus–designed golf course overlooking Table Rock Lake. Not surprisingly, the restaurant serves American cuisine, rather than meat pies and yonkapins. On a lower terrace, a metal sculpture of a buffalo is silhouetted against the lake, and outside the Top of the Rock lodge, a bronzed version of *The End of the Trail* stands in a pool reflecting pink and blue at sunset.

The Indian man in *The End of The Trail* sculpture and the buffalo are used as décor, symbols of a long-ago time.

"Memory is as important as water," Viet Thanh Nguyen writes in *Nothing Ever Dies*, his collection of essays examining the Vietnam War and all of those who were, and are, affected by it. "Nations cultivate and would monopolize, if they could, both memory and forgetting. They urge their citizens to remember their own and to forget others in order to forge the nationalistic spirit crucial for war."

I don't know what white people see when they look at the Indian man drooping on his horse. Maybe he looks benign, maybe he looks sad, or he takes them back to a supposedly simple time when Michael Landon lived with his family in *Little House on the Prairie*. In real life, Pa Ingalls had to pack up and leave the Osage Diminished Reserve around the time the railroads and settlers were fighting over Indian land, and we Osages were forced to leave for Oklahoma ourselves. Memory is as important as water.

PLAITING

Real Romantic

EDEN ROBINSON

If you like me, why bring flowers? Dead plants you can't eat or dry into tea. Bring me totes of salmon so fresh their blood smells like the sea, brined seal, shucked cockles, moose roasts. My loving gestures include gifts of wool work socks and value packs of cotton underwear. Also, jam.

*

I know that romance sells, and I would romanticize the hell out of my Indigenous culture if I had a romantic bone in my body. Even my clan is unromantic, the ever-practical Beaver clan, who are best known for their hard work and cranky disposition. I'm involved in three clan feuds with my various extended families. I didn't start the feuds; I won't end them. My job is to pick a side or have everyone involved hate me. You're here, my family reminds me, to chew the leather.

I come from potlatching cultures. We hold feasts in the sacred season, the dead of winter. Contrary to popular beliefs, we don't give away our goods willy-nilly. We redistribute them to the people who bear witness. We validate our claims publicly and your job, as a witness, is to remember accurately and repeat honestly. You tell the truth. We're matrilineal, which means I should be Eagle Clan, but I was adopted into my father's clan, the Beaver Clan (or, more accurately, the Two Beavers Sharing at the Tree of Life Clan). I have a name but haven't thrown a potlatch yet; I don't have the rank to throw a potlatch. I have to attach my business to some-one else's. My name is good but not that noble. Think Fergie rather than Diana.

A part of my duty as a clan member is to help prepare the feasts. I'm continually busted down from potato to carrot peeler during feast preps because of tardy work. When I first moved back home, this stung, to be peeling at the table with the ten- and twelve-year-olds. Women my age are usually put in charge of the soup pots for the feasts, a position of heavy responsibility. I have burnt soup. It is possible. Simply sit at your desk and type an op-ed no one's asking for and forget that you're cooking until the smoke alarm goes off.

*

My mother is Heiltsuk from Waglisla, and my father is Haisla from Ci'mot'sa, both small First Nations reserves hugging the rugged shores of the northwest coast of British Columbia. I live an hour and half drive from the Alaska panhandle, on the main Haisla reserve, a small plot of land between towering coastal mountains and the ocean. Alternately called the Kitamaat Mission, Kitamaat Village, or just the Village, our traditional name for this place, Ci'mot'sa, means "snag beach." The Kitimat River washes down tree stumps from the temperate rain forest, and they gather on our waterfront, Cthulhu-shaped roots that wander with the tide. In powwow culture, to "snag" is slang for "hook up." I think "Snag Beach" would make a great name for an Indigenous dating site where my profile would probably run something like:

Eden Robinson, 49, matriarchal tendencies. Doesn't have a pressure cooker, but knows how to jar salmon. Her smoked salmon will not likely kill you. Hobbies: Shopping for the Apocalypse, using vocabu-lary as a weapon, nominating cousins to council while they're out of town, chair yoga, looking up possible diseases or syndromes on the interwebs, perfecting gluten-free bannock, and playing mah-jongg.

Swipe right to check attached genealogical records to see if she's your cousin.

*

The only blind date I ever went on was in my twenties. I lived in East Van at the time, two blocks from my gran. She was excited, more excited than me, about the possibility I could be "marrying back" into her Heiltsuk community. She knew my date's family, their history, how they'd performed in the All Native Basketball Tournament over the years. He picked me up and we had an awkward dinner. Neither of us had dessert. Thirty seconds after I opened my door, Gran phoned, wanting to know how things had gone and where he was taking me on our second date. I said I didn't think there'd be a second date; we hadn't sparked. There was no chemistry.

"Oh, don't worry," Gran had said. "I'll talk to his mother."

Dating on the coast requires extreme vetting. When I was living in Victoria, I'd had a few dates with a man who thought I was hilarious and cute. He laughed and laughed and I marveled at how much he sounded like my uncle So-and-so.

"Hey, my dad's name is So-and-so!" he said.

As we began to connect the dots, we both realized he was a first cousin, through a relationship my uncle had had when he was a teen.

Note to self: the first question we ask cute Native dudes is not just who's your mother, but who're your parents?

*

And for those of you reading this who were taken out of your communities, who were adopted out, and now find yourself on the outside, we know this awkward dance between longing for connection and being afraid of disappointment or rejection. All the news you hear, all the stories about how broken we are, how damaged—it's true and it's not true. Yes, we have our troubles. But when you come home, you'll find us unafraid of your complexity. We get real fast. I will tell you about my inflammatory bowel disorder or my struggles with chronic depression at the drop of a hat. Any rez I've been, any urban center, any gathering, the fronting is limited. The bullshit gets called, the teasing can be rough, but we're ready to tell stories long into the night and laugh, and sing, and dance. We're messy, but fun.

The Trickster Surfs the Floods

NATANYA ANN PULLEY

I. The Inside of Animals

But the heart of the turkey is weak, I say to an innerself. My mom points to the turkey's heart and holds it under running water. She shows me how the water pumps through it. Her lips resting on the top of the heart as she blows. The tiny organ bulges and deflates. My mother says words to me that are complicated. Technical. She doesn't point to any feathers on the turkey; there aren't any. She just holds its heart, all slick and of no color that would match a crayon in my Crayola set. A red-brown-gray thing.

It is Thanksgiving and it is all that trickster coyote's fault again. The coyote Ma'ii is not around, but he must have loped through my house in the middle of the night and changed the stories and changed the words and changed the decorations around me. The world my schoolteacher painted for me this week does not fit in my home. No *Mayflower,* no cornucopia, no pilgrims. Just my Navajo mother and the cold heart she holds out in front of me.

My younger brother is oblivious—he is all hands. Slapping counters, grabbing napkins, squeezing mashed potatoes through his little fists. My mom leaves the heart on the counter and walks over to my brother. She hovers down to his ear and points at the salt and pepper turkey set on the table. "Do you know how the turkey got its white tail?" she asks. It was the

119

last to leave the Third World, and the froth of the rising water grabbed it. She says this and kisses his cheek. She says this and strokes his hair. She says these things to the little body and big soul that is new to us and raw. I think she must have said these things to me like that too. All soft lips and softer hands.

But the heart of the turkey is weak. The turkey would not leave the Third World to this world even as the water was rising up past its spur. The water says the Third World is too full, that the water monsters have claimed it for their own. The water monsters' baby has been taken by Ma'ii and hidden in his clothes. The water monsters made themselves big and flooded themselves and the area around them. So angry, the water is too loud to reason with; First Man and First Woman and all the animals must flee. The locust has the medicine from the Holy People. The medicine can save the First people and the animals. A reed is placed in the earth and it grows and grows to the Fourth World. The creatures scramble to free themselves from the water monsters' anger, but the turkey stumbles inside himself. It is too long a journey, too hard a climb, too fast a move, too loud the rush behind him, too vast a nothingness to enter, too soft a place to leave. The turkey's heart is not the heart my mother animates for me. My mom's brown skin and black eyes unlike any of my friends' and neighbors' mothers. Unlike any of my teachers. My mother with the long guttural vowels she uses when others speak from high inside the mouth. My mother with these stories whispered in my ear, but she is always holding the insides of animals out for me to touch.

We eat the turkey. My mom has chopped its heart into smaller bits to add to the gravy. She tells us how the turkey has white tips on his feathers and I push my report on the great ships in search of new land out of my mind. To make her proud, I ask her to pass the "maize" like we learned in school. But corn is called naadą́ą́' in Navajo. There are two types of corn, male and female, but that is another story. As is the story of how the water monsters got their baby back, as is the story of the great expansion over the seas to the new rock. And no story I know tells of how the scared turkey that barely made it from the Third World landed on the platter in front of us, but it must be Ma'ii's fault. The trickster. The secreter. The maker of messes and slippery slopes and oopsa-daisies.

At Thanksgiving, there are turkeys everywhere. The napkin holders. The plates. The salt and pepper shakers. The bits stuck between our teeth and the turkey in the words of my mom with its tail fan of white tips. My brother pats at his highchair tray and smiles at the turkey on the table. Ma'ii must not have gotten to him yet.

II. Mapping the Space between the Stars

I am seven and worrying the hem of my comforter threadbare with my thumb and forefinger. Ma'ii has done it again. That trickster coyote has grinned and gripped Black God's fawn-skin pouch with his teeth. He held the corner of it and tugged tugged tugged, and the pouch, which held the stars, burst open across the universe. The stars scattered and falling—some always falling—the Holy People gasp. Black God throws his maps away. His plan to sort the sky sinks and burns up as stars descend toward earth. The stars Black God placed don't dare move, but shine brightly. And the stars the coyote Ma'ii freed lay about like jacks on the blacktop, forgotten.

From the center of my bed, where I curl up and stare out the window, I imagine Black God doesn't place the stars himself but asks a young boy to help. The boy carries the stars in his beeldléí and even though the weavings carefully hung around my mom's house are wool and made with black, brown, and red threads, in my mind the child's blanket looks a lot like my green-and-yellow checkered comforter, the stars fuzzy and knotted like the purple threads tied throughout it. Always Ma'ii gets a hold of the boy's blanket and rips a hole in it. The stars fall into crevices in the heavens. They stay there, lost, forming a large gash of starlight only to be seen from below.

Not all stars fell and are falling. The ones Black God placed appear in the same position to us from below. This is why certain stars reappear or why they gather. This is why we can look at them and count on them. They tell us when to plant and harvest. When to tell winter stories and when to tuck those stories away. When and where to travel. The story is meant to do these things for the children as they huddle up to their grandfather's words—as they sit under night skies and listen to the sheep blathering about the hay and the sandy walk up the mesa and the sheepdogs that close in on them.

For me, I think: Poor Star Boy. He searches for so long his eyes are black with little glints of starlight in them. He cries stardust. His hair must be messy and greasy with cosmos and when people see him they want to give him money and send him away at the same time. I get mad at Ma'ii—it is no coyote to me because I don't live near the coyotes in Dinéland Arizona like my mom did. I live near some mixed breeds and golden retrievers and a schnauzer on a street in Utah, a street that was once named "Hindenburg Lane" but was changed to "Mountain Vista Lane" when the neighbors congregated and decided the name was too gloomy. That was the end of that story; there was no warrior twin to defeat the name. There were no Holy People to talk to the congregation or to a smaller animal. They took a vote.

In Navajoland the stars scatter and stay, and the children learn agriculture, direction, and seasonal activities. But I lie in bed, holding my comforter. I wonder how I would be able to carry it if it were full of stars, how can I carry it down the stairs? The thump thump thump of it against the stairs would wake my parents. They could hear me come back up without the heaviness of the night sky in it—no thump, but the whoosh of it along the hardwood. I try to find the words the boy might say to his parents when they don't see the stars in the sky and ask to see them in his blanket. I practice the words. Just in case I need to borrow them one day.

III. The Shipbuilder's Round-Up

The church books say it is not Ma'ii that brought about the flood, but that it was God himself. God is just one god in this story. He is all of a god and there seems to be no one for him to talk to except to shout down to the rest of us. He is angry or perhaps just moody. It is unclear to me, and the church primary schoolteacher says the world was flooded from his anger. A man was to build a ship to hold two of each animal.

Two of each! I think. A great man. A man to bring the animals together and while the book talks of the building of the ship, I think of this Great Herder, Noah. How he must have had many tin cans of special rocks to rattle and only the best of herding dogs. How Ma'ii and any other coyote friends of his must have steered clear until the very end of the round-up before sneaking onboard. What must Noah have said to the brachiosaurus and the triceratops to push them onto that ship? I think of the dinosaur prints my father was always showing us—out in the desert. My father is his own storyteller. An archeology hobbyist, my dad would track down all the ruins and remnants of the early Indians and tell us their stories. His connection from his white, Western world to my mother's family: the stories of the moving sands and ghost tools. Between stories of early Indians grounding corn and sculpting arrowheads, he'd find dinosaur tracks and point to how it must have jumped from one formation to another, landed firmly in the mud, and surged on. *See the depth of the back part of the foot? He pushed off here.* Those dinosaurs pushing off the ground onto the ramp with the Great Herder Noah jostling his tin can of magic rocks behind them. The sun cresting the mesa and the animals looking for water troughs and hay. How the Great Herder must have told many stories to the animals to keep them sleepy and learning while they sailed the Third World looking for a hole to the Fourth. Where was the little locust and his medicine bag? Where were the Holy People and how did they secret to the locust the ways of luring the reed from the ground into the sky?

I draw pictures of great ships full of dinosaurs and sheep and my neighbor's schnauzer, Sadie, and my fish creeping up a reed to the Fourth World. Noah in his beaded headband, his satchel of water, and Concho belt. His boots dusty from mesa climbing and his songs full of his adventure as Great Herder. The water monsters and God angry and gnashing behind them. Ma'ii laughing and perhaps removing spots from leopards and drawing stripes on horses to keep himself busy.

IV. A Conflation of World, Water, and Word

It is Ma'ii's fault. The way he gambles the gambler. The way he snakes the snake. All glitter and sass and up-the-sleeve magic. He's reached in my throat and pulled the words out. Ma'ii tries to teach the teacher. We come from a giant hill like an anthill! I tell her. She is wrong and the picture in our textbook of the flat and lined land is wrong. The tribes grouped and sprawled across the nation has no pictures, just names. I tell her it must be wrong. The Navajo are the Diné. We are the People. There are no humans that aren't a people, I say, so we must be all the people, including her. We came from a hole in the ground to the Fourth World. We came from a reed. A magical reed!

My friends agree with me. I'm right a lot of the time, remember? They tell her. Remember my award? My "Best Storyteller" award? I was on the playground telling the story of the squirrels. Not a story of all the squirrels or squirrels my mom knows. I tell a story that makes sense to my own self that is birthed from a truth of me—a history of me, I tell a story of a squirrel family and the lost squirrel that makes it home. I get an award. I am the "Best Storyteller" in our class. I know things. I remind my teacher of this. I tell the stories and the story is the Navajos are the People—all the people—and we came from a world above a world!

Ma'ii must have taken my words. Must have taken her ears. Must have taken the phone and made the calls to my parents. Must have kept them in the room with my teacher and principal and me in the hall. Must have chopped up the long threads of language they were speaking into bits of laughter and sighs that sound like they are smiling. The laughter like a giant water surging. I think the water monsters' baby must have been stolen again. And the sounds are the gurgling and flooding water coming from the principal's office. It will come from under the door; it will sweep through the hallway and out through the school. This world will be drowned and kept by monsters.

I must find the locust and must find the reed. I must find the Holy People and find the magic to get me free of it. They must have the answers to pull me out and away. Pull me up to them and then, if so then, I can find the Star Boy and tell him I know where the stars are! I remember them and I can help with the bad dog. We can tie him up and scold him. He will be kept from always pulling at blankets and tearing at the fabrics that hold so many celestial truths and stories of the past and ways of seeing in the night.

When I get out of here, I think, when I get away from the whisperings of my mom with her blood-and-guts hands and from the pointing and figuring and investigating of my dad as he moves across the dunes and away from the flooding of all the strange things of teachers with raised eyebrows and the things with wet and swirling arms that must be angry and searching for ways of keeping me from rising into the next world, I can get my hands on that bad dog and make him sit or lie down or perhaps even roll over.

The Way of Wounds

NATANYA ANN PULLEY

Cracks

1. Rock canoe
2. Belt
3. Canyon
4. My Canyon
5. My Hands

1. *Rock Canoe*

My grandmother's hogan is at the base of a mesa, but it's hard to tell where the mesa base begins or ends. I've started simple walks around the bottom of the mesa, sounding out the rock formations and the pockets of sand and scattered brush through an inner ear that speaks and hears the vibrations of the desert, only to find myself inclining slowly and soon ascending the mesa, past the sandy areas, finding footholds among the rock face.

Within the rock formations twenty feet north of the hogan are two stretches of slightly protruding rock. Two lips with a small gap between. My mom says this was her canoe when she was a child.

She doesn't say much more, but sometimes I picture my mom as a young girl. She is not the chatty two-world urban Navajo woman she is now, but a small thing, close to the ground. She sits in her canoe and glides herself along rough patches and the wind moves through her hair and I imagine it moves also through her head taking her bird's-nest thoughts with her.

When I saw the canoe for the first time, I saw female genitalia. I saw my mom birthed from the Arizona sands. I always see how my mom's city thoughts drain from her as we drive to the reservation. She seems to arrive in her homeland with a clear head.

2. *Belt*

My husband took off his belt, and I grabbed it from him. Folded it, but let it hang loose. In one quick move, I pulled it tight and the loud crack filled the bedroom. Broke the air. Broke my thoughts. Broke the world. Again and again.

I slapped the belt gently on my husband's skin. Playfully. Lightly. He chuckled and continued watching TV. I slapped it on my arm. Once lightly, once harder, once hard.

Then I slapped him with it.

One crack broke his skin. Broke his calm. Broke his knowledge of me. He was so surprised—too surprised and wounded to be angry.

Apologizing. Kissing the skin. Soothing it with my fingers. *I didn't mean to do it that hard.* I laughed from the look on his face. But hard was what I meant. To break or change things. To leave a sting in the air and on the flesh. To leave my mark.

3.   *Canyon*

My mother had five brothers. Two died from alcoholism and one from an alcohol-related car accident. This is the way of the reservation, some say. One brother froze after passing out in the desert; another's brain turned to mush as he lay in a nursing home and the third was hit from the side by a car. My mom tells me every time that he wasn't hit hard, just that his head was turned at the exact wrong angle and it broke his neck. When I cross the road, I try to keep my head facing forward.

My mother also has many nephews and nieces. Some died from complications and troubles. But it's no good to talk of the dead. It brings them back, I have heard. From wherever they are, they hear their once-name. They see a small spot in this world for them, and some will try to wiggle their way back to it, like shimmying into old snakeskin. Navajo way is to mourn and participate in ritual for days before sending the deceased on their way. Board up the hogan. Forget the name.

We do not talk about the dead with our Indian relatives, but sometimes my mom remembers things. She remembers a young girl. Thinks it might be a sister. But there's no way to tell. Census Man comes 'round, and only the living are recorded, and there are discrepancies. My mom has three names: Zana, Zona, and Zina depending on the records you look at. She has two social security numbers. Her birthplace is "blue canyon." She says she remembers they had a hogan there once. But she couldn't pinpoint it now. We talk of finding it.

My mother remembers one of her brothers had a young child, but the child was lost. When the kids speak of it, some say Windy Man. Windy Man took the child. Once when my brother's son was visiting the rez with my parents, they walked to a branch of the Grand Canyon from a relative's hogan, and as my nephew neared the edge of the canyon, my mom blurted, "Be careful or Windy Man will get you." She thinks now that that must be how the child died. Lost over a cliff from that terrible wind that reaches up and grabs children and rips them loose from ever being known.

I never stand close to the canyon edge. I watch from the car.

4. *My Canyon*

When I feel the world is much too heavy or much too light, when I think there's no way to push through it or that pushing through is as meaningless as not pushing through, I have a visual: a canyon. It's always midnight and the canyon walls are slate gray with tentacles flailing from the sides. The bottom is covered in bats, engines, spoiled batteries, and broken glass. At first it is easy to take a step down it; there's always a side that doesn't seem too steep. But the first step slides into four, and there's never time to catch my footing and nothing to grab at. From the bottom there is no way up.

When I feel through with things—with the pressure or the nothingness—I think of this canyon and wonder how close to the edge I am. And I take a step back. Then another.

5. *My Hands*

It happens in winter, sometimes doing the dishes, other times when I forget to moisturize: cracks in my skin. Each time I see them, I stop and stare. It's old age, I think. This here on my skin is old age. It never happened before. I could go without lotions. I could go without worrying about the dry air. Ten years ago my mom would hold my hands and slide her fingers along my skin. She'd say, "Such soft, soft hands."

Callings

1. Exotic Wallflower
2. First Daughter
3. Masked Me
4. Sister-Mom

1. *Exotic Wallflower*

I've always liked this compliment. I think of it still, pull it out from an envelope in my mind and open it up, smell it. Eighteen years after I heard it. I think of my friends and me at the mall. They flit and fuss over styles and colors and prices. I am not sure what to say or how to act. I hang back and watch. I keep looking for someone to come and tap me out. I think I still do this—expect someone to tell me I'm out. I expect to go quietly.

The salesman comes over. I think he's going to tell us to be quiet. Instead he stands next to me and says, "You are the most exotic wallflower I have ever seen." Silly to think about it now. What a perv. Me at fourteen, he was "old" back when old wasn't an age but a smallness, as if he'd been trimmed down to clean, sharp edges that would never grow. Sometimes I think of the salesman and his words and how often he repeated them and what the girls said back and what he did to himself in his car in parking lots while watching junior high girls giggle and tease as they headed home from school. I don't know when I started thinking this—when the line became "a line" and when fourteen became too young to be chatted up by salesman.

I didn't know what a wallflower was when he said it. I remember on the bus ride home, the girls twittering with the grown-upness of buying virgin margaritas at La Casita and flirting with the table of boys next to us, and me still thinking of a wallflower: a flower that grows on the wall? A flower in the wall? A flower against a wall? As if there is a world beyond that junior high world—a world of walls heavy with seeds, waiting for some great storm to penetrate them. Somewhere bulbs on walls are bursting forth and all the fragrances of cheap and expensive body washes fill the air.

2. *First Daughter*

First Daughter is her brother and sister's keeper. First Daughter inherits the world. The name. The line. The clan. First Daughter chooses the sheep to slaughter and makes it happen. She cleans the stomach and wipes sweat from her forehead without getting blood on herself. First Daughter knows it all, learned it all from stories and watching and from a locust that lives in her ear. One that knows all the medicine. Navajos are a matriarchal and matrilineal society, and First Daughter knows this. She breathes it so.

My mom is the Only Daughter. And sent from Navajoland to get an education, my mom does not know all the stories, did not do all the watching, and lost the locust for a buzzing bee. She finds out later, after the day ends, that she was to bring the corn pollen, that she was to find the holy man, that she was to step one foot in front of the other for all to see.

I am a First Daughter; I am told so. It will be my job to bury my parents. I have an older brother, but it will be my job to turn off machines, sell homes, and throw out the clutter. I learned stories. I watched the ways. I have a bee and a locust and a moth in my ear. My parents do not leave to tend the sheep, to sell the weavings, or to honor the people. They leave for days to the casino. They indulge in odds that never pay, in slots that ring them numb, and they put First Daughter in charge. First Daughter will learn the way. First Daughter will walk one foot in front of the other across the kitchen for all to see as she makes cheesy noodles for her siblings. The fourth day in a row.

3. *Masked Me*

My ex said I wear a mask, it's just that the mask is of me. I have a mask, but it looks like me? I hide behind a mask, but the mask feels like me? She must mean I made a mask—perhaps all in one day or more likely over the years, and it matched the me growing inside. Chin for chin, pore for pore. I want to ask her what I see in the mirror.

I'm pulled by these thoughts into a shapelessness, a colorlessness, a lack—it almost hurt (if things hurt there) and for a second I get it: I wear a mask, it just looks like me.

Then it is gone.

4. *Sister-Mom*

Once my little brother fell and scraped his knee. He ran into the house. My mom and I were seated on the couch and he screamed, "Mom!" but fell into my arms. I still envision the look on her face, but I'm not sure if it was really there or just my imagination.

I try to reach my siblings on a sisterly level these days. I no longer order them around. I don't meddle. But my mom still calls. "Your brother is ____, call him! Tell him he needs to _____." And sometimes I do. They listen to me.

Sometimes I wish they just were my kids, and all the years raising them would make sense. I could keep my "mom" name. It would be mine. Instead it is hyphenated or asterisked. I am their sister* (*but I took care of them daily, and my parents were gone a lot). I live a second life in a footnote. And sometimes on Mother's Day,

I suck on that scene of my brother screaming, "Mom!" and falling into my arms.

Triggers

1. Light Shining through Leaves
2. White Corn
3. Thunder
4. Split Mushroom Cap

1. *Light Shining through Leaves*

When light shines through a treetop onto the grass below, the shadows and light dance. The first flickering is a gentle reminder of natural beauty, but only for a second before my eyes double-take the event. The ground begins to roll before speeding up into a frenzy. No ground. No objects. No control. Only the quickening of light and shade and color and disorder. All of it against my corneas. Close my eyelids. Wait out the wave of vertigo.

Same thing happens when light reflects off of a lake. Light reflecting off of metal clothes racks when I walk too fast through a department store. At certain times of the day in a parking lot. At night, when cars drive past and headlights flicker through the blinds. When my husband cooks in the late afternoon and the sunlight hits the knives and metal spoons and pots and pans. When the TV or computer screen weakens for a second and then charges back to full brightness.

My eyes feel overworked. My jaw clenches. A mean and managerial me tells myself not to get a migraine. It says we cannot. It will not do. And the blood starts pumping. And soon it is en route. I become my body. Clammy, pained, nauseous, paranoid, hypersensitive, and on and on.

Sometimes it is light. Sometimes sound. Sometimes just my running thoughts. Sometimes a taste. A food. A touch. A breeze. A smell. A texture. Sometimes it is a nothing. Sometimes there is no thing that triggers, it just erupts, and those ones are usually the worst.

2. *White Corn*

"With the body of white corn my body will be beautiful," a young Navajo girl prays. She repeats the prayer with my grandfather. They face east toward the rising sun and bless themselves with corn pollen. This girl is not me. This girl is not my mom. It's a movie from the 1970s. A fifteen-minute film a grad student made of a short story in which a young Navajo girl stays with her grandparents, herds sheep, and meets another sheepherder. They make dolls from the clay and dirt along a spring.

But there is no spring near my grandparents' hogan. And I never herded in traditional Navajo dress. And I never herded them alone. And my grandparents are in the film as someone else's grandparents. And I grew up in Utah, and my mom was sent on the Indian Placement Program and lived with a Mormon family each school year and she never herded sheep in traditional dress, or made friends with another sheepherder, or built clay dolls and blessed them.

When we herd the sheep, we walk them to a certain point on the mesa. The herd and the dogs know what to do then. They come back before dark. When we do have to go get them, we take the truck to the top of the mesa. Some people use ATVs. Some still use horses. But mostly, not all homes have sheep anymore.

3. *Thunder*

I am six or seven huddled against a large rock. My father is running toward me, and I think there are dinosaurs close behind him. The rain slams us as we run to the car and I fall. The desert skies can open and drop rain like heavy nets. Flash flood, flash flood, my dad says. All is worry in the old Wagoneer as we head out of the sandy desert regions toward Tuba City.

Or is this my dad's story and I'm not in it? He was with his brother in the desert, and they had to escape the flash flood. They thought they wouldn't make it.

Or is it my dream, and there are large creatures closing in on us with terrible heavy footfalls and roars?

Or was I young and afraid of thunder and since we are always seeing dinosaur prints in the rocks when we explore, I just inserted them into the fear?

When I hear thunder, I look for a large rock to hide behind. I expect the sky is breaking and the ground will follow. And the water will rush upon me and wipe me out with gnashing teeth.

4. *Split Mushroom Cap*

He walked in front of me and pointed to a large red and pink mushroom cap that had split down the center. "It looks like a vagina," Ryan said. And I said, "Ew."

This I'd like to take back. I'd like to rip open time and space and get a solid hold on the moment and pull it from history. It'd have roots, strong roots that grew into other days and other moments and other conversations. I'd have to pull my hardest without creating too much freshly turned soil throughout the past. Without leaving sink holes, to extract that moment.

If I had to choose any of it—any of him or me or the regrets I have of him (was he a bastard or was I?)—I'd still grab that moment first. Even just the "ew." That one "ew." A traitor to my sex. To my body. To my self. Who taught me to be so mean to me?

Closures

1. Dad's Lines
2. Dead End
3. Shinaai and I
4. Drive-ins
5. The Zana Circuit

1. *Dad's Lines*

My dad's lines are closing. A nerve along his spine pinched by a disc. Blood to his heart slowed by thickened walls. His reaction time. His political views. He uses four sentences instead of two. Repeating himself. This started gradually. It's not bad, not like some. Just little things. Some medium things. Just the beginning of the cycle.

And I no longer hang on his words. They are dated now. He is wrong sometimes. He looks small and . . . normal. My dad was big once. Larger than any math. Now he calls every few days. Asks me about insomnia. Asks me about numbness. Asks me about pain.

"Is it normal?" he asks. "Is it normal to stay awake at night with your toe twitching?"

2. *Dead End*

There's a dead end at the south end of my parents' street. Abandoned houses, lots, fields of cattails. Devil worshippers. Once some neighborhood kids and I walked down that way, stood on the loading dock of a building. Pointed out where a cat was sacrificed. I don't remember who saw it. Who said they saw it. My younger brother repeats the stories. Dead animals in weird positions. Blood on the walls. Candles. Once we walked a little farther to a clearing with abandoned houses. We stood in the center of them and my brain and heart had fled the scene before my body left. A cul-de-sac of Satanists. I was sure they were watching. Watching and waiting. I thought of evil potlucks and boneyard sales.

It's all in danger of ending though. Bulldozed for more housing. My parents tell me and we sit in silence. Each of us thinking about those fields and warehouses and abandoned houses. The red paint pentagrams. Rat skulls and oils. My brother says one building has a sunken floor that is full of black water. He says he saw something move. Its slick body surfacing just in time to send the lost boys in a flurry out the door.

I think of it flattened. The creature turned to dust. The spells wiped clean. The Satanists on the street, homeless.

3. *Shinaai (older brother)*

My brother and I were once very close.

4. *Drive-ins*

I think of abandoned drive-ins. The rolling pavement broken by weeds and brush. Steel posts still at attention. Faceless. And torn screens. What I don't think of is the plot of land—the gate torn down, the poles removed, the screen pulled apart and toted away.

The drive-in by my parents' house is now just a lot. Looks smaller than the space we drove to and parked in. The space we walked backward in to get to the bathroom without losing sight of the screen. The food stand must have been mansions long for all the popcorn that spilled along those lots each summer night.

But standing there, there is just a lot. I can see across it. The new homes in the distance. That lot—I can almost not see it there under my feet.

5. *The Zana Circuit*

When I travel to the rez with my mom, we make the rounds. The Zana Circuit, I call it. My mom has seventy-five first cousins on just her dad's side. Not to mention there's no real Navajo word for cousins, and they are simply our brothers and sisters. All our family. And my mom stops by so many of them even in short two-day trips. This is not the Navajo way—to drop in and drop off goods and news and then leave. Navajo way is to sit and be. To speak only hours after settling and to help out with chores and cooking. But my mom has no time for Navajo way. And some forgive her and call her *awee* (baby) or *awee yazhi* (little baby). Others seem frustrated and see something lost in the fact of her. She is a sore to them at times.

This last visit, I saw less elders. I saw younger generations—they are frustrated with my mom, with the "Red Apple" (red outside/white inside) woman that drops in and drops off supplies but runs away and calls herself family. They don't know what to do with her. What use is she to their way—to the Navajo way? And if she is no use, is she then a threat?

And I realize when she is gone, I might not take the Zana Circuit by myself. I don't know if I'll visit or, like Zana, if I will feel comfortable dropping in on a family reunion down by the reservoir introducing myself to several people until finally finding a "brother" or "sister" among them.

To the Man Who Gave Me Cancer

ADRIENNE KEENE

I.

My cervix and I were closer friends than many. I relied on her to fight my monthly stone man, to help manage my premenstrual dysphoric disorder. I knew what she felt like at different points of my cycle. I knew when she was low and open versus high and closed; I knew what her varying types of mucus meant. I relied on those cues to know when it was time for me to start my cycles of monthly care, when it was time to take my meds, and when it was time to expect relief with the arrival of my monthly bleeding. I often marveled at how in sync with my body I had become. How I would notice the smallest changes. How learning to read myself was empowering and liberating. That's gone now, because my cervix is largely gone. Some of these signs and language of my body may come back. They may not. I've mourned and mourn their loss. You took that from me.

II.

It started with an abnormal pap smear. After decades of regularly scheduled exams and normal results, I suddenly was thrust into medical fear and uncertainty. They also tested me for HPV. It came back positive for a high-risk strain. I knew it was from you, because it couldn't have been anyone else.

I called cis female friends. Many of them have had abnormal paps. They told me what to expect, that it would be fine. That it happens all the time. But I knew in the back of my mind and from a quick google that my cells were different—they weren't squamous cells, they were glandular, and they carried more serious risk. But it was only four months after you, and I figured that wasn't enough time for anything to develop into something serious.

The colposcopy and biopsy were two hours before I had to moderate a panel at Harvard, a panel on centering Indigenous women's voices. The procedure took place in the normal exam room, my feet in stirrups, my doctor and her assistant making awkward small talk. We talked about our favorite beaches. It seemed normal and mundane. After an examination, the doctor found two sites that looked "only slightly abnormal," so decided to take "punch" biopsies with a tool that takes "just barely two millimeters of tissue." With each biopsy she paused, told me to take a deep breath, and removed a piece of my cervix. No pain medication, nothing to ease the raw pain. Just a deep breath.

I can't imagine a scenario where a white cis man would be asked to endure this type of procedure with just an intake of air for his pain.

After my doctor had completed the biopsies, I watched her place the used instruments in a plastic bag. I wasn't supposed to see, she turned her body away from me. But I saw. I saw the clear plastic streaked with my bright blood. I saw what "just barely two millimeters" produced. I cried at the injustice and the indignity, silent tears rolling down the sides of my face as I stared at the speckled drop ceiling, head on the crinkling exam table paper.

Two hours later I sat on the stage, looking a mess, having done my makeup in the car as I was driving frantically through traffic, dictating potential questions into my phone, bleeding and in pain. "Take some ibuprofen if you need it," my doctor had told me, "some bleeding and cramping is normal." But as I sat on the stage I kept thinking, *nothing about this is normal.*

Someone there mentioned you. I felt my stomach clench and I wished I could tell him. Tell him that an hour before I had made a blood sacrifice to the medical gods of settler patriarchy because of you. But I didn't. I centered our voices as Indigenous women that night, but I still couldn't tell him.

III.

The speculum was invented by a man experimenting on enslaved women without consent and without anesthesia. The tool that is so common to every experience in a gynecologist's office was a tool of a monster, designed only to push tissue out of the way and hold it there so he could get the best view. It was not designed for any patient's comfort. Not designed to ease the trauma of having a stranger stare inside of you.

The local sex shop down the street from my house has speculums in the window. They're jewel toned and meant to look pretty, displayed next to vibrators and cheeky underpants, but the last time I walked by I felt intensely sick seeing them lie there. I think they'll always make me feel sick now.

IV.

In Wisconsin, after a nightmare travel experience, exhausted, I lay on a hotel room bed, mentally running through my keynote for that evening. My email pinged with results of the biopsies. I clicked, expecting that if they had let me be notified by email it must be nothing. But it wasn't nothing. Both biopsy sites showed adenocarcinoma in situ—stage 0 cervical cancer, very early stage cancer of glands of the cervix. I couldn't breathe, I couldn't cry, I didn't know what to do.

I called my doctor and left a message. While waiting for her to call me back, I googled. The Internet is a terrifying place. Best case scenario, a cone biopsy surgery to remove a section of my cervix. Worst case, a hysterectomy—the removal of my womb. No matter what, surgery. Potential or definite loss of fertility. Potential second trimester miscarriages. Potential for preterm birth. Potential invasive cancer. ~~Potential for~~ a changed future forever.

I talked to my doctor. I cried. I called my partner and my mom. I cried. I took a shower, wiped my tears, and went to dinner with the Native students on campus. I laughed hard and deeply with them; I found healing in their stories and laughter. I did my keynote; I made my stupid jokes, answered questions, and tried to remain present. But running through my mind was a single word over and over: *cancer cancer cancer cancer cancer.*

I went straight to the doctor from the plane the next morning. I sat on the exam table, my long legs dangling, wearing the snow boots that had been necessary four hours ago in Wisconsin's freak April snowstorm. I focused on how out of place they looked back here in Rhode Island where the weather was approaching sixty degrees. I looked down at their faux fur and strong laces as my doctor drew a picture of my cervix on her clipboard and circled the large section she would be taking in the surgery, the surgery that needed to be scheduled as soon as possible.

As she left, the nurse who had assisted on my colposcopy came in and gave me a hug. "You've been on my mind all day," she said. "I'm so sorry. This was your first abnormal pap wasn't it? What a shame."

V.

I have a pseudo-tarot deck called "The Answer Deck." I use it sometimes to get clarity when I'm feeling lost. I asked it what to expect of the surgery, carefully turning the cards over in my hands as I meditated on the question. I flipped over the outcome card: "hidden enemy." I pushed the cards away in disgust and fear, interrupting the careful rows.

VI.

I wore my FEMINIST sweatshirt to the hospital for my surgery a week and a half later. It felt stupid once I got there, but that morning it had made sense. I tried so hard to be the stereotype of the "brave" and "strong" patient. I joked with everyone. My worried mom sat in the chair opposite my bed, and I tried to put her at ease. They needed four tries and two nurses to get my IV in because I was so dehydrated from fasting. It hurt, a lot, but I pretended to be fine. I even took a selfie in my purple gown (my favorite color!) and silly hat. I read my Kindle. I thanked the doctors. Inside I was a mess.

I woke up in recovery feeling OK. The nice woman nurse who had been gently easing me awake told me in my groggy state that she would be cycling off and a new male nurse would be taking care of me. He gruffly moved me from my bed to a recliner, handed me water, and left. He came back with my mom, told me it was time to get dressed, and left again. I stood up and began to bleed on the floor. I looked down at the small puddle, dark red and glistening, and was embarrassed. I looked around. He hadn't given me a pad. I asked my mom for the one in my bag. I placed my paper gown on the floor over the blood. I put back on my FEMINIST sweatshirt.

VII.

Physical recovery meant alternating anger and love. The support and love I felt from my family and friends were immeasurable. I had delivered meals, more meals than I needed. I had deliveries of growlers of hand-harvested chaga tea. I had friends praying, lighting sage, holding sweats, and putting down tobacco for me. I had a mom who flew across the country and took care of everything. I had a partner who called multiple times a day to make sure I was OK. I had a department chair and colleagues who picked up the slack for the time I was out and offered to do more if necessary.

But I was angry. So, so angry. Angry at you for hurting my heart with your actions when you had given me so much hope, angry at you for hurting my body with your virus, angry at patriarchy, and angry at myself. Angry I didn't feel well, angry I couldn't exercise, angry at the blood, angry at the pain, angry at the exhaustion, angry that I couldn't relax because I still didn't have the results. Angry at the deep shame I felt. Angry I had to miss my sister's bachelorette party, angry I had to miss my big conference and meeting with my potential book publisher because I was recovering. Angry because I couldn't write, and angry because you'll never face any career consequences for this. You'll still get tenure. People will still publish your books. You'll be fine. I'm still not fine.

VIII.

My great-grandmother gave birth to my grandmother alone in her farmhouse. She cut the cord, cleaned up, and sat nursing my grandmother when her family arrived. That farmhouse where my grandmother took her first tiny breaths now sits at the bottom of a lake, taken by colonization and a hydroelectric dam.

There is research that we can carry the historical trauma of our ancestors in our DNA, and there has been recent attention to the terrifying statistics surrounding Black women and maternal death and complications in childbirth. There are no statistics collected for Native women, but we know they are similar. Stress from living in a marked and colonized body has real effects.

Stressed and depressed women can't easily clear HPV. I have been, and am, both.

My grandma and all of my aunties on the Native side have had hysterectomies. Early hysterectomies, in their forties. A medical rite of passage—the removal of a womb that carried babies and ancestral memories into this world. My mother had uterine surgery and had her ovaries removed. These women in my family have been separated from our culture and carry little culturally of who they are, yet still carry the trauma of being Native women.

We as Native women have always been the target of settler colonialism. The desire to control Native reproduction and the legacies of forced sterilization campaigns continue. We carry that trauma. Perhaps we carry it in our wombs.

IX.

A pre-colonization world wouldn't have let this happen. A matriarchy wouldn't have let a virus that is so destructive to women go unchecked because it causes no symptoms or harm in men. I wouldn't have been made to feel so much deep shame that I didn't protect myself better. I would have been protected.

There wouldn't have been a movement to keep young girls from getting a life-saving vaccine because it may cause them to be "promiscuous." But there was. My doctor in college would have followed up to make sure I finished the series of shots. But she didn't. You would have been encouraged to get the vaccine as a man. But you weren't. Resources and funding would have been poured into curing this virus. But they're not. Because of patriarchy.

There's not even a test for you as a cis man to know if you carry this within your body. A cancer-causing poison. And your virus is special, because somehow it mixed with the stress and historical trauma of my body to move from virus to cancer in four months flat. But you can continue to spread it unchecked to other women. And it will be seen as their fault, not yours, for not protecting themselves.

X.

In situ means "in its original place." Medically it means that the cancer hasn't broken through the surface membrane, that it's not considered invasive. Yet. But one cell through that membrane, and it moves to stage 1.

To be Indigenous is to be not from a place but of a place. But I will never be *in situ*. I've been removed and disconnected. Perhaps my cancer was more Indigenous than me.

XI.

I held my breath for two solid weeks after the surgery. I didn't have a single full night of sleep. I read every medical journal article I could get my hands on that discussed adenocarcinoma, *in situ* and not. I calculated statistical percentages, read about the rare cases like mine that went from HPV infection to cancerous cells in months rather than decades, about skip lesions gone unseen and unremoved, the deaths, the instances of reoccurrence, the metastasizing and spreading. I read message boards and support sites. I thought about worst-case scenarios. I wondered if a conservative approach to preserve my fertility was smart. I didn't tell anyone what I was reading and learning. I didn't want to scare my partner or my family. So I held it all in with my breath.

XII.

Another hotel room, two weeks later. In a single week my world had clicked into place. My partner and I decided to move in together. I bought my first condo. I won a huge national fellowship. I was deeply loved and in love in a way I never thought possible, secure, affirmed in my work, and happy. So happy that I was convinced my surgery results were going to be the worst imaginable. That there was no way the universe would allow me all of that happiness. I didn't deserve such full and complete happiness.

The doctor called. I took in a sharp breath like during the biopsy, to hold the impending pain. But I was clear. They got it all. My margins were negative. There was nothing nefarious hiding beyond what they had seen. There was no hidden enemy.

I am lucky. I have good insurance, I have a wonderful team of doctors, and these cells that are often very hard to catch and like to jump and hide in healthy tissue decided to hang out on the surface where my doctor could see them and remove them. I'll have to have a pap smear and colposcopy every six months for the next four years. For two weeks a year, I will hold my breath and hope it hasn't come back. Another surgery would mean I have very little cervix left. It would mean probable infertility. It would mean that patriarchy brought by settler colonialism took my future children. But I won't think that way.

XIII.

I have no easy end to my story, no beautiful wrap-up or message of hope. I'm still deciphering the messages and lessons this journey has given me and still realizing what it has taken away. I don't know what I'll do when I see you in the community spaces I know we'll both occupy. I haven't even really said the words "I had cancer." I don't know how to process that I got away relatively unscathed when there are so many women who haven't. I don't know when I'll be able to let go of the shame of feeling like I should have done more to protect myself and that all of this was my fault, that I should have known better.

But I know that I'll keep fighting. Because that is all I know how to do.

That fighting spirit, like trauma, I carry. I will carry it in my womb, nurture it and protect it, and help it grow, to gift to the next generation. Together, they and I will carry it forward.

Self-Portrait with Parts Missing and/or Smeared

MICHAEL WASSON

So who's missing is the first question we're asked. I'm inside my ten-year-old body inside the classroom that looks out on a hill we've all rolled down during spring. Our scratched desks clustered like little ponds. I'm sitting at my desk that opens & shuts like a mouth left empty for days. My teacher asks us, *who's missing today?* My friend—who my body said last night I've fallen for—looks over at me as if finding an earring in the grass. Yesterday she asked me why I don't have a father. The roll sheet is called out. We each say *here* when the teacher says our names. My name smears and smears my lips, growing into lilies and out the crevices of piled rocks. I hear my name and say *here*. I'm here.

i.

A first day means there was a never-day. A time in which the beginning starts not at one but zero. A zero is always open for the world to see. A little number like zero will always be a space into which we empty ourselves. It is the graveyard in which we bury our relatives just as the sun rises to lift their heads to wherever it they are intended to go. I'm twelve already in this part of the sequence, after hearing someone with the same name as my great-grandmother. I'm helping my great-grandmother down the stairs, and she's yelling at me—*I can't see! I can't see!* I look into her eyes and say, *púʾx̣, can you see me?* After the daylight moves its hand from the lip of the bottom stair up to the lap of another, she sees me. She says, *I'm so sorry. I couldn't see where I was going.* I feel the music between each heartbeat because I'm the boy holding her hand in the last season of her life. Her eyes, I thought, were like zeroes. Wide enough to hold a life. To lose it.

i.

Today, I am barely more than a quarter of a century old. I am standing at the edge of the ocean watching a thunderstorm in slow motion—only because I imagine it that way. I imagine the flashes arriving like the face of someone I remember after years of trying to recollect who it is. The face has been inside every photograph I've ever carried. The skin is the organ that registers touch. We itch our skin. I ask the water reaching toward my ankles like prisoners of forced hunger, *why don't our bones itch? And why can't we just shut down our skins.* I see that I've been given my mother's hands and my father's face. So I cover my face with my palms. Yesterday, I watched a puddle and almost fell into the sky.

i.

I'm the boy again, tucked beneath long curved blades of cheatgrass. The men are looking for me. Let me say that again so you can hear me: the men are looking for me. Not who I am but my body. In their language, in their heads, in their blood courses many versions of the same message that has moved to the edge of our homelands: *the only good Indian is a dead Indian.* Some of us have learned about Ezekiel and that long valley of dry bones: their lord said, *Can these bones live?* I ask myself this as it continues to rain and rain. It's raining like a heaven of steel. Steel echoes. Echoes that can move past the walls of the body. The border—my skin—is waiting like someone holding their breath. I'm holding everything I can. I'm a nation with a language with people living and dying. My hands have merged with the dawn-colored water. Waiting for one shard—holding a stock number and rivets, a shell propelled—to splash me open. To stay. I want to stay. To carve out the exit from this one life into the next. I want the moaning to stop.

i.

He was only alive for as long as his body let him. Who is the boy standing in the living room without his socks on? I can't imagine the mouth the same way, so the face reflects a little different now. The man in the kitchen still has a warmth to him. There is body heat like an ember dying out in the woods. I'm sorry this kitchen isn't the same as we made it before: a clamshell resting on the table for cigarettes. A roll of sage we burn inside its iridescent curve to keep the ghosts satisfied—not to keep them away. The kitchen has changed again. The walls weren't so cracked. Our bodies have cracks. He was alive and *this close* to destroying all of us. Forgive me for knowing that the room shattered in one life and didn't in another.

i.

I'm a day old. Actual first name on record: Baby. Middle name: Boy. Last name: Wasson. Nice to meet you.

i.

Last week, I watched a man I knew dying in a language I couldn't fully understand. I'm at the port with the sun falling on everyone through the windows. They're inside the ship, floating like someone's springtime in bloom—so much pollen entering our lungs, swelling our throats shut. We're waiting for the village's only doctor to arrive. I reach out my arm that isn't there. To hold his wife as she's screaming in her language—*why won't he come? Why won't he come?* My arm is the shadow touching hers. I'm trying to hold her up. To let her sound enter me and rattle the cage of my body. My standing there means I'm an insect husk before the cicadas even arrive to screech like feedback filling the air. My mouth is covered as the village's only police officer tries to find the breath. Find the pulse. Pressing. *Where is it?* I'm whispering to nobody. To convince myself that a life will return here. I'm running and running. You don't need arms to run.

i.

There is an animal inside me. I swallowed all the animals because I have surrendered to my hunger. There is an animal building a fire inside me. He's climbing my ribs. Every animal is weeping about loneliness and the dark inside the body. *It's so dark here*, they are whispering between each other like I can't hear them. They're there, I know, because I saw their light and movement and inhaled every one of them. Now this little animal is inside my chest. Does he know yet? I'm a monster. I'm the monster without a heart. *'ilcwéew'cix wen'ikíse 'iin. tim'nenúut, ne'é?* There is a river running clean, trees and trees like bones rising from the earth and blossoming. There's a valley. There's no heart to cut down. What's left but the ash smearing in my belly? When I open my slick maw, smoke opens into the air like song. A song I carry as I drag my animals along the earth.

i.

The storm subsides. The rift I watched open in the sky is beginning to shut. The lightning takes its time, breathing and blinking into something like a sleeping god somewhere out over the ocean. Here I am on an island. My little location here. At the edge of the world. Nothing out there but a horizon full of stars I can no longer see. The hole is gone.

i.

I'm in your belly as it happens.

i.

So everyone's here, my teacher asks. I'm in the classroom. The sunlight at the window cooled to an ochre-like orange, failing to climb inside. Number eighteen on the roll sheet. We nod as though a chorus agreeing with everything the priest says about grace and death and life and flesh and blood.

When we are seated this way, at our desks, we are only torsos, heads, and arms. Beginning the day like any other day.

i.

There's an animal inside me, he says. He pulls the trigger.

Critical Poly 100s

KIM TALLBEAR

I began writing the Critical Poly 100s as part of an online writing group. Seven women living in different parts of the continent shared weekly 100-word pieces of writing. I now write them on my own but am thinking of starting an Indigenous women's 100s writing group. Some writers are not rigid about the 100-word limit. I personally love the discipline of it and work hard to make each piece exactly 100 words.

The concept of the 100s originated with University of Vermont English professor Emily Bernard in 2009, resulting in the founding of dozens of writing groups since that time. A writer launches her piece from an idea, phrase, single word, or anything that resonates or sparks from the previous piece. There are no limitations for form, style, or subject. Bernard explains that writers in such groups are "responsible only for our own words." The process can be understood as something akin to "a Quaker Meeting—if the spirit moves you, speak. Otherwise, let's enjoy each other's words in silence, rich and voluptuous." The introduction to a 2013 journal issue dedicated the work of one writing group, the 100-Word Collective explains:

One of the reasons so many of us are drawn to this abbreviated format is that it allows us to dialogue with other writers, even when our lives are extremely busy. We also feel freer to experiment with content, form and voice, and to risk vulnerability in our writing. 100-word pieces have been published in The Poetry of Yoga, The Paterson Literary Review, 100-word Story, and elsewhere. Some ideas catch fire and never lose their burn. This seems to be one of them.[1]

In September 2014, nearly two years into my autoethnographic polyamory practice, I started writing the 100s as a more creative addition to my blog. At that time, I lived on warm southern plains in Austin, Texas, where I was an associate professor in the Department of Anthropology at the University of Texas. In 2015 I began to also make place/body connections in my 100s writing practice. I relocated to the cold northern prairies in Edmonton, Alberta, Canada, and to the University of Alberta faculty of Native studies in August of 2015. I've continued to write 100s that draw on my experiences with both human and other-than-human loves. My land-love is the prairie; my water loves, its rivers.

In my Indigenous and Dakota translation, polyamorous multiplicity is not only about human relations. It is an ethic that also focuses on multiple relations with place and values the hard work of relating to and translating among different knowledges. In my ways of relating with human, earthly, and conceptual loves, I reject the usual definition of "promiscuity" as random and indiscriminate. In my redefinition, "promiscuous" is to seek abundance through partial connections. It is openness to multiple human loves and/or to deep connection with other-than-humans, with the lands and waters of our hearts and with different knowledge forms and approaches that enable us to flourish as Indigenous peoples. For example, in my science and technology studies (STS) work, I do not draw a hard line between so-called science and so-called traditional knowledge. I argue that such co-constituting forms of routedness between material and conceptual spaces provide an alternative ethical roadmap—one that values an accountable, responsible transgression of boundaries that by their very nature risk hierarchy and oppression. In short, being polyamorous, like being of any other sexual orientation, is not ultimately relegated to sexual relating. Multi-amorous relations are not always about sex. I love sex unapologetically and without shame. But my indigenization of the erotic does not privilege sex among intimacies. There are many ways to relate. Routing oneself respectfully between multiple bodies is another ethical roadmap. This is a different way of inhabiting the world. The 100s below are ordered in reverse chronological order. Happy reading.

28. #YEG Summer Sex (08.03.17)

Our breath slows. Ceiling fan turns the cool into a flock of birds, tiny ghosts. Their wings flutter across my outturned calves and the arch of your tapered back, the swells and concaves everywhere on you, pro-ballplayer length. Forgive me my shallow ways, I love your legs. Sweat shines in the coulee between your pectorals. They expand to my breasts, warm and soft. You will recover quickly. I am awed by your power. After twenty minutes, twenty laughs, we'll go again. I am your least strenuous exercise. In the wan Edmonton summer, the sheets stay dry, no sweat rivulets.

27. Embody (07.13.17)

His effusive e-words open, close our days. I feel them acutely from across the city, though he says he's no writer. I make a living writing and cannot word my trust or yearning. I touch it into being. "Love" lacks analytical rigor. My longing materializes in nips on his shoulder. I power rise to his belly. He opens, closes my thighs with his own. I push back hard. Not to repel him but to challenge him: *Push harder.* I refuse the idea that bodies merging is not itself love. I work my limbs strong for him—my heart, its gesture.

26. Summer Relationship Energy (SRE) (07.05.17)

No long thrust. No slow, deep cook. Summer is perceptible at 53.5 degrees north. It is when the ice mostly goes. Save occasional evening pellets when bruised clouds build, shake wind like fancy dancers in cut-glass purple, blue beaded garments. Summer's tongue traces our breasts, skims kisses across lips, down necks. We widen our eyes—silence. Summer's gone. Its ghost more present than heat of life itself. We long hard for summer in cool rooms though the horizon is pink past midnight. Summer keeps us wanting its barely attainable touch. Summer relentlessly leaves us. Summer's love is never not new.

25. Sexergonomics (06.18.17)

What is your favorite position? Dominus Blue commanded. It depends? Bodies fit together differently. I like my hair pulled but didn't know until my firefighter roped it round his wrist, a tether for rear-end thrusting traction. I thought breasts were my lubrication until hardcore Alberta cyclist neglected them, kneading instead my bottom like bread—huge hands. I didn't know I could love a smaller woman's body. Then I did. I didn't know the drug of melting chocolate with two tongues until the monogamist who kissed hard through his suffering. Before he left me and his wife for that homeschooling mom.

24. RiverSide (12.13.15)

So far, a soft winter. Snow skies are purple-pink. I am half here. How long does it take a soul to find the body when a body went thousands of miles away? I ache for that south place, for soil like a mouth's inside. The city smelled like an equator country. I fantasize of sultry air tumbling over thighs, my skirt pulled up. I left little lime popsicle lizard who lodged in a spindly limbed plant hanging under skies where a million bats fly. I had music and lovers, but long was that land emptied of all the relations I need.

23. NorthPrairieCity (12.04.15)

It is technically my ethic to share, I told him, upon hearing that women flood his world, his inbox. Blind date offers. Goddesses emerging from his past, and the woodwork. He replied: *I don't want to be shared, right now.* I do cherish days carved from our many relations of love—from dear edgy children, from big-brained companions—our sustenance, those we think, laugh, round dance, skin elk, write with. We traverse prairie highways, prairie skies, the heart of our world. I already share him, but I know what he means. Hear this though: I will not own him.

22. SouthPrairieCity (11.29.15)

I will kiss you. If we hold this embrace. In a cicada night, in a wet wrap of heat, her peppercorn eyes: *Should we? I want to.* We two covet boots, enunciations, and dresses. We never don't touch. We feed each other stories—how after years of marriage, the gaps grew wide, and we burn. Our tongues roll together, delicious like a million words in our years' long intercourse. Hands play swells under fabric. South wind too presses in. We three animate possibilities, self-forgiveness. We left good men we could no longer live with, the hardest thing we have done.

21. EmeraldCity (05.31.15)

This bit of earth has green hills sloping to plains and water arms contorting like a still dancer, bloodlife rushing within. When the rains pull in and hover, rivers spill into the city that weighs deeper each month. Water struggles in cycles of famine and feast. Crane upon crane erect glassicles into skies like a fairy-tale painting. *Oasis*, lithe white bodies jittering in crowds on the strip proclaim it. For sure, our city sparkles with dance and singing, carriages and horses, and trucks and merriment. Gems and a dewy face gain you entrance to prime real estate—the party inside.

20. HeartKing (05.24.15)

At sofa's opposite ends, sculpted fantastical like a Queen of Hearts' possession. Knees forward together, hands properly in laps, he requests I come close. But bodies touching may cloud our mediation. His anime eyes with lashes like peacock's feather edges blink, brows pop. Surely, he owes no more in our lovers' diplomatic relations? I was hostile disrupter of an orderly kingdom! My punishment was completed before he delivered his verdict. This private audience comes after exile. Accept the plea bargain. Never again protest and I may visit his realm. It is all his fancy, of course. He never executes nobody.

19. Unbreakable (04.26.15)

Like monogamy this hurts. I would take flight in skies that tower. But with lighting and artful signs and shadows, this city is a set. One can wake and sleep here, walk, eat here. But clouds beyond the Chevron, the café sign are painted. There is no expanse, no cacophony into which I can slip away from his unkind words. I think surely he has shrapnel, scars twisting his mouth. Or his incomprehensible lines that open mine, then silence my words in my throat—perhaps they are scripted of another land's lineage, another human language. And I am no code-breaker.

18. Tattoo (03.07.15)

"I thought you'd use ink and needle?" On my belly, right arm in mid breaststroke. She must have numbed me. I viewed the horror as if upon another's flesh. She forced the conical skewer in above the wrist. Like piercing a chicken's joint pre-dinner. She muscled back a prime cut of meat, carved zigzags up the arm. It was then I saw her own scars, sleeve-length, artfully sutured. Blood-soaked blankets. But I had agreed. Towels were all I could ask for. No reprieve. If I could not save the arm, perhaps the bed? "No, it doesn't matter," she said.

17. Vampire (02.07.15)

Distant centuries' stones, bricks, palatial steps, domes. Ever dewy faced offspring of those with reserves: was gold, now glowing digital number. A thousand black satchels. All these humans—bounded bags of organs, bones, flowing fluids. I've licked and listened. They drone exceptionalist visions from tongues in cafés and taverns, in wooden or glass rooms, on waves of water, sound, light ten million times over. Shallow skies stretch into dullest immensity, now etched by fire—Earth's velvet blood burned aloft. Still I watch over this world without love. 523 suns times 13 moons and counting, my lust for veins, a tedium.

16. Bay (01.24.15)

In my head a broken, descending sidewalk. Late afternoon: not cold, nor hot. Untidy fuchsia flowers like old bits of paper stuck to a wispy bush. A piano climbs slow steps inside a gray-paned front room. The bungalow is dusty pink or yellow, an egg past Easter. I can barely breathe in the city of faded light, pressed by a sky like a low glass ceiling. Thunder and lightning wisely turned back.

Formidable mountains. The ivories play a score for purgatory. I want to scream, unhinge the wan serenity. But it will not airlift me, and I will look crazy.

15. InsideOut (01.17.15)

I slice ghost clouds. Cocooned in the looming engine's roar, I know the within of time-space truncators like my own on-ground rooms, their tick-tock, their wafting perfumes. Off the great turning world, I am sky turtle. I am becoming through machines of speed and, still, I am still inside them. Flesh of my flesh, you are an Earthlier becoming—an explosion of paint silently laid by your narrow limbs to canvas. Your big-little voice infuses song precisely to air. Still you are northern plains lightning, equator rain. We have never mirrored one another. You are my—I am your—inside out.

14. IceCity (01.03.15)

A million crisp stars hung silent in blue-black depths. Zoom in: planet, city, flesh. We are noisier—mouths co-mingle laughter, syllables, breath. Warm fingers shed cocoons: touch. We will soon seek heat in the crooks of limbs. But first at the heart of the subzero city we rush to tapestried rooms luxurious with lamps and scents. The hours, the table filled with gossip, curries. Red. Neon. *Closed.* We whoosh in a salt-washed capsule through a grid of red, green, yellow. Quiet engine, cold seeps, tongues of fennel. We ascend. I straddle him. We are aloft the imperial anthem: ice-glass, alabaster.

13. Fidelitous (12.27.14)

I seek multiple tongues. Desires cross time zones. Body stretches like wings over white-light nets taut between peaks and a black, deep sea—life giver. When my first LandLoveBody sleeps on the

Twitter feed, intermittent with shots and false dreams, I turn to a European dalliance mouthing into morning headlines of violence in the streets of empire. AsiaPacific spins to the hard day's end. I am already here. Together we glitter and toast the close of year. Though we remember grief no less. My fidelity is no one-relation bliss. I won't ask everything: partial sustenance, stories forged together, shared pleasure.

12. NDNSciFi (12.13.14)

High-tech noble savage, I escape in a pod to the sky.[2] My launch obscured by planetary myths: We are mastodons, bones lodged in earth and museums, relics to adorn the living. They war for inheritance. Glued to the video feed, I peer across centuries and a field of orbiting debris. The project continues in courts and bloody streets. The eliminations, the imprisonments do not abate. Techniques, bricks shift form. Humans versus animals parsed by priests, scientists, CIA. I tried to be their citizen, but the dead cannot inherit. We're inherited. I hope relatives among the stars will take me in.

11. aMUSEd (11.29.14)

I could call him *enfant terrible*. He might roll and rise among the syllables, satisfied. Or disagree, and incisively so. He measures distances to leap between rock-faces of reason, the unlit spaces below. "Wait! Wait! I am in mid-bridge build!" My objections are not unamused. His observations compel construction. His eyes unshuttered, green, gray-blue panes. I lean in. What is there? Inside? The beauties barely shimmer, like sand-worn sea glass. His face floats up to mine from where he nests in a shelter of warm scented bends of neck and breasts. My lips touch him—I breathe: "No, not terrible."

10. Retribution (11.16.14)

Inching, braking, braking again. Collateral damage behind trepidatious cat-lady, bumper-sticker-graffitied Priuses on the streets of Berkeley. I. Am About. To Scream. I restrain myself in the back of the Yellow Cab. Dinnng. A text. From him, back on the Texas plains. "Um, did you mean to give me a hickey on my penis?" Did I? I WebMD'd it. It's like accidentally discovering you have talent for stopping time, or invisibility. He'd have to hide from his wife for days. *Wife?* I've learned a cheater's signs. Satirical celestial scriptwriters dinged him. I too hear their gentle admonition. Mea culpa.

9. Love-Couture (11.15.14)

When slipping inside a love, or a dress, your body must bend and stretch, turn into the folds and openings of thirty, or ten. If you are fortunate, you find two—three, tops?—that drape your fertile swells' downslopes and hints of bone at the edge. The best ones look woven about you—the tailor's form. You love them for years. Though many glitter, are handsomely cut, few can so enfold you. Look in the mirror. Does it work? Widen those eyes, turn to the side, look hard where it is hard to look. Ill fit? A no-fault divorce.

8. Sexorexia (11.08.14)

She summoned him. They arranged the night. She needed deep, hard, whole body contact. A withering love had turned dry and small and bitter, its leaves strewn dead about the rooms. Surprised, he obliged with his own adept form that would tend her body to a light, lush thing. From gym to bed he came, sprinkling clean sweat onto her. Her eyes soon turned from imbibing into mirrors shiny and pained with her desire: "Stop, okay?" He took her home of course. "What did I do?" "The right thing," I told him. What sorrow. Her hunger—her sustenance shames her.

7. Chichibu (11.01.14)

Once a decade or so outside my skull in air my own voice hangs. Two winters ago, two hours from Tokyo in a taxi, we rolled round switchbacks—a paved mountain road. Village lights and the train station glittered below. From the black night, from beyond cold glass my voice spoke without ado: *You may not find the one for you. You found yourself.* I grieved. I knew. Later in the house nested like a warm candle in cedar-scented hills the seer completed the vision: *He may not find another. When you grow old, you will care for each other.*

6. Malaise (10.25.14)

My speed and movements, my ingestions are calculated. Ever a risk assessor for cells and soul—a single weave inside me. But after the last encounter, or three, I fell into my head: *Was it worth the risk of opening? Entangling limbs and tongues? Is unease a vestige of when relations cohered as purity, contamination?* I despair if that story haunts me. Weary of thinking on it, I cancel on him. Instead cocoon myself in soft garments and light. I watch ghost stories. Fierce women who hunt them and burn the bad ones back to another mind's hell.

5. Sufficiency (10.18.14)

At a giveaway—we do them often at powwows—the family honors one of our own by thanking the People who jingle and shimmer in circle. They are *with* us. We give gifts in both generous show and as acts of faith in sufficiency. One does not future-hoard. We may lament incomplete colonial conversions, our too little bank savings.

The circle, we hope, will sustain. We sustain it. Not so strange then that I decline to hoard love and another's body for myself? I cannot have faith in scarcity. I have tried. It cut me from the circle.

4. Biosocial (10.11.14)

Girls teetered by in baby-doll dresses, on arms of boys in shorts with pockets. "Americans are a bit boring, you know?" His tongue formed by French. We resumed funny fighting, pearly cocktails. Strung through the bar's backyard galaxy little red suns had insects orbiting. Two decades since I inhaled inside his fine wrinkled shirts, he still teases and touches me—narrates an experiment: "You *must* have jealousy. We are animals. You provide me one storm of love to assess. I require *three*." But I fine-tuned a neurological-lightning-interrupter. Why is what we species were *factual*? Why not also becoming?

3. Austin (10.04.14)

She was not drunk. As full as her breasts was her heart. Genevieve breathed, "You're *pretty*. I'm gonna dance." She rose from where she'd squeezed between our two sets of thighs. May's palm polished her bottom. G sashayed away on so much leg and heel. Spring scent fluttered across the thrift store pearl snap of Bearded Dude at the bar. He eyed her over his Lone Star. Not one, not two, but six glossy heads followed her, undulating at fifty-five. Twelve eyes set upon her, nervous—grew embryos of horror. When they hunger over bridal magazines, Genevieve will haunt them.

2. Temple (09.20.14)

Henry is gentle. When his shirt came off, I was unprepared for the marks on his body—bites and bruises on his neck, scratches down his back and arms. Dried-blood tracks gouged and routed, criss-crossing his topography. My breath sucked in. My fingers played the air, then lightly his wounds. Did they hurt? I felt several things in quick succession. Shock, a twinge of disgust, then warming anger. Who would mark him with even a small violence? And he would submit? He apprehended the complex brew in my eyes. With a half smile, he said, "Oh, you should see her."

1. Houston (09.13.14)

My eyes are dumb apprehenders. No fine visage alone does move me. It is voluptuous sound, undulating between heavy and light, assertive and sweet. His drawl pressed back by my tongue, pushed back to the surface. His voice spilled to my mouth and ears, but didn't stay long. It needled from eardrum through neck. I arched into him. His sound looped to my belly, cut a hard path south. It was material transfer in no mundane way. His tongue's droplets dematerialized in the mechanism of sound, rematerialized within a sealed enclave of tight-skirted thighs. His voice is a teletransportation device.

NOTES

1 Strum, Circe Accurso. "100-Word Collective: Introduction," *Voices in Italian Americana* 24, nos. 1 and 2 (2013): 95.

2 NDN is shorthand for "Indian," a term Native Americans use to describe ourselves. In my experience, the use of the term by Native Americans both acknowledges the colonial genealogy of "Indian" but insists on continued use of the term in a way that connotes an insider's familiarity with its usage.

TWINING

Pain Scale Treaties

LAURA DA'

Enraged at settler atrocities and encroachments, Tecumseh stamped his foot into the ground, trampling out the fault lines of the New Madrid Earthquake. Half the nation rattled to the percussions of his dismay. The very meanders of the rivers changed. Long blades were shearing Shawnee land to the bone; sharpened nibs dripping ink were negotiating these phantom obliterations on map velum.

The loam that applauded Tecumseh's confederacy of resistance with such might grew still with the next generation's forced removal. Even now, there are traces of that sorrow that blasted the trees into crippled crescents, warping them back into the soil along the margins of those paths of exile.

Perched on the shoulders of generational trauma sit these two theses: suffering begets cruelty begets suffering begets cruelty, and pain is empathy's catalyst. When deep hurt sears, my fists and abdomen sickle inward. I compress my atoms in a futile attempt to minimize the target. When it abates, the curve of the earth returns discernably under my soles and my fingers unclench, probing and pinching the air for the velvet current of any trail home.

The last Shawnee speaker in my family was my great-grandfather. He was shipped away to boarding school as a young child, and his language slipped from story to sentence, sentence to fragment, fragment to adjective, leaving him with the sparsest scattering of nouns to pass down—a starvation harvest of syntax-starved images.

I know the words for elk and water. There are other Shawnee nouns as dense as koans with metaphor and meaning, but they remain inscrutable to me.

Following the Indian Removal Act of 1830, the Shawnee were forcibly evicted from their homelands to Indian Territory. In most cases, the removal took more than eighteen months. Primary source documents and the rare testimonials spared by history attest to the untenable conditions. Many Shawnee died on the removal road, particularly the society's most fragile members: the young, elderly, and ill. Upon arrival many more died due to disease, inadequate food and shelter, and violence.

I have an ancestor who, in the aftermath of the Civil War's upheavals, made an appeal to Congress in support of the Shawnee tribe. Articulate and intelligent, he was literate in Shawnee, English, and Latin, I am told. He was sent to Washington to advocate for the tribe in a famine winter. He spent months there, a dark shadow in the elegant Shawnee turban and clothes of his time, relegated to the chilly corners of the antechambers of antechambers.

A man of his generation would have been removed from Ohio alongside his parents and siblings in his boyhood. He would have been removed again with his own grandchildren. By the end of his life, he would have seen his nation reduced to a tenth.

Family legend claims that he waited in the Capitol for a season and a half but was met with no audience.

Historians surmise that at a peak in westward expansion, the 1830s through the 1840s, the frontier of European settlement moved at a rate of ten to forty miles a year. I used to wince at photocopies of old treaty papers—fragile shrouds from this voracious consumption.

The Shawnee, like so many of America's sovereign Indigenous nations, signed many treaties with the colonial and American government:

1786's Treaty with the Shawnee conducted at the mouth of the Great Miami River

1795's Treaty of Greeneville

1803's Treaty of Fort Wayne

1805's Treaty with the Wyandotte held at Fort Industry

1808's Treaty with the Chippewa conducted at Brownstown

1814, 1815, 1817, and 1818's Treaties with the Wyandotte

1825's Treaty with the Shawnee conducted in St. Louis

1831's Treaty with the Shawnee concluded at Wapaghkonnetta

1831's Treaty with the Seneca in Logan Country, Ohio

1832's Treaty with the Shawnee

1832's Treaty with the Shawnee made at Castor Hill in Missouri

1832's Treaty with the Seneca and Shawnee concluded at the Seneca agency, on the headwaters of the Cowskin River

1854's Treaty with the Shawnee made in the city of Washington

1865's Agreement with the Cherokee and other tribes in the Indian Territory

1867's Treaty with the Seneca, mixed Seneca and Shawnee, Quapaw, etc.

The gore of the battlefield seeps into the ground and is lost; ink on velum is its approximation.

I am laid low on a bed of dried blood, but it has been graciously consumed by the hospital's large, absorbent sheet guards and rendered into rusty shadows under the papery layers.

Any treaty is an artifact of unimaginable suffering.

Only twice do I attempt to articulate my discomfort in my own terms: once in a sham attempt at restrained stoicism, I say that it is hitting a raw nerve, then in hysterics, I whimper that I see the glint of the teeth and at once they are clamped down inside me. The third time I have learned to say that it is a seven and accept the quicksilver pulse of intravenous analgesic like a benediction.

I recognize that I have made a treaty with myself bartering the refinement of my language for rapidly delivered slivers of chemical mercy. All I need now are my hands to talk. When I hold up the numbers of the pain scale, I feel a shiver of what I have ceded with such terrified alacrity. I sign my mark in the air with my dominant hand.

A timber scribe is a small, sharp gouge designed for blazing trees. This tool, small enough to fit in a pocket, was once the first and most essential component of any surveyor's gear.

Stick is an anachronism; the traditional bellow of the surveyor as the blaze is carved into the sight-trunk and the first chain is placed.

Stick: seven marks are carved into my torso and abdomen. I meander into the territory of illness and must learn to make its land my own; my body's sovereignty evaporates.

Is it mercy or cruelty that compels the surgeon to sign her initials on the layer of skin above the first incision so that, as her scalpel begins to perforate my flesh, she is compelled to cut through her very name? A narrow conduit is surgically buried deep in my body. One end curls at the terminus of my trunk. Three inches of flexible plastic tubing droops like a tiny cannon from the side of my torso, just under my ribs—a portal that obliterates my skin's compromised frontiers.

The myth of the America landmass as virgin soil is pervasive. I don't see my former self as pure, but something integral is stripped from me just the same as I disaggregate into the numbers of disease. I am no longer a mystery. No dark stand of untouched timber is left in me. The exact equations of my survival are tallied—hourly, daily, weekly, monthly— mathematically.

I have one ancestor who surveyed in the American South just after the period of removal. I have another whose notation I once read in the Eastern Shawnee tribal library: "I don't like those lines running so close to what's mine."

Stuck: the response to the surveyor's call and the confirmation of the act of measurement.

Caribou People

SIKU ALLOOLOO

Tuktu Glow

It was Christmas break in Yellowknife, and we were celebrating. We were three Inuit women, of three generations: my cousin, whose family had been relocated from our home community of Pond Inlet by the RCMP, was one of the last to attend a residential school; her friend, like my father, was one of the last to be born and raised on the land; and me, one of the first raised outside of Nunavut and not in residential school. Like others, our lives were each threaded with an array of colonial trauma, though that evening all of this was farthest from our minds. For this brief, unexpected moment we transcended everything.

My cousin had lovingly roasted a large, beautiful piece of caribou just for us, so we sat around it with great joy. We cut pieces off with a knife and brought it to our mouths with our fingers. Tuktu was getting harder to come by, and this was my first in a long time. I chewed and the meat felt insatiably delicious in my teeth. They clenched and grinded each bite with pleasure as the flavor I was raised on dilated my every cell and brought my whole being forward to intoxicating focus. In a breath of sudden self-consciousness I looked up at the other two women and saw they were already in deep, their eyes downturned and faraway as they savored each mouthful. Without hesitating, I took another large bite. The pull carried us to an innate world. Somewhere primal, dark. Endless. Like a full moon in winter, eternity blowing in the wind across the blackness of the night. An ancient existence. A womb.

When we came back into the room, forty-five minutes had passed. Not a word had been spoken. The meat was all gone. We looked at each other.

"Holy fuck," my cousin finally said, and we all broke into laughter. "Look at us, three Inuit women, eating tuktu! What our people have eaten for thousands of years. It's so deep in our DNA that it just took us back."

We were still glowing.

"They were so incredibly tough. . . . To survive out there on their own. In the freezing cold, with only animal skins and snow houses. Traveling in the dark, no sun for months. Giving birth. Hunting for days, sometimes coming back with nothing. . . . And her, she was raised like that!" my cousin said, pointing to her friend beside me. "When all the children were being taken away, her grandmother packed her in a qamutiik and took her out into the cold. She built them an igloo and they lived there together for as long as they could, until eventually they had to go back. . . . Isn't that amazing?"

Memory of Stars

The enormous Bathurst caribou herd used to pass by my hometown of Yellowknife in the early winter when I was growing up. I remember my mom taking my little brother and me out to see them in 1992, just after she and our father split up. I was six years old; my little brother was not yet four. She was a newly single mother of four and our rock. It seemed at that time our world would be forever cast in gray, punctuated by incomprehensible heartache and confusion. *How was it possible to lose half of ourselves?* Something inside I wasn't aware of before felt exposed in its brokenness. The form I had been, that contained me, now a mess of shattered pieces. I wondered how it was possible to exist. *Was this really our life now, forever?*

She told us we were going to see something amazing as she drove out along the Ingraham Trail, a road we knew well and were fond of, as it was the way to our cabin. Halfway there, we came upon several vehicles parked along the side of the road, at Pontoon Lake. She pulled over into an open spot and turned off the ignition. We stepped out onto the ground, a bit bewildered. We had never stopped here before or seen so many people along this quiet dirt road. Rifles fired in the distance, the sharp cracks slightly dulled and resounding across the treetops below us. The air was charged with excitement, glimmering on the faces of people buzzing by.

The three of us walked down from the road into the bush, through fresh fallen snow. We kept forward through the pines, birch, and willows. Not too long and we could see through the trees, a few caribou on the edge of the clearing. Like magic. We continued on and our eyes filled with even wider amazement as we made our way to the shore. We nestled beneath the trees and watched in awe as hundreds of thousands of caribou crossed the frozen lake, just meters before us. A multitude of brown, gray, and white walking steadily ahead, their breath hanging in the air in frozen clouds, just like ours. I remember the snow on the lake, padded down by millions of hoofprints, and how special it felt to be so close to them, the three of us, like some miraculous dream. They remained calm and unhurried despite the presence of all who had come to see or hunt them. To this day, I have never seen anything so majestic.

They say the Bathurst herd was 350,000 strong that year. Difficult to imagine now, twenty-four years on, when they are down to a mere 15,000.

My dad faded out of our lives in a similarly drastic fashion at that time, like a mirrored disappearance. We barely saw him. But we would often come home to find fresh tuktu stashed outside in the deep freeze or the shed that he had dropped by for us, always, while we were away. Like so many other survivor families, we carried the fallout of all that colonial atrocity right through to our bones. Despite all the hard truths that can be said about that man, and the shatteredness of each of us, I will always cherish this: though he may not have been able to fulfill his role in most ways, he always provided us with meat. He loved us in the best way he knew how.

Years later, after our mother's death, my little brother and I were adopted into an extended Dene family. I learned that the Dené Sųłiné word for barrenland caribou (of which the Bathurst is one herd) is etthën. It is the same word for "star," and as my stepfather put it, "perhaps because there were so many." That is exactly how it was that day, like watching a million ancient beings in the snow, their light spanning across an unfathomable distance.

Or like two hindquarters appearing in the shed, a distant reminder of love. A single speck of light that managed to make it through.

"We Sew It Up"

People often speak of the north as a place of extremes and harsh realities: long and frozen winters, endless summer daylight, constant winter darkness, vast and all but uninhabited wilderness. As a northerner rooted in both Inuit and Dene cultures, the harshest extreme to me is how rapidly and far-reaching colonialism has set into our world.

Within the span of two lifetimes, my parents' and grandparents' generations have seen drastic changes both in our ways of life and our homelands. My Inuit grandparents went from freely traveling the land as our ancestors had always done to living in a permanent community. The RCMP forced Inuit into settlements in the 1950s in order to bring us under government control. They slaughtered our sled dogs so we were immobile and also split entire family groups apart, scattering us across different communities.

My father was born in a sod house in 1949 and was raised to travel the land and provide for his family from a very young age. He can navigate using constellations and landmarks, make traditional tools, build shelter in any season, attend to injuries, and his intimate knowledge of our world makes him a very skilled hunter on both the land and the sea. At the age of eight, he was able to go out for the day alone and come back with a seal to feed the family. Also at eight years old he was taken from his parents and sent to residential school thousands of kilometers away, which he was lucky to have survived.

He was one of tens of thousands of children stolen from every Indigenous nation across the country by the Canadian government and forced into assimilation schools. They knew our entire societies stem from the land, which meant we would never give it up and that we would always protect it. So for 150 years Canada stole all of our children—our heart, indeed our future—and sought to break them of our ways and collapse our societies in the process. Many of these children suffered unthinkable atrocities during their time at these schools, and thousands never made it home to our families. It is a devastating and recent history, with the last schools finally closing in 1996, and Indigenous peoples throughout the country are still working through the debilitating repercussions that persist in our lives.

The desire to dominate and exploit peoples and lands in order to create wealth—this is the driving force of colonialism and also the lifeblood of this country. If there is any hope of recuperating a sense of humanity, or of surviving the climate crisis that is rapidly intensifying throughout the world, we need to engage the reality of everything we are up against. The stakes are too high.

It is no exaggeration to say that Canada is built on racism, genocide, violence, and theft. The founding and daily maintenance of this colony depends expressly on the domination of Indigenous peoples through the illegal seizure and occupation of our territories, colonial laws and policies, police brutality, excessive incarceration, economic marginalization, gender violence, child apprehension, and the suppression of our governance systems, spiritual practices, and ancestral ways of life—all of which remain deeply rooted in our lands.

Canada is sustained by a resource-based economy—if there is any doubt as to the racism and brutality this necessitates every day, just consider: where do the resources come from and how are they obtained—are they not violently torn from the earth? And are those sites of extraction not integral parts of Indigenous homelands or crucial to animal and plant life? Why is it that most Indigenous peoples are living in extremely impoverished conditions on reserves, in remote communities, and in urban centers, whereas the resources stripped from our lands generate massive amounts of wealth for governments and corporations? Is this country not home to one of the biggest and most destructive industrial operations on the planet?[1] How many of our territories and water systems have been contaminated by hydroelectric dams, oil, gas, and toxic waste, and how many lives are being lost to new cancers as a result every year? How many community members have been harmed or arrested for protecting their homelands from pipelines and mining operations? What recourse do we have to the distinct rise in gender violence and narcotics abuse that come with intensified mining in our communities?

Treaties 8 and 11 grant permission for settlers to coexist on our lands and were contingent upon certain terms, including mutual autonomy, self-governance, and the provision of health care—but how many of our men, women, elders, and youth continually suffer violence at the hands of police officers or are denied adequate care by health providers?

These treaties were also meant to ensure that Indigenous ways of life would continue despite the presence of settlers—meaning that all of the elements that sustain life on the land would remain protected—so that our people could continue to live according to our ancestral ways forever.

Due to ongoing colonial policies, industrial exploitation, and now climate change, places where we used to be able to harvest food or medicines, drink the water, and inhabit alongside other forms of life are being turned into wastelands.

My hometown of Yellowknife was built for gold mining in 1934 and became home to one of the richest gold mines in Canadian history. Giant Mine sits on the shore of Great Slave Lake, one of the largest freshwater sources on the planet. Though the mine closed in 2004, its toxic repercussions will last forever: the deteriorating site rests upon 237,000 metric tons of arsenic trioxide, a lethal by-product of gold mining that is impossible to remediate or prevent from leaking into the surrounding lakes and atmosphere, which it is doing at a disturbing rate.[2] A study released in April 2016 showed mercury and arsenic levels to be dangerously high in lakes within a twenty-five-kilometer radius of Giant Mine; in some cases, over thirteen times the limit for drinking water and twenty-seven times the level deemed adequate for aquatic life.[3]

Canadians tend to romanticize the northern town for its remnants of a frontier history forged by sweat and gold as well as for its supposed "untouched, pristine wilderness"—but the truth is we can no longer drink the water or eat the fish in that area and now have to travel long distances to harvest foods and medicines. They say Giant Mine rests upon enough arsenic to kill the entire planet twice over—and although there have been several attempts over the years to contain the toxic waste, there has never been an adequate plan to protect the environment from contamination. For me, this is the clearest indication of western society's single-minded focus on obtaining wealth at any expense. There is no contingency plan or thought of the future or respect for any form of life. The only drive is money—and this is true of any mining operation in the country, whether diamonds or oil and gas or gold.

Today, the beautiful, vast, wild landscape of Denendeh is riddled with large-scale mining operations that have destroyed numerous lakes and river ecosystems, as well as the migration and calving grounds of caribou—an essential source of sustenance for both Inuit and Dene alike since time immemorial. We are caribou people, and the widespread decline of this ancestral relation is a source of deepening loss across the north.

There are many stories of the generosity and benevolence of caribou, how they offer themselves in times of need. Dene and Inuit peoples would not exist without the caribou: its hide has given us warmth and protection from the cold, its meat our main source of nourishment, its bones and antlers our tools, its skin stretched on drums that carry our songs and spiritual connection. It was the caribou who taught us how to honor our kinship and practice ways that sustain us both. A growing anxiety throughout our communities is, *What happens when there are no more caribou? Are we still caribou people? If we can no longer practice our culture in all of the ways that depend on the caribou, are we still Dene or Inuit?*

Protecting the caribou was once a major rallying point for northerners. It's what galvanized us to stand strong against the Mackenzie Valley

Pipeline and assimilative government policies in the 1970s and also work toward self-determination. Since then both the caribou population and our anticolonial nerve have been in steep decline. We have veered quite far from the unified vision we once fought hard for to ensure that our homelands would remain grounded in Indigenous principles, values, and ways of life well into the future.

Last spring I spent some time with a very knowledgeable and beloved elder, Ethel Lamothe. We were at Dechinta Bush University—a northern organization based outside of Yellowknife that delivers Indigenous education on the land and one of the saving graces in my own educational journey. I was helping her scrape her moose hide in preparation for tanning, and as our hands worked we talked about womanhood, spirituality, and bush medicines. She told me about the work she and others did in previous decades to advance decolonization, social transformation, and healing in Denendeh and also shared insight about the challenges. I had been troubled lately about the gap between elders and young people, the cultural inheritance being lost, the growing alienation I see in current generations, and the complexity of overcoming all these challenges when we are starting from such fragmentation. At one point Ethel stopped and said: "Our society is full of holes now, like the ones in this hide. So we have to sew them up. Where there's a hole there instead of a mother or a father, an aunty or grandparent steps in to raise the kids. We have holes in our spirituality and culture, how we relate to each other and deal with things, so we have to find ways to relearn that. You know, we lost some of our own ceremonies and ways of praying, but we can learn from other cultures who still have it. You don't have any grandmothers to teach what you need to know as a woman, so you adopt a new grandmother who can teach you. So we do it like that. We sew it up."

The Elders Kept Heart

In 2015 I led a project with elders and youth on the land near Fort Smith to study how climate change impacts ancestral foods and ways of life. The changes are drastic: massive declines in animal and plant populations, erratic weather, disrupted seasonal patterns, diminishing quality of snow and ice, disappearing sources of fresh water. The land is growing more dangerous to travel. People are having to go farther to search for food, medicine, and materials, and everything is less abundant. Etthën, for example, have not passed through this territory in over fifty years.

It is very difficult to face the extent of these changes, to realize how much everything our cultures depend on is bearing the brunt of climate change and industrial development, the same way we as Indigenous peoples are bearing the brunt of colonialism in our everyday lives. It was especially difficult for the youth, whose entry point to their culture and territory came with the disappointment of realizing how much is being lost. The elders kept heart. They stressed the importance of survival skills, encouraging us to become self-sufficient and adaptive on the land—the same way our peoples have always had to be. They said that though we are unable to stop the changes, we must continue on and not be afraid.

Beautiful, wise Ethel also taught me to cut upward when harvesting plants for medicine. "Because life goes *up!*" The same way my brothers honor their kill by setting its ears in the direction it was headed so its spirit can go forward. Everything is done with respect to the natural flow and continuation of life, even when taking life, because we exist as a continuum. The essence that we come from will always carry through us, and beyond us.

Though the birds no longer black out the sky as they migrate and the fish no longer teem and the river no longer breaks up in thunderous crash of six-foot-thick sheets of ice, the elders remain in close connection to the land as it is now; they continue to live in our ways despite unprecedented changes and endlessly destructive forces. They lead us younger ones to fortify from within, from the richness of our cultures, from the sources that strengthen, connect, heal and affirm. An understanding of how potent our lifeways remain begins to emerge—lifeways meaning ways of life we belong to and also ways that give life. Those old ones knew it was always about both.

So when we experience something that breaks through the haze, like eating caribou meat or spending time on the land, we meet a profound and undeniable truth: that our ancestral connection is alive, embodied, and easily reawakened.

NOTES

1   See Environmental Defence's report, "Canada's Toxic Tar Sands: The Most Destructive Project on Earth," February 2008, https://environmentaldefence .ca/report/report-canadas-toxic-tar-sands-the-most-destructive-project-on -earth.

2   See Clark Ferguson's *Shadow of a Giant* (2015), which "is an interactive web documentary that tells the story of one Canada's largest environmental disasters, Yellowknife's Giant Mine. https://vimeo.com/100450687.

3   Ivan Semeniuk, "Lakes Near Yellowknife Contaminated with Arsenic, Mercury after Mine Closing," *Globe and Mail*, April 6, 2016.

Part One

Redeeming the English Language (Acquisition) Series

TIFFANY MIDGE

When did he first say, "Ugh!"
When did he first say, "Ugh!"
In the Injun book it say
When the first brave married squaw
He gave out with a big ugh
When he saw his Mother-in-Law.

—FROM WALT DISNEY'S *PETER PAN*

.

1. Etymology of "Ugh"

From the *Online Etymology Dictionary*, "ugh" is listed as—

"Imitative of the sound of a cough; as an interjection of disgust, recorded from 1837." And from *Wiktionary*: "used to express repugnance, disgust, boredom, annoyance, tiredness, or horror." Such as: *When I saw how the stuff in the larder had gone moldy all I could think of to say was, "Ugh."*

"Ugh" might also have its origins from an 1872 memoir about a Creek Indian council held in 1825. Michael Johnston Kenan, who assisted US treaty commissioners at Broken Arrow in the Creek Nation, remembered:

I was particularly surprised by the simultaneous—& clearly,
Expressed responses or guttural "ugh's," of the entire Council—
This appeared to be the word of assent or approval that every
member uttered, as the speakers rounded or clinched as it
were, their statements or inferences—It was as much as "yes"—
"that's so," or their equivalent meaning.

But it was not until the very popular frontier adventure stories of James
Fenimore Cooper that "ugh" was successfully injected into the mainstream
vernacular in relationship to all things *injun*.

1.1 Acronym as Acrostic Poem

Uncivilized.
Grunting.
Heathen.

1.2 Language Acquisition (Overwritten)

As a small child I rarely spoke. I didn't have to. My older sister did all the
talking for me. When adults asked, "What is your name?" my sister
answered for me, "Her name is Tiffany." I was a ventriloquist's dummy to
my big sister's act. I broadcasted my thoughts through a telepathic wave
we inexplicably shared, and she, the willing conduit, became the vehicle
for my every toddler whim. I had no need for articulation because I didn't
have to. I probably owe a lot to my sister. It was through her enabling of my
chronic speechlessness, my Harpo to her Groucho, my yin to her yang, that
contributed to my preference for writing—a silent activity—over speaking. She was the mystical channeler, my personal J. Z. Knight, open and
receptive to the three-year-old entity I unleashed at her disposal. I was the
putty and she was the hand, and if it was not for her, I may have ended up
being a talker instead of a writer; one who runs loudly at the mouth rather

than one who purrs quietly at the keyboard. Language came to me in the form of drawing and coloring—reflections of an artistic savant—and gradually evolved into writing. "Ugh" could easily have been my first utterance. But it could just as easily have been _____.

Universally, across cultures, most every baby's first word is "mama." In Dakota we say *Ina*.

1.3 Phonology

I grew up with extra sets of grandparents. Like luggage, extra sets of grandparents are fortunate and sometimes convenient things to have. This is not so unusual a thing in Native communities (extra grandparents, not luggage). The lineage can be confusing so I won't bother to draw you a diagram. Suffice to say, I grew up with three Indian grandmas (Eliza, Ethel, and Charity), and though Eliza tragically died in a car accident before I was born, she remained a constant presence throughout my childhood because Grandpa Dick (her husband) lived with our family. All of my grandparents grew up speaking their tribal languages and retained it into their advanced years. A common occurrence in my house: after dinnertime, my mother seated with my grandpa around our yellow Formica table, practicing Dakota.

Linguists who study American Indian English describe the dropping of final voiced obstruents in standard American English. They call this *final devoicing*. It is commonly known among social scientists that the loss of a language is on par with the loss of a species; when a language dies, a piece of humanity dies with it. Indigenous languages are in danger of extinction. Native American languages and cultures are inextricably linked because the ideas of a culture are anchored within the language; it is not just a reflection of a culture but *is* the culture. Native cultures have their own set of realities, their own particularities of expression and distinct perceptions of being in the world, and those realities are conveyed through language.

I *still* do not speak my tribal language. Just a smattering of words.

1.4 Literacy Acquisition (Example of Dramatic Irony or Running Counter to Expectation)

(Spelling Bee, 1972) My sister competed against the entire student body at the Snoqualmie Valley Elementary School Spelling Bee and won by successfully spelling words like *incendiary, vacuum,* and *hors d'oeuvres.* She went on to compete with the other schools in our district—middle school and high school combined—and won those competitions too—*myrrh, ingenuous, obsequiousness.* When she went on to compete against the winners of the neighboring district, she lost. The word that cost her the competition was *rhythm.* She was a nine-year-old Indian girl with dark skin and braids who out-spelled and out-performed more than two hundred white (WASP) students, many of whom were several grades ahead of her, and she lost to the word *rhythm.*

The drum is the heartbeat of our nation. It remains resistant to English interpretation, to translation. As well as it should, because how can you translate a heartbeat?

2. The Use of "Ugh" in American Literature

There are numerous references to "ugh" in James Fenimore Cooper's *Last of the Mohicans.* This may well have been the birth of "ugh" as it applies to Native Americans. However, "ugh" was originally scripted as "hugh," which was later refined by subsequent authors to "ugh" so as not to confuse readers with the man's name "Hugh," which is English in origin and means "bright mind."

From *Last of the Mohicans* (1826):

> "*Hugh!*" exclaimed Chingachgook, who had been occupied in examining an opening that had been evidently made . . . "I would wager fifty beaver skins against as many flints, that the *Mohicans* and I enter their wigwams within the month!" (205).

When his son pointed out to the experienced warrior the situation of their dangerous enemy, the usual exclamatory *"Hugh!"* . . . Hawkeye and the *Mohicans* conversed earnestly together in Delaware for a few moments (71).

"Hugh!" exclaimed the young *Mohican*, rising on the extremities of his feet, and gazing intently in his front, frightening away the raven to some other prey, by the sound and the action (270).

. . . out to the experienced warrior the situation of their dangerous enemy, the usual exclamatory *"hugh"* burst from his (161).

2.1 Addendum: December, 2014

NBC's three-hour-long musical production of *Peter Pan Live* (not to be confused with Disney's animated version) attracted 9.1 million television viewers. Due to the offensive Indian-speak gibberish of the "Ugg-a-Wugg" musical number, a Chickasaw composer, Jerod Impichchaachaaha' Tate reimagined the song and renamed it "True Blood Brothers"; the "Ugg-a-Wugg" chorus replaced with "OWA,HE," the Wyandotte word for "come here."

While this redo of an inflammatory musical number might appear to represent some nod toward progress, it more accurately conveys a kind of compromise. What might seem an effort for cultural sensitivity smacks to me as something more like a bargain. As in, *We'll revise the guttural-Injun-speak just so long as we can still sensationalize and dehumanize actual Native peoples by presenting these antiquated, stereotypical, racist representations.* In fact, the updated version made the costumes, choreography, and staging all the more garish, contributing even further to the grotesquerie. It seemed all the more insulting.

3. Stages of Language Development (PEPSI)

Level I: Pre-production Stage (Silent Period). Minimal Comprehension;
No Verbal Production.

I keep a photograph of what I believe is of my grandmother Eliza, taken during her boarding school days. In the photo are eight little Indian girls and eight little Indian boys posing on a shady lawn beneath the branches of a large tree. The little boys are attired like George Washington: white wigs, ruffled blouses, cummerbunds and breeches, while the girls are posed as elegant debutants replete in flowery lace and wigs. The children are linking their arms together in uniformed sequence as if curtsying before a waltz or cake walk. Is it strange that the faces of the children in this photograph are downcast and ominous? Of course most photos taken during the 1920s appear this way, except the context forces one to interpret it in a different, more loaded way. It was common to shear children's hair, forbid traditional clothing and customs, and punish children severely for speaking their tribal language. To speak one's own language was an obstacle for acculturation. Although I imagine the children must have cried in their beds after the lights were turned out, whispering *Mama* in their tribal language.

Level II: Early Production Stage. Limited Comprehension;
One/Two-Word Response.

In the sixth grade I rejected the principals of "liberty" and "individualism" by becoming a conscientious objector. Our three classrooms consisted of seventy-five children, all white with the exception of one black boy, a Mexican boy, and myself. We weren't exactly a melting pot. Our three teachers brainstormed a self-esteem program and titled it "Especially-Special-People." The incentive-designed program listed specific criteria for membership, such as extending good deeds, cleaning blackboards, and turning in extra credit assignments. Once a potential "ESP" completed the checklist—much like earning merit badges—they were celebrated in an awards ceremony, given their diploma, and given a bright red ESP button to wear.

Probably the best privilege of being an ESP was entry into an elite organization with exclusive benefits such as being allowed to chew gum, purchase soda from the teacher's lounge, and have extended recesses. For several months I repeatedly resisted becoming *just another* ESP. Every student in our three classrooms, one by one, met the criteria and were indoctrinated and rewarded as Especially-Special-People. All of seventy-five children, except for two: myself and the Mexican boy, Ricky. On the last day of class, before we were let out for summer break, all of the students left school grounds to a nearby park and were treated to an extravagant picnic replete with games, activities, hotdogs, and ice cream. One of the teachers was forced to stay behind in the hot, stuffy classroom with just Ricky and myself, as we sat quietly at our desks for the rest of the afternoon.

Level III: Speech Emergence Stage. Increased Comprehension;
Simple Sentences; Some Errors in Speech.

(1971, Christmas) Her name was Tamu (Swahili for "sweet") and I had picked her out of the toy section in the Sears catalog. What I did know is that when I pulled her talking string she spoke the phrases:

- My name is Tamu.
- Cool it, baby.
- Do you like my dress?
- Sock it to me.
- I'm sleepy.
- Can you dig it?
- Let's play house.
- I love you.
- Tamu means "sweet."
- I'm hungry.
- I'm proud, like you.

But what I didn't know were Tamu's origins. She was created by Shindana Toys, a division of a company called Operation Bootstrap, Inc., founded as part of a set of initiatives in South Central Los Angeles in 1968 following the 1965 Watts Riots. A goal of the company was to raise black consciousness and improve self-image. I pulled on Tamu's talking string with such frequency that I ended up breaking her, and she never spoke again. Later that same year my mother unearthed her old "talking" baby doll. Suzy had a cracked porcelain head and most of her original, silken yellow hair had fallen off. My mother told me that Suzy would gurgle and fuss when she was laid down, that Suzy would say *Mama*. But she was very old, a 1940s-era doll, and had also become mute with age. These were the only baby dolls I ever wanted, or ever kept, my grandmother told me, because I was *ina was'te*, a "good mother."

Level IV: Intermediate Fluency Stage. Very Good Comprehension; More Complex Sentences; Complex Errors in Speech.

(1963) Frank Wing, my sister's biological father, waited in a doctor's office with his young wife, our mother, and received the grim news that complications from his type 1 diabetes were rapidly progressing and that he should not expect to live beyond six months. It was a Friday, November 22, the same day President Kennedy was fatally shot while riding with his wife, Jacqueline, in a presidential motorcade. My mother and Frank heard the tragedy broadcast on the car radio after the doctor visit. *Where were you when you heard?* Their breath would have expelled in frosty plumes, like smoke, as they waited for the engine to warm. My mother would have reached over with her gloved hand and switched off the radio.

My sister was almost three months old when Frank and my mother were confronted with the prognosis. Yet despite the news that he was terminally ill, and despite having gone blind, Frank continued his studies in the Education Department at Northern Montana College. My mother read out loud from his textbooks each evening, going over every lesson, while they drank cups of black coffee at the yellow Formica table.

Apocalypse Logic

ELISSA WASHUTA

My great-great-great grandfather Tumalth, headman of the Cascades, was hanged by the US Army in 1856, a year after signing the Kalapuya Treaty. He was accused of treason, but he was innocent. I feel like I should say I'm tired of writing this again. I am always writing that Tumalth was hanged a year after signing the Kalapuya Treaty. I am always writing that his daughters were taken to Fort Vancouver when the Cascade leaders were hanged. I am always writing about the resistance of the women who hung tough along the Columbia River for generations, even after the disruption of the systems of hunting, fishing, and gathering our family maintained for thousands of years. Actually, I'm not tired of writing about this, and I may never be, but sometimes when I say once more that *my great-great-great-grandfather was hanged by the US government* I can feel someone thinking, *God, she's back on that.*

X

The last time I watched television, a man kept touching a screen with a red-and-blue map on it. After a while, I was nauseous and my whole body felt held up by metal rods. *Stop putting your hands on that map*, I wanted to tell him. I was in a huge room full of people who were booing, crying, and drinking heavily. *Termination*, I thought. *They are going to terminate my tribe.*

They are going to finish what they started. I am certain that I was the only person in the whole venue—a concert space—thinking about tribal termination. I am always in this room, and I am always lonely.

X

From 1953 to 1968 the US government tried to wipe out some tribes by ending their relationships—withdrawing federal recognition of these tribes as sovereigns, ending the federal trust responsibility to those tribes, allowing land to be lost to non-Natives. The tribes terminated, for the most part, were those the US government considered to be successful because of the wealth within their tribal lands: timber, oil, water, and so on. Terminating a tribe meant fully forsaking all treaty responsibilities to them.

X

In 1993 Donald Trump testified in front of the House Native American Affairs Subcommittee:

> If you look, if you look at some of the reservations that you've approved, that you, sir, in your great wisdom have approved, I will tell you right now—they don't look like Indians to me. And they don't look like the Indians. . . . Now, maybe we say politically correct or not politically correct, they don't look like Indians to me, and they don't look like Indians to Indians.

Earlier that year, Trump had made efforts to partner with the Agua Caliente Band of the Cahuilla Indians as manager of their proposed casino near Palm Springs. The tribe declined.

In 2000 Donald Trump sent a gold-monogrammed letter to the Cowlitz Indian Tribe, of which I am an enrolled member. Hoping to partner with us, he toured our proposed casino site, which he said was the most incredible site he'd ever seen. In 2002 Trump submitted a proposal to partner with the tribe in developing the casino. The tribe declined.

In the letter he sent us in 2000, he wrote, "I want to assure you and all of the members of the Tribe that I do now, and always have, supported the sovereignty of Native Americans and their right to pursue all lawful opportunities."

Our casino will open in April. By then, Donald Trump will have a hand in determining what's lawful.

X

While I watched television and listened to the pundits talk about the man who loves revenge, I began having a panic attack that, as I write this, is eight days deep, the longest I can remember in my decade of PTSD, which I developed and cultivated as a response to multiple rapes, sexual assaults, threats of violence, and acts of stalking that accumulated over the years. For me, a panic attack is dread made physical, an embodied trauma response: nausea, insomnia, a pounding heart, headaches. My psychiatrist said my triggers are many because I went years without PTSD treatment.

In *The Beginning and End of Rape*, Sarah Deer writes, "Colonization and colonizing institutions use tactics that are no different from those of sexual perpetrators, including deceit, manipulation, humiliation, and physical force."

I watched the man touch his hand to the map and knew what my body was trying to tell me: the sexual violence against my body has been carried out in response to the settler state's instructions to its white men, and now the instructions would be delivered clearly, from behind no screen. Maybe my triggers are many because to live in the United States of America is to wake up every day inside an abuser.

X

Boston is the chinuk wawa word for *white* (adj.) or *white person* (n.).
Boston-tilixam also means *white person*, or *white people*.
Siwash is the white people word for *savage Indian* (n.).
I saw the word *siwash* attached to a photo embedded in a wall in a park
    in the Seattle suburbs.
I know only a few words in chinuk wawa:
Mahsie is *thank you.*
Klahowya is *hello.*

Some people say chinuk wawa, also known as Chinook jargon, isn't a real language. This, I think, is because, before the boston-tilixam had us speak English, the jargon was the assemblage of words we used to talk to each other, all up and down the coast.

X

A few days after the last time I watched television, I went to a community response forum in my neighborhood. A line of people hugged the side of the building, waiting to enter. Two boston-tilixam asked the people in line behind me, "Is this the line to get in?" When they heard that it was, they went to the front of the line. Inside, a volunteer said that people who live north of the ship canal would meet in a gallery down the block; people south of the ship canal would stay here and would split into groups by neighborhood. A group of boston-tilixam didn't want to be split up. The volunteer assured them that it wasn't *mandatory* that they separate. The boston-tilixam, relieved, chose a group they could all agree upon.

X

Chief Tumalth's daughter Virginia Miller (my great-great-grandmother's sister) was photographed by Edward Curtis, a boston best known for his sepia-toned portraits of unsmiling Indians posed in their ceremonial dress. Curtis interviewed Virginia, who spoke through an interpreter about traditional Cascade life and her father's hanging. And she told Curtis this, presented here in his words:

> An old man dreamed and announced that new people were coming, with new ways, and the Indians would die. He made them put coyote-skins over their shoulders and two by two, men in front and women behind, march in a circle, while he sang his song of prophecy. The old woman who told [Virginia] about this said it happened when she was a little girl. She took part in the dance, and laughed at the flapping tail of the skin on the girl in front of her, and the old man seized her by the wrist, flung her aside and said, 'You will be the first to die.' As it happened, she outlived all the others.

X

The US has been a party to many treaties.
Some bind the US to its allies: an armed attack on one member of the
    alliance is considered a threat to the other members, who agree
    to "act to meet the common danger."
Some are with other international sovereigns, settling all sorts of
    agreements.
Some are with tribes; all of these have been broken.
One is with my great-great-great-grandfather and a bunch of other men,
    some of whom were hanged for treason.
The US did not enter into treaties with tribes in order to create alliances.
This feels like a logic game that I am too tired to play.

X

Now I see I'm inclined to write, again, about how my great-grandma gave birth to my grandmother with no help but from scissors and string because she didn't want any boston woman messing with her. Like I do in all my essays, I try to explain that she did this at a time when boston-tilixam were stealing Indian babies because it was the quickest and easiest way to turn Native people into boston-tilixam: turn their tongues before they take on an Indigenous language they'll have to unlearn, keep them sheared so there will be no braids to cut. I am alive because of the scissors and the string, because of the everyday resistance that led my great-grandmother to turn away the boston ladies who wanted to help her learn to do white lady things like crochet.

I am most thoroughly colonized by the desire to have the boston-tilixam like me. I look like them, and I try to use this to say things that wouldn't be tolerated from someone who doesn't look like them. But sometimes my desire silences me. Sometimes it speaks so loudly that I can hardly hear the ancestors' instructions for surviving genocide.

X

I sleep less than before. I wake up before sunrise and research things I don't understand. The river where Edward Curtis photographed Virginia Miller with her canoe, the river that is home to salmon and smelt and steelhead, the river where my family lived for ten thousand years—I am forced to imagine it covered in oil. I learned about environmental impact statements and tribal consultation ten years ago, when I was in an entry-level position with the USDA Natural Resources Conservation Service, making best practices flowcharts and compiling resource manuals, but I abandoned that to become a writer.

Boston-tilixam keep asking me, "What can we do?" and I explain that the Lower Columbia River Estuary—our tribal homeland—is threatened by a proposed oil terminal, methanol plant, and coal terminal that could bring major environmental disaster and undermine ongoing habitat restoration efforts. The US Army Corps of Engineers is ignoring tribes' concerns despite active tribal involvement in the consultation process. The coal terminal's environmental impact statement says, "As it currently stands, the tribes exercise their treaty fishing rights in Zone 6, which is outside of the NEPA scope of analysis for this EIS." The focus here is narrow and fails to respond to concerns about coal train dust. This would be the largest coal export terminal in North America.

I tell my Facebook friends that the public comment period is still open. I wonder whether there will be a point at which direct action like the water protection at Standing Rock would be needed, but it's too early to know.

I am wedged inside a small window in the boston people's attention, and I am screaming.

X

In James Welch's novel *Winter in the Blood*, white men gather in a bar alongside the Native American narrator. "But you're mistaken—there aren't any goldeyes in this river. I've never even heard of goldeyes," one of the white men tells the (unnamed) narrator. Another one says, "There are pike in the reservoir south of town. Just the other day I caught a nice bunch." They continue to disagree. The narrator asks, "In the reservoir?"

I want to know whether he thinks there are fish in the river, or in the reservoir, or anywhere, but instead he studies the white men in suits and listens to them talk about the sunfish and the goldeyes and the "clarity of the water" until the subject changes.

X

In 1957 Celilo Falls, part of the Columbia River near where my family is from, was the oldest continuously inhabited community in North America, with archaeological records dating Celilo village sites to eleven thousand years ago. This was once an important site for trade and fisheries, but the opening of the Dalles Dam created a reservoir that flooded Celilo Falls and Celilo Village to make Lake Celilo. Last year, the Army Corps of Engineers thought it might be neat to lower the water for a couple of weeks to reveal Celilo Falls again. Susan Guerin (Warm Springs) wrote of the idea, "My people can't return to Celilo Falls to fish. It won't mend the broken hearts of my family from whom the Celilo Falls were taken. The study will tear off wounds long scabbed-over, and for what: the benefit of spectators?"[1]

X

I used to like to keep safety pins attached to my messenger bag because I used them to clean pepper out of my teeth when I was out of the house.
I used to drink water straight from the tap.
I used to have no idea what my blood quantum was because nobody had ever thought to tell me something like that.

I began to carry floss.
I began to drink from cups.
I began to tell people my blood quantum when they asked, even when I didn't want to.

Somewhere, someone wearing a safety pin on her jacket is saying to someone else, *I'm so sorry for what your ancestors went through. May I ask, are you full Native?*

X

Boston man: white man.
Boston klootchman: white woman.
Many white fur traders, the first whites to occupy the Lower Columbia River Plateau, were from the city of Boston.
Boston Illahee: The United States of America.

I am the descendant of Chief Tumalth of the Cascade people. The United States in which I live is the descendant of the Boston Illahee in which Tumalth was hanged under orders of Philip Sheridan—"The only good Indians I ever saw were dead"—and his daughters were taken by the military to Fort Vancouver.

Why I have used *boston* in this essay when I am talking about *white people*: for the white people who have already made up their minds about their own whiteness; for the white people who have forgotten that their whiteness is new here, that whiteness is not a phenotype but a way of relating; for the white people who don't believe me when I say that the most thorough answer to the question, "What can we do?" is "Remove your settler state from this land and restore all governance to its forever stewards."

X

At the end of *Dances with Wolves*, Wind in His Hair shouts down to Lt. Dunbar from a cliff. The English subtitles read, "Do you see that you are my friend? Can you see that you will always be my friend?"

Because I don't want boston-tilixam to think I am a *nasty woman*—there is already a word for this when applied to Native women, a word we don't use, which is *squaw*—I want to explain that I love many boston-tilixam. Some are relatives; some I love so much that they are family to me; this has nothing to do with anything, and I'm embarrassed that I even feel the need to say it. There are some boston-tilixam I don't like, but it's not because of their whiteness. Sometimes, it is about the things their whiteness motivates them to say and do, but none of that is really my business. The boston-tilixam are responsible for their own whiteness.

When the boston-tilixam came here, we traded at the river.

When they wanted our land, representatives of Boston Ilahee killed and relocated us.

I am descended from many boston-tilixam, and I hold them inside my Indigenous body. I look like them. I have never said that I "walk in two worlds." I walk in the world in which Native nations welcomed visitors who responded by creating a government on our forever land whose mistreatment benefits them.

I don't know of a chinuk wawa word that translates exactly to *whiteness*, maybe because we experience it not as an abstract noun but as an action verb. None of us can choose the legacy we are born within, but all of us choose our alliances. We make and reinforce our commitments with every action.

The problem: that Indigeneity is viewed by the boston-tilixam as a burden while whiteness is not.
The result: some boston-tilixam pour energy into defending the wearing of safety pins.
The weather forecast for Standing Rock: blizzards.

X

"You're an old-timer," the narrator of *Winter in the Blood* says to a man he meets in a café. "Have you ever known this river to have fish in it?" The old man only says, "Heh, heh," before he drops dead, face-down into his oatmeal.

My students, at times, used to struggle with the fish motif. Maybe that happened because I couldn't guide them through seeing the river as symbol. How can we speak in metaphor when we need the river to be seen as literal?

X

For a while I thought that because my work had me at energetic, physical, and emotional capacity, I was doing enough. I was writing, teaching, and informally educating. I changed my mind last week. I found more energy; it had been tucked into night hours I used to use for sleeping. I want to rest, to comfort myself, to meditate, to relax, to practice self-care, but I have a sick belly and a sunken face now. I would like to take a break from the work, but my nausea is telling me that I don't really have a choice. I can't let myself stop with small steps—a Facebook post, a retweet—when Native people are being teargassed, shot with rubber bullets, and threatened with live ammunition for doing the thing the ancestors are still— from within my body, from the other side of genocide—doing: committing to the river.

I want to hold the scissors. I want to tie tight, constricting knots with the string. I want to inhabit my body so fully that I know how to use it to protect the people and the land I love. Because I, too, am asking, *How can I help? What can I do?* And my ancestors tell me clearly, *Find us in your body, and we will show you.*

X

When the Cascade leaders were hanged, some of the people went onto reservations and some remained in the homelands by the river. These people, like my family, were called renegades. To be a renegade is to have betrayed an alliance. Who is betrayed by the act of staying alive in the place where one has lived for ten thousand years?

Tumalth signed that treaty with his X that meant he and his fellows would *acknowledge their dependence on the government of the United States, and promise to be friendly with all the citizens thereof, and pledge themselves to commit no depredations on the property of such citizens.*

If my survival is a betrayal, make no mistake: I'll betray.

X

Tyee is chief. *Tumtum* is heart. *Klushkakwa* is not a word I can translate for you but you might hear me say it instead of *goodbye*, which is not what it means. Instead of *goodbye*, my mom says *toodle-oo* because saying good-bye isn't done, just like stirring batter counter-clockwise, just like walking on the parts of the cemetery where there are graves that could cave in. If this doesn't make sense, don't think about it. Don't try to find explanations consistent with what might be called *logic*. Know that, if you are not from a post-apocalyptic people, you may not be familiar with these strategies we use to survive.

If you are a boston and, when you hear me mention that my tribe's casino will open in April, your first impulse is to say it's a shame that we're doing that, try this instead: trust that we are doing what we believe will help us survive your nation. Instead, say it's a shame that we are still forced to react to the settler state built upon intentional efforts to kill us all.

X

During the summer of 1829, four-fifths of the Cascade people were killed by a white disease. The year before Tumalth signed the treaty, there were only eighty Cascade people left.

Apocalypse comes from an ancient Greek word that's supposed to mean *through the concealed*.

Apocalypse has very little to do with the end of the world and everything to do with vision that sees the hidden, that dismantles the screen.

We have known for a long time that they intend to kill us. I have spent almost every moment of my life in an America that will not rest until I am either dead or turned boston klootchman. I make my way in an America that wants to assign me whiteness because that will mean they've exterminated the siwash they see in me.

It doesn't work that way, and it never has.

Boston-tilixam ask me, *What can I do?* And I talk about the river.

Klushkakwa.

NOTE

1 Tom Banse, "Proposal to Resurrect Columbia River's Celilo Falls Draws Flak," April 16, 2015, on Northwest News Network, www.nwnewsnetwork.org/post /proposal-resurrect-columbia-rivers-celilo-falls-draws-flak.

Women in the Fracklands

On Water, Land, Bodies, and Standing Rock

TONI JENSEN

"Who is responsible for and to this woman, her safety, her body, her memory?"

I.

On Magpie Road the colors are in riot. Sharp blue sky over green and yellow tall grass that rises and falls like water in the North Dakota wind. Magpie Road holds no magpies, only robins and crows. A group of magpies is called a tiding, a gulp, a murder, a charm. When the men in the pickup make their first pass, there on the road, you are photographing the grass against sky, an ordinary bird blurring over a lone rock formation.

You do not photograph the men, but if you had, you might have titled it *Father and Son Go Hunting*. They wear camouflage, and their mouths move in animation or argument. They have their windows down, as you have left those in your own car down the road. It is warm for fall. It is grouse season and maybe partridge but not yet waterfowl. Despite how partridge are in the lexicon vis-à-vis pear trees and holiday singing, the birds actually make their homes on the ground. You know which birds are in season because you are from a rural place like this one, a place where guns and men and shooting seasons are part of the knowledge considered common.

Magpie Road lies in the middle of the 1,028,051 acres that make up the Little Missouri National Grasslands in western North Dakota. Magpie Road lies about two hundred miles north and west of the Standing Rock Reservation, where thousands of Indigenous people and their allies have come together to protect the water, where sheriff's men and pipeline men and National Guardsmen have been donning their riot gear, where those men still wait, where they still hold tight to their riot gear.

If a man wears his riot gear during prayer, will the sacred forsake him? If a man wears his riot gear to the holiday meal, how will he eat? If a man enters the bedroom in his riot gear, how will he make love to his wife? If a man wears his riot gear to tuck in his children, what will they dream?

Magpie Road is part of the Bakken, a shale formation lying deep under the birds, the men in the truck, you, this road. The shale has been forming over centuries through pressure, through layers of sediment becoming silt. The silt becomes clay, which becomes shale. All of this is because of water. The Bakken is known as a marine shale—meaning, once, here, instead of endless grass, there lay endless water.

There, just off Magpie Road, robins sit on branches or peck the ground. A group of robins is called a riot. This seems wrong at every level except the taxonomic. Robins are ordinary, everyday, general-public sorts of birds. They seem the least likely of all birds to riot.

When the men in the truck make their second pass, there on the road, the partridge sit their nests, and the robins are not in formation. They are singular. No one riots but the colors. The truck revs and slows and revs and slows beside you. You have taken your last photograph of the grass, have moved yourself back to your car. The truck pulls itself close to your car, revving parallel.

You are keeping your face still, starting the car. You have mislabeled your imaginary photograph. These men, they are not father and son. At close range, you can see there is not enough distance in age. One does sport camouflage, but the other, a button-down shirt, complete with pipeline logo over the breast pocket. They are not bird hunters. The one in the button-down motions to you out the window with his handgun, and he smiles and says things that are incongruous with his smiling face.

II.

The night before, in a nearby fracklands town, you stand, with your camera, in your hotel room doorway. You left Standing Rock for the Bakken, and the woodsmoke from the water protector camps still clings to your hair. You perform your fracklands travel protocol, photographing the room—the bedspread and desk, the bathroom. In your year and a half of research for your novel, of driving and talking to women in the fracklands, you have performed this ritual, this protocol, dozens of times. You upload the photos onto a website that helps find women who are trafficked, who have gone missing.

The influx of men, of workers' bodies, into frackland towns brings an overflow of crime. In the Bakken at the height of the oil and gas boom, violent crime, for example, increased by 125 percent. North Dakota attorney general Wayne Stenehjem called this increase in violent crime "disturbing" and cited aggravated assaults, rapes, and human trafficking as "chief concerns."

In each place, each frackland, off each road, you wait until checkout to upload the photos of the rooms. In the year and a half of driving and talking and driving and talking, if you've learned nothing else, you've learned to wait. Because it is very, very difficult to sleep in a hotel room once you learn a woman's gone missing from it.

III.

In the Marcellus Shale in Pennsylvania, a floorhand shuts the door to his hotel room, puts his body between the door and a woman holding fresh towels. A floorhand is responsible for the overall maintenance of a rig. The woman says to you that he says to her, "I just want some company." He says it over and over, into her ear, her hair, while he holds her down. She says it to you, your ear, your hair. She hates that word now, she says, *company*. A floorhand is responsible for the overall maintenance of a rig. A floorhand is responsible. But who is responsible for and to this woman, her safety, her body, her memory? Who is responsible to and for the language, the words that will not take their leave?

In a hotel in Texas, in the Wolfcamp Shale, you wake to the music of the trucks arriving and departing. This hotel is shiny tile and chrome bathrooms. It is a parking lot overfilled with trucks, with men from the fields who have an arrangement with management. An arrangement can mean flowers in a vase. An arrangement can mean these men pay for nothing, not even a room. In the morning, the parking lot is all trashcan. Beer bottles and used condoms and needles, the nighttime overflow.

In a hotel in Texas, in the Permian Basin, you report to the front desk re: the roughneck in the room above. You dial zero while he hits his wife/girlfriend/girl he has just bought. You dial zero while he throws her and picks her up and starts again. Or at least, one floor down, this is the soundtrack. Upon his departure, the man uses his fist on every door down your hall. The sound is loud but also is like knocking, like hello, like Anybody home? You wonder if he went first to the floor above but think not. Sound, like so many things, operates mostly through a downward trajectory.

At a hotel where South Dakota and Wyoming meet, you are sure you have driven out of the Bakken, past its edge, far enough. That highway that night belongs to the deer, and all forty or fifty of them stay roadside as you pass. You arrive at the hotel on caffeine and luck. The parking lot reveals the calculus of your mistake—truck after truck after truck, and a hotel clerk outside transacting with a young roughneck. Their posture suggests a shared cigarette or kiss or grope—something safetied through vice or romance or lust. You'd take it. But here the posture is all commerce, is about the positioning of the body close so money can change hands. You are in a place that's all commerce, where bodies are commerce only.

When two more roughnecks stagger into your sight line, the hotel clerk and her partner are heading inside. She meets your eyes like a dare. The staggering man is drunk, the other holding up the first while he zips his fly. This terminology, *fly*, comes from England, where it first referred to the flap on a tent—as in, Tie down your tent fly against the high winds. As in, Don't step on the partridge nest as you tie down your fly. As in, Stake down your tent fly against the winter snow, against the rubber bullets, against the sight of the riot gear.

The men sway across the lot, drunk-loud, and one says to the other, "Hey, look at that," and you are the only *that* there. When the other replies, "No. I like the one in my room just fine," you are sorry and grateful for *the one* in an unequal measure.

You cannot risk more roadside deer, and so despite all your wishes, you stay the night. A group of deer is called a herd; a group of roe deer, a bevy. There is a bevy of roe deer in the Red Forest near Chernobyl. The Bakken is not Chernobyl because this is America. The Bakken is not Chernobyl because the Bakken is not the site of an accident. The Bakken is not Chernobyl because the Bakken is no accident.

IV.

On Magpie Road, the ditch is shallow but full of tall grass. With one hand, the button-down man steers his truck closer to your car, and with the other, he waves the handgun. He continues talking, talking, talking. The waving gesture is casual, like the fist knocking down the hotel hallway—hello, anyone home, hello?

Once on a gravel road, your father taught you to drive your way out of a worse ditch. When the truck reverses, then swerves forward, as if to block you in, you take the ditch to the right, and when the truck slams to a stop and begins to reverse at a slant, taking the whole road, you cross the road to the far ditch, which is shallow, is like a small road made of grass, a road made for you, and you drive like that, on the green and yellow grass until the truck has made its turn, is behind you. By then you can see the highway, and the truck is beside you on the dirt road, and the truck turns right, sharp across your path. So you brake then veer left. You veer out, onto the highway, fast, in the opposite direction.

Left is the direction to Williston. So you drive to Williston, and no one follows.

At a big box store in Williston, a lot sign advertises overnight parking for RVs. You have heard about this, how girls are traded here. You had been heading here to see it, and now you're seeing it. Mostly, you're not seeing. You are in Williston for thirty-eight minutes, and you don't leave your car.

You spend those thirty-eight minutes driving around the question of violence, of proximity and approximation. How many close calls constitute a violence? How much brush can a body take before it becomes a violence, before it makes violence, or before it is remade—before it becomes something other than the body it was once, before it becomes a past-tense body?

V.

Q&A

Why were you there on the road?

Because Indigenous women are almost three times more likely than other women to be harassed, to be raped, to be sexually assaulted, to be called a *that there*.

Because when the governor of North Dakota made an order to block entrance into the camps at Standing Rock and then rescinded it, he said the order was intended toward "public safety." Because in his letter to the Standing Rock tribal chairman, the commander of the Army Corps of Engineers said he was "genuinely concerned for the safety and well-being of both the members of your Tribe and the general public located at these encampments."

Because these statistics about trafficking, about assault, are knowledge considered common, but only if your body is not considered a general-public body.

Because you're a Métis woman.

Because you and they and we misunderstand the danger at Standing Rock, the danger of this pipeline going in there or elsewhere or everywhere. Because you and they and we misunderstand the nature of danger altogether.

Because each person in Flint, Michigan, for the foreseeable future, is rationed four cases of bottled water per week. Because you can see this future upriver or down. Because everywhere is upriver or down.

Because your first memory of water is of your father working to drown your mother. Because you are four or five, and you need to use the bathroom, but instead, find yourself backing out the bathroom doorway and down the hall where you sit on the rust-colored shag. Because you wait for your father to quit trying to drown your mother. It seems crucial in the moment not to wet your pants. It seems crucial to hold the pieces of yourself together. If you make a mess on the carpet, if your father doesn't kill your mother, then she will have to clean the carpet. It seems crucial not to cause any trouble. So you sit. You wait. You hold yourself together.

Because all roads used to lead back to that house, and it is a measure of time and hard work that they no longer do. Because all roads lead to the body and through it. Because too many of us have these stories and these roads. Because you carry theirs and they carry yours, and in this way, there is a measure of balance. Because you are still very good at holding yourself together. Because these times make necessary the causing of trouble, the naming of it.

Because to the north and west of Magpie Road, in the Cypress Hills of southern Saskatchewan, in 1873, when traders and wolf hunters killed more than twenty Assiniboine, mostly women and children in their homes, the Métis hid in those hills and lived. Because they lived, they carried the news. Because they lived, you carry the news. Because the massacre took place along the banks of a creek that is a tributary that feeds into the greater Missouri River.

Because these times and those times and all times are connected through land and bodies and water.

What were you wearing, there on the road?

Not riot gear.

Why didn't you call the police?

See the water cannon on the bridge at Standing Rock. Listen to the sheriff's department men call it a "water hose" like this makes the act better. See also: Birmingham, Alabama. See the dog cages constructed outside the Morton County Sheriff's Department to hold "overflow." See the overflow—the water protectors, Dakota and Lakota women and men in cages. See it all overflow. See the journalists arrested for trespass and worse. See the confiscated notebooks, the cameras they will never get back. See the woman struck by a teargas canister. See how she will no longer be able to see through her right eye. See the children whose grandmothers and grandfathers are hospitalized with hypothermia. See the elder who has a heart attack. See how science newly quantifies what some of us have long known—how historical and cultural trauma is lived in our bodies, is passed down, generation to generation, how it lives in the body. See the fires that elders light to keep warm. See the water extinguish those fires. See the children seeing it.

Why were you by yourself?

On a road like this, you are never alone. There is grass, there is sky, there is wind. See also: the answer on historical and cultural trauma. See also: Cypress Hills. See also: the everyday robins who are in formation now. See also: their ordinary, general-public bodies in riot.

What did you do, after?

You drove north and west and sat in rooms with friends, old and new. You hiked and ate good meals and talked about art. You wrote things down. You began the work of stitching yourself back together. You did this on repeat until the parts hung together in some approximation of self. In Livingston, Montana, you made use of the car wash. You left the tall grass there.

Further questions should be directed toward: Proceed to the Route. Upon arrival, pick up loose, roadside threads. Use them to stitch shut the asking mouths.

VI.

At Standing Rock, the days pass in rhythm. You sort box upon box of donated blankets and clothes. You walk a group of children from one camp to another so they can attend school.

The night before the first walk it has rained hard, and the dirt of the road has shifted to mud. The dirt or mud road runs alongside a field, which sits alongside the Cannonball River, which sits alongside and empties itself into the Missouri.

Over the field a hawk rides a thermal, practicing efficiency. There on the road, in the mud, three Herefords block progress. The cow snorts to her calves, which are large enough to be ambulatory, young enough for the cow still to proffer protection. She places her body between you, the threat, and her calves. She stamps her hooves into the mud, and they stick in a way you imagine unsatisfactory.

In that letter to the Standing Rock Tribal Chairman, the Army Corps commander wrote that the people must disperse from camp "due to the concern for public safety" and because "this land is leased to private persons for grazing and/or haying purposes."

A cow holds public hooves whether stuck in mud or otherwise. A cow is not a concern to public safety. But what of these children? Are they considered public or private? If they don't graze or hay, if they cannot be leased, what is their value, here on this road, in this, our America?

That day, there on the road, once the mother cow allows safe passage, you walk on. After school but before the return walk, the children and you gather with hundreds to listen to the tribal chairman speak of peace, to sit with elders to pray, to talk of peace.

On this day, it is still fall. Winter will arrive with the Army Corps's words—no drilling under Lake Oahe, no pipeline under Lake Oahe. The oil company will counter, calling the pipeline "vital," saying they "fully expect to complete construction of the pipeline without any additional rerouting in and around Lake Oahe." The weather will counter with a blizzard. After the words and before the blizzard, there will be a celebration.

A gathering of larks is called an exaltation. Even if it wasn't so, you like to think of them there, like to think of their song, there with the people in the snow, there, alongside the river.

Back in the fall, you walk the children home from school, there on the road. You cross the highway, the bridge, upon your return. This bridge lies due south of the Backwater Bridge of the water cannons or hoses. But this bridge, this day, holds a better view. The canoes have arrived from the Northwest tribes, the Salish tribes. They gather below the bridge on the water and cars slow alongside you to honk and wave. Through their windows, people offer real smiles.

That night, under the stars, fire-lit, the women from the Salish tribes dance and sing. Though you've been to a hundred powwows, easily, you've never seen this dance, never heard this song. You stand with your own arms resting on the shoulders of the schoolchildren, and the dancers, these women, move their arms in motions that do more than mimic water, that conjure it. Their voices are calm and strong, and they move through the gathering like quiet, like water, like something that will hold, something you can keep, even if only for this moment.

Goodbye *Once Upon a Time*

BYRON F. ASPAAS

On Thursday we left Colorado Springs and drove north toward Denver, where I connected to Interstate-70—a part of the interstate I never experienced before. My green car rolled over green mountains, capped with winter, and excitement arose with new images, new memories, and a new voyage with parts of the Rockies we had never seen.

The Colorado River, thick and wide, wove itself, over and under, as we raced toward the west to beat the sun. By evening we emerged in Grand Junction—near the Utah border. The desert welcomed us and embraced us. With wide-open spaces painted with brown horizons, we watched clouds stretch themselves across open skies as we veered through desolate lands of rock pushed through ground, plateaus risen high into sky, arroyos scraped deep with dryness, and patches of rain shadowed through shrouded clouds—my car filled itself with scents of familiarity.

Home, a memory, just an hour, maybe two, south of us. *Dinétah.*

At Highway 24, we drove south and noticed the sun's painting of a different ending to the day as goblins stood guard below the castles of clouds that formed high above in the sky. Night soon hugged twilight, enveloping the land in one gulp. Within the hour, an almost full moon climbed into the eastern horizon as Hanksville glittered in the south.

I stopped to fuel my car at Hollow Mountain—a convenience store carved into stone. Not long thereafter, we drove into a darkened canyon curled with cottonwood. Darkness swallowed the headlights when silhouettes began to stir in shadows. The moon shined above the desert and woke monstrous mesas. Rocks and walls of sandstone stood ground as we wove and veered through unknown territory; up and down small hills, emerging before twin shadows. Twin boulders, placed side by side, guarding the entrance to Capitol Reef, stood at my destination.

I don't know how to begin this story.

Initially, I wanted to share this experience that included a tale of the coyote. As a child, my first introduction to the character was a story I plagiarized from an English textbook. In seventh grade, my version of the text, that included coyote, was placed high upon the wall with other great stories that my science teacher asked for: *How do you think stars formed?*

For decades, guilt has sat itself upon the walls of my heart knowing coyote is who I had become—a liar, a fake, trouble.

How do I begin this story?

With a new laptop in front of me, I sometimes wonder, how did I ever get through school? At thirty-three years old, I placed myself into a class that evolved into classes that evolved from one semester to multiple semesters, and then I finished with a bachelor's degree in creative writing. Soon thereafter, I followed up with a master's in creative writing.

What was I thinking?

I do feel the beginning of this story calls for an exposition—an interjection, a small fact about me—explaining how writing was my worst subject as a child. My first book involved a tape player by Fischer Price, which included a read-along, *The Tawny Scrawny Lion*. It came filled with pictures and music of rabbits who converted the tawny scrawny lion into becoming a vegetarian. They lived happily ever after.

For years, I feared reading without the aid of song.

My first diary was a small booklet of papers. My eldest brother wrote in a diary. My dad wrote in a diary. I wanted a diary, so I made one. For a few days I wrote inside the booklet I made, stating how much I missed my family. I spent six weeks in Illinois during the summer of 1993. The Mississippi overflowed. Houses were submerged in water. The river knocked at the doors of the St. Louis Arch. I never wrote about those sightings, but I can tell you of the ache I felt about missing family. Being a sixteen-year-old junior, almost senior, who spent forty-two days at the University of Illinois was a first for me.

I hated writing. Probably because I wasn't consistent.

My spelling was embarrassingly corrected in seventh grade. During a spelling bee, my teacher asked me to sit down when she realized I could not spell *balcony*. I was placed in remedial English until tenth grade. I faked my way around the English language and placed myself into Honors English by twelfth grade, but my stutter continued to follow me when asked to read in front of my peers, and I feared asking the teacher what a run-on sentence was when written on returned papers.

My hatred for reading was accompanied by embarrassment, but karaoke helped me sing along and overcome the fear of standing in front of those who listened and cheered as my stutter disappeared.

As an undergraduate student, I learned a story has three parts: a beginning, middle, and end.

In graduate school, I fumbled with that narrative arc, also known as the hero's journey.

Where is the conflict, inner-conflict, the climatic point? Why are you not writing a linear story?

These phrases I heard constantly—and as anxieties of the English language resurrected, my stutter resurfaced.

A hero never stumbles—or do they?

In the following morning, I woke in Capitol Reef, where a canyon of red surrounded me. Red rock, red sand, red me. I met with my writing group, writers from all over the country. Julie and Hannah, our tour guides, helped those to load their baggage onto the truck provided. Julie, a tall blonde with long legs, wore a ball cap and glasses with long yellow hair placed into a ponytail. She helped me load my bags, while Hannah helped others with theirs.

We drove east, toward the rising sun. We passed the twin boulders that greeted me the night before, one larger than the other, but almost identical. Both red and round and statuesque, they stood guard as we entered the canyon, where a campsite hid inside behind an army of cottonwoods. We set camp.

Hannah, an elvish princess with brownish-red hair, flew my way with questions about me. Her soft princess voice captivated me, and her knowledge of the woods enchanted me. As the elvish princess of the woods who could sing as well, she cooked alongside her blonde ponytailed queen who guided our writing excursion each day.

Dr. Herbert Benally is a former teacher who shared his insights about history and story and kinship with me and others in our Diné culture class. My older sister and I sat quietly, next to one another, as he spoke. *K'é* was introduced to me, then. I was twenty-three years old when I asked my parents about *K'é*. What did it mean to each of them?

Mom said *K'é* was like family. Dad had something similar in translation. His explanation leaned more toward clanship.

"What about *Sa'ah Naagháí Bik'eh Hózhóón?*" I asked.

For a moment, I think my mom almost fell over when the phrase flowed from my mouth.

"*Ha'át'íí?*" she said.

Both she and Dad looked at each other in disbelief and smiled.

"Where are you learning this?" she asked.

"Navajo culture class," I said.

∴

In March of 2016 I drove home to visit family members of the Four Corners region. My family resides in the northwest region of New Mexico where twenty-nine years of my life happened. Currently, my life is in Colorado Springs, Colorado, with my partner, Seth. It seems recently my car has driven this path more times than it had in past years. In February I lost a good friend in an unfortunate accident. I went home to mourn beside friends and family of hers who mourned her death uncontrollably. In January I left to recalibrate parts of me by re-centering my own self-being. I went home to mourn by myself and sobbed uncontrollably.

Who had I become? Where was I going? When did I lose me?

For a year and I half I had worked as a barista at a small coffee shop on the campus of Colorado College. The students and I had formed a friendship, unknowingly. With each drink ordered through me, bits of them were served through lattes and americanos and mochas where conversations occurred between me and them, between 7:30 a.m. and 3:30 p.m., Monday through Fridays.

As a much older person, I kept parts of me—namely my sexuality—secret from them in hopes to never scare them away. Being employed at a progressive college, where progressive students spoke more progressively than other colleges I had experienced elsewhere, kept me hidden like I had hidden myself my whole adult life.

For spring break, I had ten days off from work. Seth suggested I go back to my family's home, a home I feel I abandoned almost ten years before. Bits of me felt I needed to return to my childhood, return to a family I feel I am forgetting and a culture slipping from my now aging mind, but more importantly, return to find me.

In preparation, I gathered two bags: one blue and one gray. In the blue bag I packed tightly a week's worth of clothes where pants were rolled seductively inside the arms of the T-shirts and color pressed itself upon color and legs touched shoulders. Underwear hid themselves inside the pockets of socks and tucked themselves inside and below. In the gray bag sat my laptop with books propped up against its front end and the toothpaste kissed the toothbrush inside plastic containers while the toiletries kept themselves separate and snuggled deeply inside darkness.

With my partner home, our family of dogs and cats and fish will be watched over while I am away, and Seth reassured me he would be okay.

Go, he said. *Visit your family. You need this.*

Confusion ached with pain filled inside the sadness of my body. Fresh and raw and exposed, I left reluctantly.

It will be good for you to go home, he said. *You need to go.*

For miles, "Cowboy Take Me Away" escaped my mouth. As the Front Range listened and rolled past in long strips of Rocky Mountains, I watched the sun dangle in the west on that late Saturday afternoon, and my little green tugboat drifted down I-25, where the sight of the Spanish Peaks indicated that I set my sails due west, where *Tsisnaajiní*, the doorway to *Dinétah*, glimmered white—*shighaandi*.

"What do those rocks represent to you," Hannah asked.

She pointed to two monolithic figures that stood before us, almost identical. We stood looking east, where a cathedral of rocks stood behind us. The sun glared high, above, jutting shadows along cliffs of the rocky mesas. The company in my presence became red from the southern Utah sun, while I darkened to a more Navajo brown, darker than the red desert surrounding us.

"What do you mean?" I asked.

"The one on the left is the Temple of the Sun," she said, "the one on the right is the Temple of the Moon. I have seen these rocks many times before, but never asked anyone who is Indigenous to these lands. What might they mean to them?" She pointed.

"They look like twins," I said.

"Interesting," she said.

The wind pushed against our backsides toward the group ahead of us. A butterfly trimmed with black that dotted the orange of its wings held its footing on dried sandstone. What looked like a monarch was not a monarch butterfly, but maybe it was. I am not sure. The wind pushed against it harder. Wings fluttered frantically. Pockets of clay crinkled beneath our feet as we stepped forward, crinkled as bits of me ruminated in panoramic surroundings. What seemed lifeless in the valley seemed like home to me. The desert.

My childhood community had shifted. What were once dirt roads are now paved with loose gravel; the elementary school I attended is no longer standing—a sandy mound of ghost-memory remains with skeleton trees mourning the past.

In the darkness, a new school stands erected, tall, like a double-layered cake decorated with concrete. Its bright lights flicker upon a once darkened neighborhood, that I remember, where we once gathered clay to make pies that banked and crinkled under the desert sun.

Dad was not home when I opened the door.

Since Mom died, I am told Dad is never home, and the porch light is always kept on. So I waited and listened to the silence of the house as the refrigerator sang a hymn of memories. The motor coughed and echoed down the hallway, into the room, where I lay wrapped in remembrance of mother and son.

≈

I have marveled over my young nephew since his birth. He is the last grandchild my mom held inside her frail arms. He does not remember her because he was only six months old when she left. There is a picture on the refrigerator of he and she, and he is reminded of she, daily.

At almost age three, many presumed my nephew was deaf because words could not find him. In preparation of hand movements for sign language, his mother, my younger sister, comforted and nourished her only son until words soon dribbled from his mouth and soon happiness sprung in leaks of sounds.

"Water," he said, cupping the sides of Seth's face as they stood on the sides of the Animas River in Durango—baby palms trickled and motioned waterfalls as fingers sprinkled down Seth's cheeks. "Water," he repeated and smiled a half smile to Seth.

Within a month, my nephew turned three and my sister called. Her voice brightened with news that showered our conversation with her baby's progression.

He speaks in sentences, she said, *his words flow nonstop.*

Flooding my ears with her excitement, my younger sister sounded relieved. Throughout the years, I've listened to my nephew grow. His language is remarkable. Now, at age six, his vocabulary continues to grow uncontrollably.

He's surpassed his classmates, my younger sister said.

Paragraphs have puddled like pondwater, filling with questions, which have overflowed and seeped out of the mind by way of words through my nephew's mouth, articulating curiosity with critical thinking, mixing stories with imagination that swirled stars into galaxies creating unlimited stories. His mother, my younger sister, was bewildered by his exponential growth in voice and so was I. I wanted to learn from him.

For ten years I have been away from my family. For six years I have introduced myself and reintroduced myself to my nephew, who grew without me, and repeatedly asked his mom: *What's his name again?*

≈

I spent an afternoon with my nephew.

As a treat, I told him we were going on a hike. The evening sun touched the five o'clock sky when we parked at the base of the basin, where clay hills stood before us. He asked me, again, what we were about to do. *Hike,* I said. Before long, my nephew was on hands and knees, climbing up dried clay hills, and I followed, clambering behind—like a sheepherder, he steered me to the top.

Along the rim of the rocky basin, we hugged a faded trail that strung high above the desert valley.

Uncle, are we on top of the world? he asked.

My stomach twisted at the height we emerged into. *Sit here,* I said, placing him upon the sandstone ledge. *Do not move,* I said, and panicked. I gripped onto the sides of the pebbled cliffs. Rocks fell at the touch of my fingers and sand shifted below each shoe. Fear streamed down my spine knowing my younger sister would not be happy with me right now. *Do not move,* I repeated. My arms trembled as I positioned one foot upon the ledge and repositioned myself from south to north.

The wind touched my face, touched my hands, and skimmed coolness down my backside as wetness touched air. Serenity settled upon us while the crows glided below. My nephew planted himself quietly—positioned in full-Lotus form—eyes closed, spine elongated, legs wrapped within each other, fingers pinched to the sky, and both forearms bloomed toward the sun.

The wind brushed his child eyelashes as his chest exhaled life through tiny six-year-old lungs.

Yes, sonny, we are on top of the world, a new world, I whispered.

Standing before two monolithic sandstones, memories of Monument Valley, of Chaco Canyon, of the Burnham Badlands flooded me like monsoon rains—rushing through the caverns of emotion as pinks flushed into reds and grays darkened to purple with moisture from silver clouds sewn to the hems of the horizons, pillowed reflections of desert. Southern Utah painted stories—*Diné Bikéyah*.

For thirteen years, my dad worked as a heavy equipment operator. For thirteen years, I watched Dad leave for his job at the Pittsburg Midway Coal Company. For thirteen years, Dad left on Sunday evenings only to return Friday afternoons—sometimes before school ended, sometimes in the evening. Each weekend began with surprises, but then it ended with sadness in goodbyes. For thirteen years, my dad traveled a hundred miles away to live on a dragline as big as our house. He operated its crane for money, scooping coal for the home he did not occupy. For thirteen years, he worked the night shift and Mom became Dad while Dad became a creature of the night—working the twelve-to-eight shift—his eyes red with no sleep. For thirteen years, Mom began to show her age while Dad remained ageless.

Because of nightmares and fear of sleeping at home, I began to travel with Dad to his worksite. Once, Dad snuck me into the coal pits, and I watched the crane move slowly—a brontosaurus dipping into a lake of bedrock. I slept in the back of my older sister's Turismo, wrapped in Dad's blankets, listening to the moan of the machinery howl into the night. I was nine years old.

Upon driving home one morning, I watched the sun color the desert bright yellow and brown. I then noticed the white lines of the road drift to the middle of the car. *Dad*, I screamed. Dad's eyes opened as he repositioned our vessel to the right side of the road.

We were fifty miles away from home on a two-lane highway, located between Gallup and Shiprock, New Mexico. Highway 666 was known for its head-on collisions—maybe those who crashed were just as tired as Dad was—who knows?

Do you think you can drive, son? Dad asked.

I can try, I said.

It's almost like the motorcycles at home. All you need to do is steer. I'll have my foot on the pedal, he said. *Sit on my lap, son.*

Okay, I said.

For fifty miles, my dad held his foot on the pedal. My foot rested upon his foot to add pressure to the gas, if needed. With one eye closed, he kept watch on the asphalt river ahead. With me positioned at the helms, my guidance was trusted as I steered us home, down the highway and through the windy dirt roads of the Burnham Badlands.

At age ten, my foot reached the pedals of my sister's car with the aid of pillows behind my back. No longer a pirate with one eye closed, Dad began to sleep comfortably. As I continuously drove my dad home, landscape became recognizable by different shapes of purple mounds within the badlands of Burnham. Each form became a different story, as well as a map. Scattered rocks, red from fire, revealed truths of a story I heard of Monster Slayer and his sibling fighting evil in Burnham. Story markers of red rocks appeared in Dad's version, a version he could not remember fully—but monsters were mentioned.

Pittsburg Midway Coal Company devoured mountains while Dad remained employed with them. Behind our home, the Navajo Coal Mine nibbled at the Burnham Badlands. For thirty years, I watched stories scraped from land because food is what the monsters need: food for our cars, food for our homes, food for our electronics.

We have learned to consume like monsters.

While on spring break, I sat inside my dad's room and read Facebook posts. A question was posed to me: *Byron what is your view on this?* Attached was a link titled: Obama's Clean Power Plan Will Destroy Navajo Nation Jobs. It stated: "Under the president's power plan, certain Indian territories are especially singled out." This site was created by the Heritage Foundation.

Within the website, there was a YouTube video.

In this video, a young Diné girl shared her story of a castle with three chimneys. She said the castle was visible from her window, near Page, Arizona, I believe. She continued to say a warrior needed armor to enter the *castle*. Her voice was innocent and soft.

> *Ałkidą́ą́*—it was ritual to watch Dad prepare each Sunday as he placed armor onto his worn body. When Dad returned on Friday afternoon, the scent of Dad returned, also. The combination of coal mixed with sweat, splashed with coffee, presented itself when Dad staggered into our home, drunk-like—eyes red with fatigue— he slumped onto Mom's bed, exhausted. I used to think my dad never aged. His hair was always black like mine, but then my brother died from leukemia, and then the coal mine stripped Dad of his armor and removed Dad of his valiant dragline, the dragline Dad used to dip into the earth, the one that fed us. Not long after his termination, Dad could not sleep. Dad roamed our house until four each morning, reading or watching TV or probably overthinking *why was I let go?* His hair began to wither with silver strands. Sadness overwhelmed him and made Mom cry in quiet rooms. The scent of coal mixed with sweat, splashed with coffee, stained Mom's room for a very long time.

In this video, a young Navajo man said he wanted to give back to the community. He said he wanted to follow in his father's and grandfather's footsteps while working at the power plant. As this is spoken, landscapes of the red desert panned to wild horses running freely and Horseshoe Bend reflected the beauty of sky—tranquility is released with Native American flute songs.

> *Ałkidą́ą́*—like my father, my dad, *shizhé'é*, I wanted to give back. I wanted to give back because that's what we were taught as children. Like my father, my dad, *shizhé'é*, I wanted to work and make money

as an engineer, so I can be someone of stature of dignity of respect, but my degree was never completed. I left school in 2003. It was my second attempt at college. I was a junior with credits in civil engineering. But before leaving, I was an intern at the Bureau of Land Management. I spent two summers in Rawlins, Wyoming. I was nothing like my father, my dad, *shizhé'é*, who was only drunk on tiredness—and unlike my father, my dad, *shizhé'é*, I learned to be drunk and became overweight and squawked "Cowboy Take Me Away" at a shithole bar that smelled of piss and cigarettes while my tiredness was mixed with beer and bad karaoke.

In the video, Arizona state senator Carlyle Begay said the natural resources of the Navajo Nation was a blessing—namely coal. With well-spoken English and a voice of an educated man, Begay sat situated with a mauve-collared shirt and a fuchsia polka-dotted tie. As he spoke, truths about coal unfolded and he revealed coal's integral connection to the community. The tone in Begay's voice was as sincere as the somber look upon his face. As the video played, Speaker of the Arizona House of Representatives, David M. Gowan Sr., exhibited the relationship between Arizona and the Navajo Nation. He spoke of the importance of the Colorado River and its vital role in creating energy. As the video came to an end, employees stated their experiences with the power plant. An elder Navajo man spoke certainties that smoke is not smoke, but the smoke those see from the plant is *only* generated steam, *only* water. He said, those who *do not* understand power plants should ask questions, not assume. The last employee was, maybe, thirty. His story included economic concerns. His eyes filled with sadness before the video faded to black.

Ałkidąą—as children, we were raised to believe coal benefited us. Yes, financially, we were given the security our grandfathers and grandmothers, our fathers and mothers, worked for as coal miners. As children, we were raised and taught to buy and spend and buy more, never asking where money came from, and we wanted more.

As children, we were given securities within our homes, our cars, our belongings, and we were fed to believe coal mines lived forever. As children, we were given the security of benefits, benefits that aided those who spent time in hospitals with diseases, like leukemia, that pulled families away from school, a school system that taught *Diné* children to devour and consume and take and eat and throw away— but never question: *What if it all goes away?*

The little girl in the video was told the power plant was the heart of the land. *Its heartbeat can be heard by many,* she said. *It's been beating for a long time,* she said. *More likely longer than mine,* she said. *It will probably live to be at least 120,* she said.

Ałkidąą—I grew up in a house where two castles with multiple chimneys stood outside my bedroom window. At night, I watched lights sparkle like orange stars that blipped with a timed cadence. Sometimes, I sat in my parents' HUD home and watched a milky way of lights brighten the valley below. Sometimes, the natural gas company's torch lit up the cloudy desert sky and I pretended Lady Liberty stood below in New York—but there was no Lady Liberty, no New York, just dirty air, and my hand over heart.

What happens in 120 years when all is gone and scraped away?

Ałkidąą—I grew up in a house where two castles with multiple chimneys stood outside my bedroom window, and I watched their eyes glow with bellows of clouds weaving its story of gloom into the sky and the land rumbled from its hunger.

My invitation to this writing workshop allowed me to engage in deep conversation with those I met while in Capitol Reef. At dusk, I witnessed the hollowed eyes of the canyon walls listening to the stories we shared with one another. At night, the full moon invited itself inside my tent, and the cold air nestled with me inside my sleeping bag. But, before slumber, I secretly watched shadows cascade off the cliffs as the moon climbed over sandstone vistas.

With it being late May, the Utah nights were still cold from winter's breath, while the days were heated by summer's draft. Cotton blew from cottonwood trees, resurrecting dormant desert allergies I had forgotten about since moving to the greenness and moisture of Colorado.

On December 28, 2016, President Barack Obama's proclamation came as a shock to many when he used the last days of his presidency to name Bears Ears as a national monument. In recent decades, Bears Ears was once an extraction site for uranium mines. When monsoon rains came, the Male Rain flashed unearthed minerals into the San Juan River, a vital vein of water resource for *Diné*, the people, my people.

On August 5, 2015, the Gold King Mine triggered a major spill of toxic waste into the Animas River, creating a flow of yellow water that snaked its way from Durango to Aztec to Farmington and through *Dinétah*. It slithered into the San Juan River, incongruent to the La Plata River—*Tóta'*: Three Waters, Three Rivers, a confluence of three. *Tółitso*, Yellow Water.

In the 1960s the San Juan River had a stream of lifeless fish floating westward. It was said, kids of that time noticed the fish and jumped into the river to retrieve them. It was said, most husbands worked in those pits and came home, dusted in yellow, while their wives washed their dusty clothes with the family's dirtied laundry, and the children swam and brought fish home to eat. It was said, no one explained the dangers of working in those pits, in those uranium mines. It was said, no one explained the risks of mixing yellow dust with water, which made yellow batter, which became known as yellow cake to the *Diné*. *Tółitso*, Yellow Water.

On January 24, 2017, the elected president signed an executive order to rescind Obama's halt on the Keystone XL Pipeline. A minute later, he signed an executive order to restore life to the Dakota Access Pipeline. He breathed life into snakes thought dead.

On February 15, 2017, the elected president announced to America: "The state of Israel is a symbol to the world of resilience in the face of oppression. I can't think of no other state that's gone through what they've gone, and of survival in the face of genocide, we will never forget what the Jewish People have endured."

On February 23, 2017, Sacred Stone was evacuated, forcibly. Those who stayed were gassed with chemicals and shot with rubber bullets and jailed and removed and charged with trespassing. This is a state, a symbol of the world, that reflects resilience during a time of oppression. I can't think of no other people who have gone through what they've gone, and are survivors of genocide. How can you ever forget, America?

On February 28, 2017, the elected president addressed those at his congressional speech, saying, "America must put its own citizens first because, only then, can we truly make America great again." During this speech, he added concerns for clean air and clean water, when earlier that day, he began the process of rescinding the Clean Water Rule—a ruling to protect drinking water for 117 million US citizens—a rule supported by Obama's Clean Power Plan.

Tó éí ííná

Water is Life

"Mni Wiconi," jíní

Upon leaving Capitol Reef, I decided to visit my dad in New Mexico. Our writing group dispersed and I said my goodbyes to my new friends. In the company of great writers, I am blessed and reassured I was taking the right path of the journey through life.

Along Highway 95 south, I drove along the cliffsides of dry air and flakes of cottonwood. I stopped at the twin boulders to examine the scenic beauty of the red landscape all around. There was no information of the twin boulders, no story, no hints to Indigenous *myths* or *legends*—just geological fact and scientific jargon about sedimentary cake layers.

Sa'ah Naaghái Bik'eh Hózhóón is said to be the duality within each of us—both male and female counterparts nestled into one another, wrapped and swirled inside *us*, awaiting to present themselves if needed. *Sa'ah Naaghái*, the male presence, becomes recognizable as the protector and the aggressor of the two forces, suggested Dr. Benally; *Bik'eh Hózhóón*, the female equivalent, nourishes and heals those with health, strength, and sustenance. Both are considered negative and positive entities (not in the literal sense), Dr. Benally mentioned, but they are complementary energies that create one that exists wholly, never separately. Without one or the other, one would never be balanced, *jíní*. Together, they are the power of creation.

"We are made of male and female," Dr. Benally said to the class.

Sa'ah Naaghái Bik'eh Hózhóón is a harmonious action between male and female; therefore, this balance becomes us. It should be performed throughout one's life and used within the universe as a positive and negative (male and female) form. One should establish a serenity toward all beings, not just human beings—but *all* of earth's entities. To achieve *Sa'ah Naaghái Bik'eh Hózhóón*, one needs to practice it daily, ritualistically, and find beauty within themselves because *Sa'ah Naaghái Bik'eh Hózhóón* will transpose them toward peace of mind and help establish an emotional stability where inner strength forms and helps those to become ecologically aware.

This process begins with *K'é*—family. It begins at home.

My car's fuel gauge read over three-quarters full when I drifted down Highway 95. Dixie Chicks blasted my speakers, giving life to the landslide of memories that cascaded down canyon walls—red brushstrokes of stained water—smeared recollections of Wyoming, Arizona, Colorado, and bad karaoke. There were no clouds over the Utah desert, but signs of water colored the edge of a lake green. Hite Overlook, the sign read. An umbilical cord of the river below fed into a body of water. Large rocks peaked and poked and stood around the horizons of the birthplace of Lake Powell. The Colorado River pulsed.

I continued forth, only to stop and go and stop and go, again, to take photos of the cathedrals and temples and basilicas of the desert—places I have never visited before. My fuel gauge sank below half with seventy-nine miles to Blanding.

Arroyos of Navajo sandstone carved deep by Male Rain guided the Colorado River west while asphalt roads wound deeper east, through Chinle canyons and yuccas and cedars. A sign pointed to Jacob's Ladder, a tabletop butte sitting on the north side of the road. It read:

ON JULY 15, 1881, A U.S. CALVARY SCOUT NAMED JOSEPH S. WORMINGTON AND A COWBOY NAMED JAMES "ROWDY" HIGGINS WERE KILLED IN A BATTLE WITH INDIANS AT NEARBY PAIUTE PASS. THESE MEN WERE PART OF A POSSE OF CATTLEMEN AND SIXTH CALVARY TROOP SOLDIERS FROM FT. LEWIS, CO., WHO WERE CHASING A BAND OF RENEGADE UTE AND PAIUTE INDIANS LED BY MANCOS JIM. THE INDIANS HAD STOLEN 150 HEAD OF HORSES FROM THE ROUND-UP GROUNDS IN VERDURE, UTAH, AFTER A 75-MILE CHASE THE UTES AND PAIUTES LED THE POSSE AND SOLDIERS INTO AN AMBUSH. TWO MONTHS AFTER THE BATTLE, PROSPECTORS CASS HITE AND JOE DUCKETT FOUND AND BURIED THE REMAINS. THE UTES AND PAIUTES WERE WATCHING THE U.S. GOVERNMENT ABSORB THEIR HOMELANDS. THEY FOUGHT BACK IN THE ONLY WAY THEY KNEW HOW. THE SOLDIER GAVE HIS LIFE IN THE SERVICE OF HIS COUNTRY. THE COWBOY

DID THE TOUGH JOB HE WAS PAID TO DO AND A LITTLE MORE.
ALL OF THEM PLAYED OUT THEIR HEROIC ROLES IN THIS EPOCH
STRUGGLE TO SETTLE THE OLD WEST.

I left with no acknowledgment, no empathy.

A large butte sat on the north side of Highway 95. A sign read, The Cheese Box. I tried to envision a vintage cheese box with a handle centered on its top, but nothing came to mind, because my family had never owned a cheese box. We never knew much about the variety of cheeses because our cheeses came in one size and one color, never circular, or in fancy boxes. Our cheese was supplied by the US government. It was rectangular and encased by flimsy cardboard, which was thrown away, and stamped: *USDA Approved.*

As I drove away from the Cheese Box, the reflection grew smaller and tinier in my review mirror: *Images In Mirror May Appear Closer Than They Are.*

The sun dwindled, turning sand into deeper shades of red, and shadows began to appear behind the wall of piñon and cedar trees. The road curled northeast, where two buttes sat high above the landscape—one slightly larger and pointed; the other, small and flattened in comparison.

My fuel gauge was just below a quarter of a tank when I reached a sign that read Blanding 38.

After finishing graduate school and working as a barista and not writing because I wasn't disciplined or consistent enough, I fell into darkness. After losing my best friend, after trying to re-center my life, and after questioning my own self as a writer—am I really a writer—I revisited a home I had missed.

Asleep on the couch, I woke to an invitation to Writing by Writers.
I woke.

I feared the English language. Sometimes, I still think I do. I did not grow up speaking the *Diné* language, but it was embedded inside me at a young age. My mom told me so. She said, *In preschool, you spoke* Diné bizaad. She said, *After preschool, it faded.*

"Maybe that's why you picked it up easily?" she said. "It lives inside you."

I tried to blame my dad for our lack of knowledge of the *Diné* language. His bluntness made me realize maybe it was my fault and not my parents', who retaliated and said, "It's not my fault you were too damn stubborn to listen."

He was right. We were stubborn. We were raised much different. We were spoiled. We expected things. Kids, like me, learned to consume and poke fun at those who were fortunate to grow up within a *Diné* home because I did not.

When *K'é* was introduced to me, I began to listen. I began to question and tried to make understanding of who I was as a person. Dr. Benally mentioned *Nádleehí* during a lecture and spoke about the identity of Child Born for Water—the twin to Monster Slayer—a child born of fluidity. A sexuality unknown—non-binary—no pronoun.

Today, many identify Child Born for Water as a boy because he's identified as a twin to Monster Slayer. Moreover, probably because of conservative outlooks by conservative Navajos who are now Christian and no longer *Diné*.

Monster Slayer is identified as the older brother, the powerful one, the one most likely bigger of the two, who continued to slay because hypermasculinity is what's expected in story roles of postcolonial story-telling methods.

But what about the fluid one? What's become of them?

Tóta' is where my story begins, a small reservation border town,
where some of my earliest memories have filtered into reflections
of my own personal journey, a stream of consciousness, a place
where three waters meet, *Tóta'*

When I drove through southern Utah, I noticed the red landscape. I noticed twins appear everywhere—place markers with different stories—like the night I entered Capitol Reef, or the moments I spent with Hannah who pointed out the Temple of the Sun and Temple of the Moon, or the twin buttes that overlooked the landscape near Blanding.

Twins appeared timeless, in forms of rocks, all throughout *Diné Bikéyah*, our home, and yet we are still identified as the villains of our own epoch battles by those who invaded and stole and punished and shot and gassed and poisoned those who chose to protect.

I told Hannah, while we walked through the cathedral of rocks, the formations reminded me of *Naayéé' Neizghání áádóó Tóbájíshchíní*, son of *Jóhonaa'éí*, the sun, and child of *Tóneinilí*, the water being.

They are the Monster Slayers of the *Diné*, our protectors, I said.

What I noticed throughout southern Utah were misidentified place-names. Where I saw the Cheese Box as *bihooghan*, the female hogan—the nourisher, the healer, the one who provides strength for those who are inside her—*Bik'eh Hózhóón*.

To *bilagáanas*, I was driving around Bears Ears when my car's fuel gauge dropped below a quarter tank. To *bilagáanas*, the rocks were not Twin Warriors, like I thought, but rocks with ears, ears of the bear, the *shash*, the powerful one with minerals inside its belly.

Why do we live with given names? How can we take back those names? When can we tell our stories of lost names? Who have the Diné'e become? Where are the Monster Slayers?

It wasn't long ago that I began to write. Because my mom was nearing the end of her life, I enrolled myself into a school that crafted me into a master of creative writing. Every day I begin by questioning my ability to convey story from thought: *Am I really a master?* With grammar and spelling as the villains of my story, I began to rewrite a narrative introducing my inner conflict with obvious sources of weaknesses. I presented new characters by introducing a powerful, older brother, who I lost long ago to a monster living inside him. I bring to life a mother my nieces and nephews will never know—namely, my six-year-old nephew, who has emerged into a world of questions, a world of judgement, a world of greed, and a world of identity.

I began to write for *shizhé'é* because his stories included me—I am a child born of two waters: *Táchííníí áádóó Tódich'ííníí nishḷ́.*

I began to write for my sisters and brothers who are my stories.

I began to write for the landscape and lost stories scraped away by those who colonized the people the land the language and the story.

I began to write to help rewrite a literary landscape reworded by a grand narrative that did not include a language of our own.

I began to write to reclaim voice.

I began to write, so I can heal and I do not want to hide my identity anymore.

I wanted to begin this story with a coyote tale, but I figured this whole story is filled with coyotes with multiple tales. I am a coyote who has learned from errors put along his trail. Every day, reverberations of the coyote pulse inside each of us, whether we like it or not; we are all tricksters. We are all survivors. We learn from our stories—our past mistakes.

In *Diné* stories, there were monsters, *jiní*. Those monsters destroyed the people and shook the land from within. In *Diné* stories, the people were misguided by a powerful gambler, who lied and cheated and stole people, making them slaves—the gambler has returned. In old *Diné* stories, we prevailed and banished and celebrated by giving back to the land because the land is what takes care of them.

Jiní, that which is said.

✦

I don't want to pretend I want to live in castles anymore—goodbye *Once Upon a Time*.

As night began to rise in the east, my eyes picked points in Monument Valley that I recognized. Smog settled like fog around the pinnacles of knuckled rocks within the valley—pollution was clearly visible and present.

Up and down beautiful desert hills, we coasted into Blanding, where I held my breath, not knowing where the needle pointed upon the fuel gauge. Somewhere between mile thirty and twenty, I covered the gauge with my phone and drove in hunger.

I am no different than a monster who consumes.

My green car is the color of a monster.

We depend on one another.

It is my friend.

My twin.

We.

I Am Chopping Ivory or Bone

JOAN NAVIYUK KANE

How many Eskimo words are there for *white people*? How many Eskimo words are there? How many Eskimo?

*

My mother told me to attach the string to the claw and the string to the wood: "take the claw and put a string with a little piece of wood." I must have asked her something or paused for her to continue. Or she paused, and then continued.

"You swing it and try to put the piece of wood through the claw." I asked her what kind of crab claw. "Crab from King Island."

*

There is a game my mother played as a child at King Island Village. You attached a crab claw with a string to a small stick (wood being not easy to come by) and tried to catch the claw on the stick. I asked her what kind of crabs. I think she said something about king crabs or kinds of crab, but she definitely said the words "King Island." I asked my husband later that day where he thought she got the wood.

*

How many miles from the nearest tree is King Island? How many Eskimo words for *tree* are there? How many Eskimo words? How many Eskimo? How many?

*

The evening following this conversation with my mother, which was also the evening following that with my husband, my children and I joined my parents for dinner at Mexico in Alaska, an Anchorage restaurant we've frequented for forty-one years. I asked her where she was when she played this game. "King Island." Then I asked her where she got the wood. "It was around," she explained.

*

She remembered another game involving crab claws. *If it landed one way, it was a seal. If it landed another, it was a polar bear.* What do you mean? I asked. I meant, which way does it have to land for it to be a seal? For a polar bear? And what does *was* mean? She repeated, word for word: *If it landed one way, it was a seal. If it landed another, it was a polar bear.*

Does this mean a hunter would get a seal or a polar bear? Or that the crab claw held the innate *inua* of a *niqsaq* or a *nanuaq*? Asking these questions in English, substituting three Inupiaq words for three English words, didn't prompt any further explanation or conversation. Is the use of Eskimo words an event?

*

There are two modes of narrative in the tradition of Inupiaq literature: *quliapyuk* and *unipkaaq*. Yaayuk Alvanna-Stimpfle translates *quiliapyuk* as "story" and *unipkaaq* as "legend." Larry Kaplan, director of the Alaska Native Language Center and a linguist fluent in the King Island dialect of the Inupiaq language, explains that the former "includes oral history and personal reminiscence, usually relating something the storyteller or someone he knows has experienced," and that the latter "is an ancient myth" one that "tells of events, often with supernatural aspects, which occurred long before anyone can remember." My mother and most of my other relatives have the habit of speaking about experiences on King Island in the third-person past tense, which aside from being accurate (most King Islanders left the island altogether in 1959, no one has lived on the island year-round since 1965, and the number of surviving King Islanders born after 1974 who have been to the island could probably be counted on two hands) always troubled me with its emphasis on fixing hundreds or thousands of years of inhabitation of the island in the distant and impersonal and irrecoverable past.

Part of this has to do with the translation of the suffix -*guuq*, which translates most passively into English as "it is told" or "it is said." In the context of a conversation, or storytelling session, to hear this verbal terminative would be a way to reaffirm the preceding utterance's legitimacy by having the authority of its assertion rest outside of the subjective and limited perspective (and perhaps motivations) of the speaker. It would be a way for the speaker to remind the listener that these words were spoken. They happened. They are real and connect the listener to some kind of truth. They're not an invitation to historicize, to impel the speaker to use an active voice, to needlessly distort or omit.

*

There are two books I need to mention as long as I have your attention: Joseph Senungetuk's *Give or Take a Century* and William Oquilluk's *People of Kauwerak*. The former, a memoir of the author's formative years in Nome, Alaska, and his family's history and engagement with the land around Wales, Alaska, was published in 1971, and I could not imagine being a writer without this book. The latter was published in 1973, and I would not be alive without this book, which chronicles with vivid detail the five historical disasters the Inupiaq people have survived and continue to survive.

I was with Joe's brother Ron once at his house in Homer. Both Ron and Joe were taught things about carving walrus ivory as young men in Nome. "The kind of Inupiaq your grandfather spoke," he told me, "was like Shakespeare's English."

William Oqilluk, along with my maternal grandmother and her two sisters (and hundreds of other Inupiaq children), was orphaned in the 1918 influenza pandemic and raised by Ursuline nuns at a Catholic orphanage on the grounds of Pilgrim Hot Springs on the Seward Peninsula of Alaska. The virus traveled from village to village with postal service delivery from Nome. Death letters.

*

Back in the last century, I was one of the first employees of the Alaska Native Heritage Center, where we were given a script that was written (by a white anthropologist) for us to deliver in the third-person past tense to an audience that consisted largely of cruise-ship tourists. Paradoxically, the heritage center is owned by a regional Alaska Native corporation, one that's developed most of its local land—the boreal forest in Anchorage— into big box stores and strip malls. Anyhow, the script was comprehensive and detailed, and not to be whimsically spruced up with the interruption of personal narrative.

I was a college student, slightly bored and wondering what my friends in NYC and Boston were up to. What my relatives were doing on the tundra or the swelling tides of the Bering Sea, in the endless light of summer's white nights. I needed to depart from the script for the sake of my sanity, even though we were monitored and reprimanded for such departures. One of the things I was required to do was to demonstrate "Eskimo yo-yo" in order to increase the sales of authentically handcrafted yo-yo products in the heritage center's gift shop. Once I got the tourists interested in how fun and rewarding it was to master their use, I would tell the tourists the real story of how my mom and uncles and most other King Islander kids would learn how to use them in order to later learn how to use bolas to catch and kill migratory seabirds. There were millions of birds that nest on King Island. I didn't understand that in any language until I went to King Island. That is another story, all those birds and all the things and places and people that are still there but soon may be vacant.

I imagine the cliffs bare. And then: "Mom," I ask, after a good interval of conversation where we both repeat things to each other we already know, "is there a word you know for seabird?" Maybe she doesn't want to disappoint me. "*Imaani*: ocean. *Tiŋmiat*: bird. *Imaani.tiŋmiat*," she answers.

*   *   *   * *   *   *   **   *

How many oceans full of seabirds were there?
　How many oceans
　How many words

　　　many oceans once full of seabirds
　　　few words to describe them

　　tiŋitkaa:
　　　　it blew away

　　a particular constellation containing many stars:
　　　　siġupsiġat

　　siġvauraq: young guillemot
　　it is empty: *imailaq*

　　imiktuq: it is echoing

　　　　　qayuktuŋa

Blood Running

SASHA LAPOINTE

My great-great-aunt Comptia, I've been told by my mother, was a strong woman. My mother reminds me constantly, "You come from a strong lineage, you're my daughter, and their blood runs through your blood."

I'm twenty-two years old and I am shivering behind a dumpster in an alleyway behind my house. The snow on the pavement is a murky, brown, city snow, glittering with squashed beer cans and discarded needles. I've run out in such a hurry I've forgotten to grab a jacket and have to hug myself tightly. I tremble and consider not breathing, out of fear of the wispy shapes of my breath giving me away. I watch for the drummer's form in the light of our window. He staggers across the dining room, stumbles out of view. I think of this so-called strong blood in my veins, but behind the dumpster, I am alone in the cold, nothing in the bloodstream but fear and shame.

Years later, over coffee on the couch with my mother, she retells the story. My great-aunt Comptia, a Chinook woman in the lower Chinook region, married young. A Scottish captain had come over from Shetland, in hopes of setting up a prosperous life in the New World. In 1844 when Captain James Johnson arrived along the banks of the Columbia River he learned that a married man gets twice the allotment of land as a single man. He chose to marry my aunt, settled into his 640 acres, and built himself a large house. "Your aunt wasn't allowed to live with him, in the main house," my mother tells me, and stirs her coffee, "he made her live out back." Comptia spent her days in a drafty shack on the property line, with dirt floors and only a single window. Most nights she sat, eating haggis alone by lamplight, watching the windows of the grand house go from black to golden, as the captain's silhouette moved by candlelight up the stairs and to bed. "Even when she gave birth to the captain's sons," my mom, gazing into her coffee, sighs and continues, "he still made her live out there."

Behind the dumpster I hesitate, out of fear of being found. I can hear his footsteps on our deck, the weight of his drunken lumbering making the old wood creak and sway. I don't want to go back inside, despite my goose-bumped skin. Inside, there are holes punched in doors. Broken things. Inside, I might find him again, slumped on the bathroom floor, the cord of my blow-dryer wrapped around his throat, eyes bulging and wet with tears. Inside, I might have to call the police again, or at least threaten to. I shiver, a cornered fox in the night, coward, the word hangs in my mouth, balances in my throat.

My great-aunt, who birthed the boys in dirt, on the floor of her shack, said goodbye to her sons each morning as they disappeared down the river with their father. She would kiss them goodbye; she would walk the stony path from the river, each day, alone. My mom picks up her mug and it leaves a little ring on the glass coffee table. I let out a long, exasperated moan. The kind of noise you make as a child.

"But," I say, wiping the coffee away with the back of my hand, "if she was so strong, why didn't she just leave?" I kick my foot up onto the table and recline back against the sofa. My mother looks over her mug, to me, her eyes fixed in a way that shows she is also pondering this. I swallow the last of my coffee and think about strength, the strength it takes to stay, the strength it takes, to finally leave.

Hesitating, in the shadow of the dumpster, I look up at the light. Snow falls quietly around me. He has gone back inside, pacing in the dining room. Each shaky step I take up the stairs of our porch is a trembling protest. The door pushes open, my feet, cold and damp, squeak and slosh across the wood floor. He's on the bed now, the sandwich I had made before the fight is in a pile along the wall, where it had missed my head and landed. I tell him I'm going out. I think, then rephrase. I tell him I'm leaving. I grab a jacket, make a phone call, and even though it is cold and icy out, run fast. Run down the alleyway, past the church and past the grocery store, toward the headlights of a friend who has come for me. In the dark, behind homes lit up and warm, in the chilled winter air, I smile, quicken my pace, and I don't look back.

The days she spent alone, weaving, harvesting, humming songs and stories to herself, my great-aunt waited to greet her sons when they returned with their father each night. In town, the people talked. Rumors of the captain's piracy floated down river, reaching the small village where they lived. She knew about the strange imported furnishings in the main house and let the villagers have their stories of buried treasure, of chests with gold coins.

There was no fantasy when it came to the captain's bootlegging. During a time when it was illegal for any Native persons in the village to consume alcohol, the captain was a provider. Distilling different gins and bourbons, he profited as the villagers staggered each night to his doorstep in search of booze. My aunt, from her small square window, watched her cousins, friends, and elders walk away from the house and into the woods, mason jars of whiskey in their hands catching the moonlight.

An anger surged in her, though she found peace in daily tasks. Preparing fish for eating, cedar for weaving, she rooted herself to the earth, she tried not to forget her Chinook name, Comptia, though everyone in town had begun to call her by her English name, Jane.

Comptia grew up along the Columbia River in the Lower Chinook region of what is now considered southern Washington. In 1829, when Comptia was only nine years old, a great flu epidemic hit the Columbia basin region, nearly wiping out the entire Indigenous population. She survived the epidemic that ravaged the villages in the area for three years. Some considered her lucky, the women of my family believed it was her strength that helped her survive. When she died at the age of thirty-four, the cause unknown, the women of my family believe it was her heart. It had finally been broken. Comptia, too strong to live as a captive, left this world to travel to the next. When her boys were old enough, and she knew they'd be strong enough to move through the world on their own, she let herself go, finally to freedom. Shortly after her death, the captain, now a widower, left with two boys and a big white house on 640 acres of Chinook land, died alone at sea, too weak to go on without the woman he kept like property.

I take my mother's coffee cup to the sink, rinse it, and put it on the rack to dry. As my mother gathers her purse and jacket, I consider, for a moment, telling her about the night in the alleyway, in the cold of winter, the night I made my own choice to finally leave. But she mutters something about the traffic, and I know my story will have to wait until next time, or perhaps even until one day, when I have a daughter of my own.

A Mind Spread Out on the Ground

ALICIA ELLIOTT

He took his glasses off and rubbed the bridge of his nose the way men in movies do whenever they encounter a particularly vexing woman.

"I'm really confused. You need to give me something here. What's making you depressed?"

His reaction made me think briefly of residential schools, though at the time I couldn't understand why. Maybe it was the fact that he operated his therapy sessions out of a church. That certainly didn't help. I wasn't sure what to say. Can a metaphor or simile truly capture it? It was definitely heavy, but could I really compare it to a weight? Weight in and of itself is not devastating; depression is. At times it made me short of breath, and at times it had the potential to be deadly, but was it really like drowning? At least with drowning others could see the flailing limbs and splashing water and know you needed help. Depression could slip in entirely unnoticed and dress itself up as normalcy so when it finally took hold others would be so surprised they wouldn't know how to pull you away. They'd stand there staring—good-intentioned but helpless. Empathetic, perhaps, but mute. Or, in the case of this particularly unqualified therapist, angry and accusing. Not that I necessarily blame them. I've done the same thing.

My family of seven lived in a two-bedroom trailer on our rez—my sister and I in the smaller room, my three younger brothers in the master bedroom. My parents had no bedroom, no bed. They slept in the living room on the couch and recliner. As one may assume of such circumstances, privacy was precious, if it existed at all. Doors never stayed closed for long; at any moment someone could barrel in unannounced. This meant there was no place for my mother to hide her illness.

She'd been diagnosed and re-diagnosed many times. Postpartum depression, manic depression, bipolar disorder, schizophrenia. Most recently, my mother's been officially diagnosed as having post-traumatic stress disorder or schizoaffective disorder, depending on which doctor you talk to. None of these phrases gave her relief. In fact, they often seemed to hurt her, turning every feeling she had into yet another symptom of yet another disease.

What these words meant to my siblings and me was that our mother's health was on a timer. We didn't know when it would go off, but when it did, our happy, playful, hilarious mother would disappear behind a curtain and another would emerge: alternatively angry and mournful, wired and lethargic. When she was depressed, she'd become almost entirely silent. She'd lie on our brother's bottom bunk and blink at us, her soft, limp limbs spilling onto the stained, slate-colored carpet. I'd sit on the floor beside her, smooth her hair—bottle red with gray moving in like a slow tide—and ask her what was wrong. She'd stay silent but her face would transform. Damp, swollen, violet, as if the words she couldn't say were bubbling beneath her skin, burning her up from the inside.

Terminology is tricky. Initially, depression was known as *melancholia*, a word that first brought to my mind a field of blue cornflower and golden hay. Its trochaic meter gave it an inherent poeticism, an ingrained elegance. It was delicate, feminine. Hamlet's doomed lover Ophelia definitely did not suffer from depression. When she floated down that river, decked in garlands, stones in her pockets, she was in the throes of *melancholia*.

The term first appeared in Mesopotamian texts in the second century BCE. At the time, they considered melancholia a form of demonic possession. They weren't alone: ancient Babylonian, Chinese, and Egyptian civilizations all attributed mental illness to demons overpowering the spiritually weak. Exorcism—which often entailed beatings, restraint, and starvation—was the only known "cure." Even during the Renaissance, when thinking about depression began to reflect the more progressive views of early Greek physician Hippocrates, a heavily Christian Europe had another way to describe those with mental illness: witches. They were "cured" by burning at the stake. Sometimes, as part of their trial, suspected witches underwent an ordeal by water. They were tied to a rope and thrown over a boat. If they sank they'd be pulled back to a safety of sorts; their innocence proven but their illness unchecked. If they floated, like Ophelia, they were considered a witch and summarily executed.

My quite Catholic mother believes demonic possession is a real danger. She pretty much used the 1973 film *The Exorcist* as an instructional video for my siblings and me. It was mostly effective. I played with a Ouija board only once, reluctantly, and though I remained firmly in control of my body, I still try to avoid the game (and pictures of Linda Blair) at all costs. I know demonic possession is impossible, probably, but it still scares me more than I'd like to admit.

So when my mother told me she was hearing "demonic voices" and thought she needed an exorcism last year, I was legitimately terrified. Not because I thought she was actually possessed—she didn't mention anything about floating above her bed, and her voice sounded totally normal. I was scared of how scared she must be. She actually believed demons were real and could take control of the spiritually weak. If she thought she was being overtaken by these demons, logic would dictate that *she* was spiritually weak. As if her depressed mind didn't have enough to guilt her with.

She wouldn't tell me what the voices were saying to her. She just reiterated over and over that she was a sinner, that she had impure thoughts, that she hadn't been going to church enough. None of this seemed to me like enough reason to call in an exorcist.

Evidently her priest down in Florida disagreed. He said it did, indeed, sound like she was in the midst of a spiritual battle, that she should contact the church about sending an exorcist right away. Though he himself was part of the Catholic Church, he never offered any assistance with her "spiritual battle," never offered to bring in an exorcist to slay her inner demon. He just gave her his half-baked opinion like a torch and watched as she caught flame.

As far as analogies go, comparing depression to a demon is actually a pretty good one. Both overtake your faculties, leaving you disconnected and disembodied. Both change you so abruptly even your loved ones barely recognize you. Both whisper evil words and malformed truths. Both scare most people shitless.

*

According to Diane Purkiss's *The Witch in History: Early Modern and Twentieth-Century Representations*, European colonists widely considered Indigenous peoples to be devil worshippers. In fact, during the infamous Salem witch trials, the people of the Sagamore tribe were blamed—described by early Puritan minister and mastermind of the witch trials, Cotton Mather, as "horrid sorcerers, and hellish conjurors . . . [who] conversed with Demons."[1] One person on trial claimed to have attended a black mass with the *Sagamore Indians*. Mercy Short, another accused witch, took it one step further: she claimed the Devil himself was an *Indian*, describing him as "not of a Negro, but of a tawney, or an Indian colour."[2]

This literal demonizing of Indigenous people was a natural extension of the tactics used to move colonization along. In 1494 the Treaty of Todesillas declared non-Christian lands could be colonized under the Papal Doctrine of Discovery. Since the entire "New World" was apparently peopled by "devil-worshippers," this essentially gave Christian monarchs the right to claim all the land they wanted, regardless of the Indigenous people already living on it. It was such a tantalizing, seemingly guilt-free justification for genocide, even Secretary of State Thomas Jefferson decided to adopt it as official policy in 1792—and we all know how much Americans wanted to distinguish themselves from Europe at the time.

The Doctrine of Discovery is still cited in court cases today whenever Canada or the United States want to shut up Indigenous tribes who complain. In an attempt to stop this lazy, racist rationale, a delegation of Indigenous people went to Rome recently to ask the church to rescind these papal bulls. Kahnawake Mohawk Kenneth Deer says after hearing their concerns, Pope Francis simply looked him in the eye and said, "I'll pray for you."

"Can you imagine going to a funeral every day, maybe even two, for five to ten years?" the chief asks. He's giving a decolonization presentation, talking about the way colonization has affected our people following contact. Smallpox, tuberculosis, even the common cold hit our communities particularly hard. Then, on top of that, we had wars to contend with—some against the French, some against the British, some against either or neither or both. Back then death was all you could see, smell, taste, or hear. Death was all you could feel.

"What does that type of mourning, pain, and loss do to you?" he asks. We reflect on our own losses, our own mourning, our own pain. We say nothing.

After a moment he answers himself. "It creates numbness."

Numbness is often how people describe their experience of depression.

I was sixteen when I wrote my first suicide note. I was alone in my room, for once. It was cold; the fire in our wood-burning stove must have gone out. I was huddled beneath the unzipped sleeping bag I used as a comforter. I was listening to the only modern rock station my ancient radio could pick up. The songs washed over me. My brothers laughing, crashing, and crying washed over me. My mother half-heartedly yelling at them while she watched a movie with my sister washed over me. My father's absence washed over me.

Even though the trailer was full, I was alone. I was alone, and I felt nothing, and it hurt so much. More than grief, more than anger. I just wanted it to end.

Tears fell on the paper faster than I could write. It was hard to read in parts. I didn't care. As long as it reassured my family they shouldn't blame themselves, it would do the trick.

I looked at the knife I'd smuggled from the kitchen, pressed its edge to my wrist. Nothing happened. The blade was too dull. I'd have to stab hard and slash deep just to break the skin. I was crying so hard.

I re-read my note. I looked back at the knife. Even though it could hardly peel a potato it scared me more than the void I felt.

I laid back down, disgusted with myself and my lack of resolve. I tried to listen to the radio. I couldn't hear anything.

Though suicide was quite rare for Onkwehon:we pre-contact, after contact and the subsequent effects of colonialism, it has ballooned so much that, as of 2013, suicide and self-inflicted injuries are the leading cause of death for Native people under the age of forty-four. Suicide and depression rates for our people are twice the national average. For Native youth from fifteen to twenty-four, the suicide rate is five to seven times the national average. Suicide attempts among Native peoples are about five to seven times the national average, depending on gender. For LGBT2S Onwkwehon:we no data exists.

Interestingly, the Centre for Suicide Prevention has found lower rates of depression and suicide among those communities that exhibit "cultural continuity." This includes self-government, land control, control over education and cultural activities, and command of police, fire, and health services. In other words, the less Canada maintains its historical role as the abusive father, micromanaging and undermining First Nations at every turn, the better off the people are.

Lower instances of suicide were also found in communities where over 50 percent of the people spoke their Indigenous language. This probably isn't much of a surprise to an Indigenous person. We know our cultures have meaning and worth, that the culture lives and breathes inside our languages.

Canada knew that, too, which is why they fought so hard to make us forget them.

There are two scientific designations for depression. The droller, more scientific term for melancholia is "endogenous depression." In contrast to exogenous, or reactive, depression—which stems from a major event such as divorce, job loss, or death in the family—melancholic depression has no apparent outside cause. In other words, it comes out of the blue. This is a rather ridiculous way of putting it when you consider depression itself is sometimes referred to as "the blues." The blues coming out of the blue. Go figure.

I've heard one person translate a Mohawk phrase for depression to, roughly, "his mind fell to the ground." I ask my sister about this. She's been studying Mohawk for the past three years and is practically fluent. She's raising her daughter to be the same. They're the first members of our family to speak the language since priests beat it out of our paternal grandfather a handful of decades ago.

"Wake'nikonhra'kwenhtará:'on," she says. "It's not quite 'fell to the ground.' It's more like, 'His mind is—'" She pauses. She repeats the word in Mohawk. Slows it down. Considers what English words in her arsenal can best approximate the phrase. "'His mind is—'" She moves her hands around, palms down, as if doing a large, messy finger painting. "Literally stretched or sprawled out on the ground. It's all over."

She explains there's another phrase too. Wake'nikonhrèn:ton. It means, "The mind is suspended." Both of these indicate an inability to concentrate. That's one of the signs of depression. I know because I've checked it off in the copy of *Mind Over Mood* I took out from the library.

It says I'm currently 32/57 depressed, or 56 percent. Not the worst. At least I'm not considering suicide. Suicidal thoughts is number ten on the checklist.

There is nothing in the book about the importance of culture, nothing about intergenerational trauma, racism, sexism, colonialism, homophobia, transphobia. As if depression doesn't "see" petty things like race or gender or sexual orientation.

"We're all just people, man," melancholia mutters, pushing its dreads aside as it passes me a joint.

*

I've heard people say that when you learn a people's language, you learn their culture. It tells you how they think of the world, how they experience it. That's why translation is so difficult—you have to take one way of seeing the world and translate it to another, while still piecing the words together so they make sense.

Lately I've been thinking a lot about the fact that there is no Mohawk word to differentiate between reactive and melancholic depression. No scientific jargon to legitimize and pathologize. Just wake'nikonhrèn:ton, and wake'nikonhra'kwenhtará:'on. A mind hanging by a thread, and a mind spread out on the ground. A before and an after. What does that mean about our culture?

Though the two phrases differ in severity, perhaps, when you think about it, they're referring to the same thing. Maybe all words for those feelings are—endogenous, exogenous, depression, melancholia. All in their own way describe a person in pain who needs help to heal.

Is there a language of depression? I'm not sure. Depression often seems to me like the exact opposite of language. It takes your tongue, your thoughts, your self-worth and leaves an empty vessel. Not that different from colonialism, actually.

In fact, the *Mind Over Mood* depression inventory checklist could double as an inventory for the effects of colonialism on our people. Sad or depressed mood? Check. Feelings of guilt? Check. Irritable mood?

Considering how fast my dad's side of the family are to yell, check. Finding it harder than usual to do things? Well, Canada tried to eradicate our entire way of being, then forced us to take on their values and wondered why we couldn't cope. Definite check. Low self-esteem, self-critical thoughts, tiredness or loss of energy, difficulty making decisions, seeing the future as hopeless, recurrent thoughts of death, suicidal thoughts? Check, check, check.

And if colonialism is like depression, and the Onkwehon:we suffering from it are witches, then I guess it shouldn't surprise anyone that our treatment has always been the same: to light us on fire and let us burn.

I know now why that therapist in that church reminded me of residential schools. When I think of that man sitting across from me, chastising me for not saying the right words, the words that made it easy for him to understand me and cure me, I think of how my grandparents and great-grandparents felt when priests and nuns did the same to them. The difference is that therapist was trying to cure me of being depressed; those priests and nuns were trying to cure my ancestors of being Indian. In some ways they succeeded. In many they did not.

Both depression and colonialism have stolen my language in different ways. I know this. I feel it inside me even as I struggle to explain it. But that does not mean I have to accept it. I struggle against colonialism the same way I struggle against depression—telling myself I'm not worthless, that I'm not a failure, that things will get better.

Our Haudenosaunee condolence ceremony was originally created by Hiawatha to help a person in mourning after a death. Whoever is conducting the condolence recites the Requickening Address as they offer the grieving person three strands of wampum, one at a time.

One: soft, white deer cloth is used to wipe the tears from their eyes so they can see the beauty of creation again.

Two: a soft feather is used to remove the dust from their ears so they can hear the kind words of those around them.

Three: water, the original medicine, is used to wash away the dust settled in their throat, keeping them from speaking, from breathing, from reconnecting with the world outside their grief.

I know this is supposed to be a ceremony for people with reactive depression caused by a death. As far as I know there is no condolence ceremony for those Onkwehon:we suffering from melancholia—those who are, in effect, mourning themselves. There's no collective condolence ceremony for our people either—those who need help to see our beauty and hear our songs and speak our language.

But maybe, one day, there can be.

Things that were stolen once can be stolen back.

NOTES

1 Philip Jenkins. *Dream Catchers: How Mainstream America Discovered Native Spirituality* (London: Oxford University Press, 2005), 23.
2 Alden T. Vaughan, ed. *New England Encounters: Indians and Euroamericans, ca. 1600–1850* (Boston: Northeastern University Press, 1999), 173.

ACKNOWLEDGMENTS

The editors gratefully acknowledge Regan Huff, Larin R. McLaughlin, Rebecca Brinbury, Nicole F. Mitchell, and all other past and present members of the University of Washington Press who assisted in the production of this book. We also thank the MFA program in creative writing at the Institute of American Indian Arts for its role as a confluence point where relationships are made and new work is created.

Unless otherwise noted, all essays are reprinted with permission of the authors.

"Caribou People" by Siku Allooloo was previously published by the *Malahat Review*.

"Pain Scale Treaties" by Laura Da' was previously published by the *Rumpus*.

"A Mind Spread Out on the Ground" by Alicia Elliott was previously published by the *Malahat Review*.

"Women in the Fracklands: On Water, Land, Bodies, and Standing Rock" by Toni Jensen was previously published by *Catapult*.

"Letter to a Just-Starting-Out Indian Writer—and Maybe to Myself" by Stephen Graham Jones was previously published by *Transmotion*.

"Blood Running" by Sasha LaPointe was previously published by *Portland Review.*

"Fairy Tales, Trauma, Writing into Dissociation" by Sasha LaPointe was previously published by the *Rumpus.*

An excerpt from *Aunt Susie Sampson Peter: The Wisdom of a Skagit Elder*, transcribed by Vi Hilbert, translated by Vi Hilbert and Jay Miller, and recorded by Leon Metcalf, was reprinted with the permission of Lushootseed Research in Sasha LaPointe's essay, "Fairy Tales, Trauma, Writing into Dissociation."

Excerpts from "Girl Machine" by Kenward Elmslie were reprinted from the book *Routine Disruptions: Selected Poems and Lyrics, 1960–1998* (Minneapolis: Coffee House Press, 1998) in Chip Livingston's essay, "Funny, You Don't Look Like (My Preconceived Ideas of) an Essay." Used with the permission of Coffee House Press.

"Fear to Forget & Fear to Forgive: Or an Attempt at Writing a Travel Essay" by Bojan Louis was previously published by *Mud City Journal.*

"Nizhoní dóó 'a'ani' dóó até'él'í dóó ayoo'o'oni (Beauty & Memory & Abuse & Love)" by Bojan Louis was previously published by *As/Us.*

"I Know I'll Go" by Terese Marie Mailhot was previously published by *Burrow Press.*

"Little Mountain Woman" by Terese Marie Mailhot was previously published by *BOAAT.*

"Fertility Rites" by Tiffany Midge was previously published by *Quarterly West.*

"Part One: Redeeming the English Language (Acquisition) Series" by Tiffany Midge was previously published by the *Toast.*

"Tuolumne" by Deborah A. Miranda was previously published by *World Literature Today.*

"The Great Elk" by Ruby Hansen Murray was previously published by the *Rumpus.*

"The Trickster Surfs the Floods" by Natanya Ann Pulley was previously published by *Fugue.*

"The Way of Wounds" by Natanya Ann Pulley was previously published by the *Florida Review.*

"Real Romantic" by Eden Robinson was previously published by *Hazlitt.*

"Critical Poly 100s" by Kim TallBear was previously published by the *Critical Polyamorist.*

"Apocalypse Logic" by Elissa Washuta was previously published by the *Offing.*

"Self-Portrait with Parts Missing and/or Smeared" by Michael Wasson was previously published by the *Rumpus.*

CONTRIBUTORS

Siku Allooloo, an Inuit/Haitian Taino from Denendeh, Northwest Territory, holds a BA in anthropology and Indigenous studies from the University of Victoria. Winner of *Briarpatch*'s 2016 creative nonfiction contest, she has published in the *Guardian* and *Rabble*.

Byron F. Aspaas is Diné. He earned his BFA and MFA from the Institute of American Indian Arts. His work is scattered throughout various journals and anthologies. His clans are Red Running Water; born for Bitter Water People. He resides with his partner, three cats, and six puppies in Colorado Springs.

Billy-Ray Belcourt is from the Driftpile Cree Nation. He is a PhD student in the Department of English and Film Studies at the University of Alberta. His debut collection of poems, *This Wound Is a World*, was published by Frontenac House in 2017.

Laura Da' is a lifetime resident of the Pacific Northwest. Da' studied creative writing at the University of Washington and the Institute of American Indian Arts. She is Eastern Shawnee. Her first book, *Tributaries* (University of Arizona Press, 2015), won a 2016 American Book Award.

Alicia Elliott is an award-winning Tuscarora writer living in Brantford, Ontario, with her husband and daughter. Her writing has been published in the *Malahat Review, Room,* the *New Quarterly, CBC, Globe and Mail, Vice,*

Maclean's, and other outlets. And her book, *A Mind Spread Out on the Ground*, was published by Penguin Random House Canada (2019).

Alaska State Writer and Tlingit Kaagwaantaan **Ernestine Hayes** was born in Alaska Territory. At the age of fifteen, she moved to California, where she lived for twenty-five years before returning home. She is associate professor of English at the University of Alaska Southeast, and her published works include *Blonde Indian* (University of Arizona Press, 2015) and *The Tao of Raven* (University of Washington Press, 2015).

Toni Jensen's story collection, *From the Hilltop*, was published in 2010 through the Native Storiers series at the University of Nebraska Press. Her stories and essays have been published in journals such as *Ecotone, Catapult,* and *Denver Quarterly* and have been anthologized in *New Stories from the South, Best of the Southwest,* and *Best of the West: Stories from the Wide Side of the Missouri*. She teaches in the programs in creative writing and translation at the University of Arkansas. She is Métis.

Stephen Graham Jones is the author of seventeen novels, six story collections, and so far, one comic book. Stephen has been an NEA recipient and has won the Texas Institute of Letters Award for Fiction, the Independent Publishers Award for Multicultural Fiction, the Bram Stoker Award, and a few This Is Horror Awards. His work has also been listed among Bloody Disgusting's Top Ten Horror Novels. Stephen is the Ivena Baldwin Professor of English at the University of Colorado, Boulder.

Joan Naviyuk Kane is Inupiaq with family from King Island (Ugiuvak) and Mary's Igloo, Alaska. She was raised in and attended public school in Anchorage, Alaska, where she currently raises her sons as a single mother. A 2018 Guggenheim Fellow in Poetry, she has authored five collections of poems and one book of prose, *A Few Lines in the Manifest* (Albion Books, 2018). Her most recent poetry collection, *Sublingual*, was published in 2018 by Finishing Line Press. Visit thejoankane.com for links and no scarcity of context.

Adrienne Keene is a citizen of the Cherokee Nation and assistant professor of American studies and ethnic studies at Brown University. Her research areas include college access, transition, and persistence for American Indian, Alaska Native, and Native Hawaiian students, including the role of pre-college access programs in student success. She is also dedicated to pushing back against stereotypes and misrepresentations of Native peoples on her blog, *Native Appropriations* (nativeappropriations.com), which has received national and international attention as a voice on contemporary Indigenous issues.

Sasha LaPointe is from the Upper Skagit and Nooksack Indian Tribe. Native to the Pacific Northwest, she draws inspiration from her coastal heritage as well as from her life in the city of Seattle. She writes with a focus on trauma and resilience, ranging on topics from PTSD and sexual violence to the work her great-grandmother did for Coast Salish language revitalization to loud basement punk shows and what it means to grow up mixed heritage. Her work has appeared in *Hunger Mountain*, the *Rumpus*, *Indian Country Today*, *Luna Luna* magazine, the *Yellow Medicine Review*, the *Portland Review*, *As/Us*, *THE Magazine*, and *Aborted Society Online Zine*. She recently completed an MFA through the Institute of American Indian Arts with a focus on creative nonfiction and poetry.

Chip Livingston is mixed-blood Creek and the author of the novel *Owls Don't Have to Mean Death* (Lethe Press, 2017); a short story and essay collection, *Naming Ceremony* (Lethe Press, 2014); and two poetry collections, *Crow-Blue, Crow-Black* (New York Quarterly Books, 2012) and *Museum of False Starts* (Gival Press, 2010). His writing has appeared on the Poetry Foundation's and Academy of American Poets' websites, and in journals such as *Ploughshares, Prairie Schooner, New American Writing, Cincinnati Review,* and *South Dakota Review*. Chip teaches in the low-res MFA programs at the Institute of American Indian Arts and at Regis University. He lives in Montevideo, Uruguay. Visit his website at www.chiplivingston.com.

Bojan Louis is a member of the Navajo Nation—Naakai Dine'é; Ashiihí; Ta'neezahnii; Bilgáana. His first collection of poems is *Currents* (BkMk Press

2017). He is the author of the nonfiction chapbook *Troubleshooting Silence in Arizona* (Guillotine Series, 2012). He is poetry and production editor at *RED INK: An International Journal of Indigenous Literature, Arts, and Humanities*.

Terese Marie Mailhot is from Seabird Island Band. She is the *New York Times*–bestselling author of *Heart Berries: A Memoir* and winner of a 2019 Whiting Award. Her work has appeared in the *Best American Essays* 2019 and elsewhere.

Tiffany Midge is the author of the collection *The Woman Who Married a Bear* (University of New Mexico Press, 2016), which won the *Kenyon Review*'s Earthworks Prize for Indigenous Poetry and a Western Heritage Award. Her work is featured in *McSweeney's, Waxwing, Okey-Pankey, Moss, Indian Country Media Network*, and *World Literature Today*. Tiffany is an enrolled member of the Standing Rock Sioux (Hunkpapa Lakota) and aspires to be a writer in residence at Seattle's Space Needle.

Deborah A. Miranda is an enrolled member of the Ohlone-Costanoan Esselen Nation in California. Her book *Bad Indians: A Tribal Memoir* (Heyday Books, 2012) received the PEN-Oakland Josephine Miles Literary Award, a Gold Medal from the Independent Publishers Association, and was short-listed for the William Saroyan Literary Award. Miranda is professor of English at Washington and Lee University.

Ruby Hansen Murray is the winner of the Montana Prize in Creative Non-fiction, fellowships at Hedgebrook and Voices of Our Nations Arts Foundation. Her work appears in *Cutbank, World Literature Today*, the *Rumpus*, and *Apogee*. She is a citizen of the Osage Nation with West Indian roots on her mother's side and lives along the lower Columbia River.

Natanya Ann Pulley is a Diné writer of fiction and nonfiction with outbreaks in poetry and collage. She has published work in numerous journals including the *Collagist, Drunken Boat, Entropy, McSweeney's, Waxwing*, and *As/Us*. Her essays have been anthologized in *#NotYourPrincess: Voices of Native American Women* (Annick Press, 2017); *Women Write Resistance* (Hyacinth Girl Press, 2013); among others. A former editor of *Quarterly West* and *South Dakota Review*, she is currently the founding editor of the Colorado College literary journal, *Hairstreak Butterfly Review*. Natanya is assistant professor of English at Colorado College, where she teaches Native American literature, fiction writing, and experimental forms in ethnic literature.

Eden Robinson is a Haisla/Heiltsuk author who grew up in Haisla, British Columbia. Her first book, *Traplines* (Henry Holt, 1996), a collection of short stories, won the Winifred Holtby Memorial Prize and was a *New York Times* Notable Book of the Year in 1998. *Monkey Beach* (Houghton Mifflin, 2000), her first novel, was short-listed for both the Giller Prize and the Governor General's Literary Award for fiction in 2000 and won the BC Book Prize's Ethel Wilson Fiction Prize. Her latest novel is *Son of a Trickster* (Alfred A. Knopf Canada, 2017).

Kim TallBear is associate professor, faculty of Native studies, at the University of Alberta. She mixes anthropological approaches with community-based research, including arts-based research and performance. She co-produces Edmonton's sexy storytelling show, *Tipi Confessions*, which is modeled on the popular Austin, Texas, show *Bedpost Confessions*. *Tipi Confessions* has also been staged in Ottawa, Saskatoon, and Vancouver. There are plans for shows in New Zealand and the United States. Kim is a citizen of the Sisseton-Wahpeton Oyate in South Dakota. She blogs at www.IndigenousSTS.com and www .criticalpolyamorist.com. She also tweets @KimTallBear and @CriticalPoly.

Theresa Warburton is a non-Native scholar who is a Mellon Postdoctoral Fellow in Native and Indigenous Literatures at Brown University. She is also assistant professor of English at Western Washington University, where she is affiliated faculty in women's, gender, and sexuality studies and Canadian studies. Her scholarly and community work focuses on both the historic and potential relationships between literary production and radical political intervention.

Elissa Washuta is a member of the Cowlitz Indian tribe and a Cascade descendant. She is the author of two books, *Starvation Mode* (Future Tense Books, 2015) and *My Body Is a Book of Rules* (Red Hen Press, 2014), and is assistant professor of creative writing at the Ohio State University.

Michael Wasson is the author of *This American Ghost* (YesYes Books, 2017). The recipient of the 2017 Adrienne Rich Award from *Beloit Poetry Journal*, his poems have appeared in *American Poets, Drunken Boat, Kenyon Review, Poetry Northwest, Narrative, Bettering American Poetry,* and *Best New Poets*. He is nimíipuu from the Nez Perce Reservation in Idaho.